"Love Him For Us"

By Barbara Marquart Johnston

"Love Him For Us"

Copyright (c) 2020 Lutheran News, Inc. All Rights Reserved.

No portion of this book may be reproduced in any form, except for quotations in reviews, articles, and speeches, without permission from the publisher.

Library of Congress
Lutheran News, Inc.
684 Luther Lane
New Haven, MO 63068
Published 2020
Printed in the United States of America
IngramSpark, TN
ISBN #978-0-9864232-8-4

DEDICATION

This book is dedicated to the memory of
my beloved late husband, Kurt E. Marquart.
The stories will explain why.
I would also like to dedicate it to all
those sisters in the Faith throughout
our Church, all around the world,
who are living with pastor/husbands.
May the Lord of the Church bless
you and yours richly.
Thank you!
For all those of you who are in
the process of preparing for the public Ministry,
I hope you will enjoy this little effort,
and that it will give you encouragement
and hope for good things ahead!

Barbara Marquart Johnston

Love Him for Us is like a warm cup of the Queen's tea and tasty tarts with whipped cream! Marvelous and meant to be shared with others! Barb Marquart Johnston does a fantastic job taking you through the fascinating and encouraging journey of her life including her own great happiness, sacrifices, rewards, struggles, and tremendous joys. What a splendid encouragement to pastors and their wives who serve Christ's Church now. These memoirs remind us that the Lord's hand is truly guiding us in our life on a day to day basis and He has a plan for each of us! Readers will smile, cry, and laugh throughout because of the honest account of church work life we all face as a pastor's family, especially the pastor's wife! Yet, Barb Marquart Johnston cheerfully reminds us to find joy, not just in the daily adventures, but in the ultimate truth that we ALL, as God's people, have forgiveness and grace in our Lord and Savior, Jesus Christ. Thanks be to God for wonderful, selfless, pastors such as Dr. Marquart, who preach and teach Christ crucified!

—Mrs. Sarah Bibb

In the short time that I have known Barbara as her Pastor and in all our correspondence from the beginning, she is a lady of great courage and honor, with the same witty insights and deep convictions of the late Dr. Marquart. I wonder if he picked some of that up from her? Either way, there is certainly a common thread between the two, and how fitting for it to be her in writing such a book. — Rev. James Gier

Barbara and Kurt

Love Him for Us by Barbara Marquart Johnston is, simply put, a book that I would recommend for every Lutheran pastor's wife – and her husband as well. Barb (as she is called) was the wife of one of the great Lutheran theologians of our time, Professor Kurt Marquart. Hidden in the mystique of this towering intellectual was a human being who was known best by his wife. Other pastors' wives will find in this book, written from a wife's perspective, an assurance that their vocation as wife, while never easy, is truly to be a servant of Jesus Christ.
—Dr. Daniel Gard

I haven't known of any books written by a Lutheran pastor's wife about her life that includes counsel to parish pastor's wives. Until now! Mrs. Johnston has written the perfect book on the subject, which I highly recommend to clergy wives and their husbands, as well as seminarians and their wives, and couples thinking about the ministry. Mrs. Johnston's observations are frank, and her counsel is right on target. Along the way we get the author's memoirs, including life together with Professor Kurt Marquart, which are worth reading in themselves.
— Rev. Martin R. Noland, Pastor of Grace Lutheran Church, San Mateo, California

Tony, Kurt, Barry, Danny - Barry's wedding at Ascension

ACKNOWLEDGEMENTS

This little book comes as the result of life among wonderful Christian family and friends who have been instrumental either in their influence in my life, or have provided the on-going and necessary nagging and support that has given this result!

In my youth, the first person to inspire me to write was my Mother. The second one, in Grade Nine, was Mrs. Leonard, my English teacher! I don't think I understood what all the lectures were about, why they thought I should write, when none of my friends seemed to care about writing. As time passed, and I actually developed opinions about anything important, it dawned on me that writing was the only way to express those ideas in a world congested with so much rubbish. As well, since I was not a teacher, or anyone who had the status to influence others, I had no platform. Gradually, it occurred to me that writing might provide that.

Thus, you have it.

Along the way, the others who played the most dominant part in all this were the dozens of seminary student wives, and even some of their husbands, who repeatedly begged me to give them some resources, since there didn't seem to be much available on the market in the particular field of clergy couples, and wives in particular. Pat Nuffer can take credit for living in my conscience all these decades, because she made me promise to do it someday.

I would be remiss, then, if I didn't thank all the folks who have continued to prompt me to get this done. Part of my motivation was to also share an aspect of the life I enjoyed with your friend and colleague, Kurt Marquart. He provided so much of what I think of as important to me now; he is largely responsible for who I am today.

There is yet one person who finally gave me the final shove, and without her wonderful help, we would still not have this book. She volunteered hours of her time editing the various stages of manuscript and has been largely responsible for the final product. Thank you, Vary Fischer! She has been a wonderful partner in all this.

My dear husband, Robert Johnston, can take credit for having sacrificed so much that was necessary to allow me to spend the necessary time to complete this project. Never doubting that I would finish this, he is the one who provided the tranquility, confidence, and opportunity to achieve this completion. Thank you Bob!

Nearly every day, for so many years, I have asked God for His support of this project. My motto was, "If He wants it to get done, He will make it happen." So, if there is anyone to praise for this, it is our Lord Himself!

TABLE OF CONTENTS

Note: The chapters in this book were written over a prolonged period of time. Therefore, they are not necessarily listed in the order of occurrence. While the emphasis may appear to be directed towards clergy couples, it is my belief that most of the material will be of interest to everyone. While listed somewhat in order of interest and topic, I intentionally arranged things the way I did so that we are reminded that in the midst of the ordinary, extraordinary things happen. Primarily, these stories are intended to not only share a particular culture or vocation, but for those of you who knew Dr. Marquart, I believe you will enjoy being reminded that he was everything you thought he was, and more. Enjoy!

INTRODUCTION

Labor Pains 1
"Love Him for Us" 3
Why This Book 4
Things I Learned 7

I
LIFE BEFORE KURT MARQUART

Mother – Daughter Relations 9
Good Shepherd Sunday 17
Hang On, Little Peter! 20
First Marriage 23

II
BARBARA & KURT

The Courtship 29
In the Journal - "To This Time" 31
Okay, Now Let's Hear His Side of the Story . . . Maybe? 41
New Beginnings 48
The Wedding Day 52

III
LIFE IN AUSTRALIA – 1961 – 1975

Youngest Pastor's Wife in the District 60
Toowoomba - Garden City of Australia 66
Sylvia 72
It Must Have Flowers 75
Mrs. Margate 78
Second-Hand Children 82
Minnie Bradhurst, Ugly Duckling 84
Undeserved Adversaries 88
Pastor Perry Mason 93
Aboriginal Relations 95
The Tropic of Capricorn 96
First Years of Marriage 100
The Petition 110

Sanctity of Life 112
It Takes a Lifetime 115
Good News! There is No Typical Pastor's Wife 126
Forgiveness is Costly 133
The Greatest of These 134
Bringing Up Children in the Parsonage 136
Acceptance 141
"The Proppa Banner" 144
Unexpected Houseguest 147
My First Trip to New York 149
Great With Kids 153
Overheard 156
The Lord Is On Your Side 159
Funerals - Why We Go 160

IV
LIFE IN THE ACADEMIC WORLD
1975 – 2006

Acapulco 163
Seminary Calls/Rescinds Call To Teach 167
Gleen How 171
What If Something Should Happen? 177
Vienna 177
Four Star Hotel It Was Not 183
The Russian Project 186
O, Canada! 188
911 192
Dealing With Adversaries 194
Marquart For President 195
Unlikely Reunion 200
Erik Christopher 205
Hands 207
2000 or Y2K 209
How Do I View Retirement? 211
International Year of Women - 1975 215

V
LAST STRUGGLE

The Emperor's New Clothes 219
What Do You Feel Like Doing? 221
Always In His Shadow 223
Last Moments 225
Give to Him Who Asks of You 229
Into His Nearer Presence 232
Final Reunion 235
Students Recall Dr. Marquart 237

VI
MORE NEW BEGINNINGS

It All Began with a Christmas Card 242

INTRODUCTION

Labor Pains

Some folks who have known me for a long time know that for decades, I've promised to attempt this book. In the beginning, it was at the request of some women married to seminary students during the 1980's, who begged me to put something together for clergy wives.

These ladies had heard me present at one of their classes and wanted a session in one of their homes where they could visit and ask all kinds of questions. They invited me to one of their Bible study meetings. So, I went. Trouble was, I got laryngitis earlier in the day, and by the time I got there, I could just whisper! It was sad for all concerned. But at that time, they begged me to write a book for them, and I promised I would.

I had already, while in Australia, had ideas about writing, but had not decided which way to go. As time passed, so did life, with its crazy derailments and distractions. The book was always being written in my head, because I have always carried a tangible love for my sisters in the Faith who walk at the side of clergy husbands. Putting it into print had so many false starts, you would not believe it.

Rather like discovering you are expecting your first child, it seems as if you have tons of time to prepare. Before you know it, you are at the point where you just want to get on with the delivery. That's the way it's been with this book. Suddenly, I find myself an old woman, and as we all know, only God knows how much time is left. As I approach eighty years of age, (Yes, I know. It doesn't seem possible.) the pressure is on!

It reminds me very much of the time when my late husband, Dr. Kurt Marquart, received the Call to teach at Concordia Theological Seminary, when it was still located in Springfield, Illinois, after fifteen years in parish ministry. There were three months from the time he accepted the Call until we finally left the shores of Australia. We were "farewelled" by every national, district and local entity, painful in itself, until at last, we just wanted and needed to move on.

While I have been very close to executing this effort many times, there have been numerous periods during those years when I would become so totally disillusioned by the actions of some in the greater body of the church, that I didn't feel as if I could honestly espouse serving her. Sometimes my health would become precarious for a while, and the energy it costs to write was just not there. Other times, domestic issues were so overwhelming that I didn't feel I had any business advising anyone! Part of me kept hoping someone in our circles would beat me to the punch and put something out there that was so good I needn't bother at all. After all, as one friend once told me, "Why bother, when there is nothing new under the sun. You can't write anything that hasn't been written before." Or, as another nagged, "Leave it alone. They'll figure it out when they get out there." Well, it seems to me as if many are not figuring it out. And it is obvious that times are different now than they were thirty years ago, when this was but a glimmer in my eye.

Our culture, our church, the attitude of the congregations to their pastors and their families are all different than they once were. The feminist movement and "women's studies" have given women so many crazy ideas about what it means to be a wife and mother, much less a pastor's wife. There is, as they say, no absolute truth anymore. So, your idea is as good as the next guy's as to how we are to try to live. Perhaps it is helpful, then, to attempt some plain common sense to some things. Shall we try?

I'm not anxious to ruffle feathers, make judgements, dictate, or shove anyone into or out of any point of view. Any negative responses to this manuscript will not be answered nor debated. I am putting it out there for you all to take or leave, agree with or hate. It matters not. I am fulfilling a promise to many women, who through the years thought I had something to say about these issues.

At one point, most recently, when I read some really unkind, cutting criticisms about an effort by some other women, who, by the way are much more learned than I, I put all my articles in a box and decided I was not going to open Pandora's Box by offering my version of help to the women of the church. The very next Sunday, I was slammed between the eyes with the Old Testament reading for the day. After reading it, I figured I'd better try again. Here it is:

"Whoever corrects a scoffer gets himself abuse, and he who reproves a wicked man incurs injury. Do not reprove a scoffer, or he will hate you; reprove a wise man and he will love you. Give instructions to a wise man, and he will be still wiser; teach a righteous man and he will increase in learning. The fear of the LORD is the beginning of wisdom, and the knowledge of the Holy One is insight." Proverbs 9:9-10

More than once, during our years together, Kurt impressed upon me these words: "The only thing that remains behind when we are gone is what we write." This, then, is my gift to you.

"Love Him for Us"

Not long after the laryngitis affliction, while attending a faculty reception at the seminary, quite unexpectedly, a pastor who was one of the guests came up behind me, and in a brief whisper said, "Love him for us."

It was a time during which several of the seminary faculty were embroiled in a critical battle for the Truth, and it was perceived that my husband, then a professor at the seminary, was one of the leading forces behind holding the line against dangerous encroaching trends. Because I knew the young man who whispered to me, I took his words to mean, "Your man is one of God's warriors in our army. He will be in this war until the finish. And at the end, you may be the only one left at his side. We can pray for him, and we can encourage him. But you alone can love him in the way that is needed. Apart from God, only you can provide what he needs so that he can continue to serve God, and us."

Before I could turn around, he was gone. But his words stuck with me, and for days their implications swirled around in my mind. *(After all, he was, as many of us knew him, "the bishop of the world".)* While I knew them to be applicable to our own situation, I grew convinced that those words were appropriate for all pastors' wives, and that someday they would serve as the title for my book, if and when I got around to writing it.

Every pastor is a foot soldier in the Church Militant. Many times, each of them will seem to be left standing alone. Some folks think "church militant" means that Christians are continually fighting among themselves. It certainly can appear that way sometimes. Much more importantly it means the Church in this world is in perpetual battle against the principalities that would destroy Her and who militate against Her and Her children with great and deliberate evil. The pastor's family is a prime target. The pastor and his wife will face conflict in the congregation and in their family, as Satan's efforts are directed at disrupting the work of the Lord, and to preventing the saving Gospel from doing its work.

To that end, this effort is written for the women who have been chosen by the Lord of the Church to stand at the side of those men who are the stewards of the mysteries of God. It is my hope that just talking about, crying over, and laughing about life in the parsonage will encourage and help to lift spirits and give hope for each day — to be loving wives, faithful mothers, and tender friends to the sheep under their husbands' care.

Why This Book

During the early evolution of this book, I happened to be vacationing in another state, when it became my pleasure to visit with the man who was serving as District President of that area in the Lutheran Church-Missouri Synod. In his role, it had fallen to him to visit congregations and pastors, to counsel and affect reconciliation throughout his district. As a result of his contact with those in his charge, he had become acutely aware of the pain and conflict that was in the homes of some of the pastors and their families, as well as the flocks they serve.

When I mentioned to him my hopes of writing a book that might be helpful to women in the parsonages across our Church, he was very encouraging, saying that to his knowledge, this kind of help was not readily available on the market. (Most of what is on the racks of "how to" books rarely speak to the unique situations and difficulties that can effect life in the parsonage, and the pastor's wife in particular.) I was grieved to learn from him that in his district alone, at least 50% of the problems in the congregations he visited had been either created or exacerbated by the pastor's wife.

This fact bespeaks a population of presumably devout Christians in unspeakable unhappiness and crisis. The mind boggles to imagine all those pastors attempting faithful labor among God's people, living under the cloud of misery at home, torn with guilt either way they turn. It reveals a situation where hundreds of women, young and old, are suffering spiritually and emotionally, often in secret, yet in a way that many times undermines and destroys the very work the husband is doing. It explains why many children raised by clergy couples grow up disenchanted with the church, because they have seen what they believe is the result of an untenable home life.

It is my prayer that we can address some of the problematic behavior of both clergy couples and parishioners. Perhaps we can shed some light on why and how pain and unhappiness are sometimes self-inflicted, that some conflict is the result of miscommunication or a misunderstanding of what really happened, one's possible determination to be a martyr, or another's longing to get "a pound of flesh" back every time someone offends.

Can an action mean two totally different things, depending on one's perception? Do we incite conflict with an attitude of "entitlement"? Is it possible that some clergy couples really believe they are there to be served, rather than to serve? As well, why is it that some clergy couples are very happy in their vocation, have a passion for living and working with fellow Christians, and raise children who later believe they too would love to be pastors and pastors' wives?

Someone asked me, "Are there really clear rules and guidelines for the pastor's wife that don't apply to all Christian women?" Initially, I thought, "no". But I was mistaken. While we all know that only God creates Faith, if we are conscious of our husbands being the business of leading folks to eternal life through his work, we hope to be able to enhance, not be an obstacle, to that effort.

So the pastor's wife will work hard to create and maintain a peaceful home, where the children feel loved and secure, especially when the dad must often be absent. She will support him, even when it means self-sacrifice. She will refrain from "suffering at the hands of the church", so that her children will grow up to be happy, loving Christians.

One cannot automatically assume that problems in the parish are due to the pastor's wife. That's absurd! There are hundreds of combinations of circumstances that crop up when there are groups of sinful humans trying to work together. We are all familiar with the insidious undercurrents that can be raging just below the surface that prevent the work of the Gospel from succeeding. Many pastors walk into an unknown quagmire of landmines, and the nightmare of sorting out the real problems can take a large portion of each day for a long while. This can take a big toll on the couple, especially as they begin in a new place.

As silly as it sounds, there is sometimes an unrealistic idea among the people that their pastor is, or should be, infallible. If it is true that the pastor can do no wrong, then if there is trouble, it might (must) be the wife! It would not occur to the congregation that he could be in any way lacking. Therefore, anything that is amiss must be laid at the feet of his wife. If, on the other hand, all is going well in the congregation, let's give credit to a warm, friendly and wise and loving pastor's wife! See how unfair that is, and what a troublesome burden it places on life in the parsonage?

In a gathering of student wives, one lady declared to the gathering that she believed the pastor's wife should be friendly, able to rally the women, a leader. I asked her, "What if she is not inclined to be an outgoing person?

What if it is simply not within her to be a cheerleader?" We must not assume that every pastor's wife, no matter how much she might wish to be, is going to fit that model. It's simply not realistic, nor even loving.

This book was intended to help and encourage those women who live under the fearful cloud that they will somehow threaten the effectiveness of their husbands. I've listened to many women over the years who worry that they are too loud, or less than poised. They've covered this fear by stomping into the new congregation with an obvious attitude of "What you see is what you get; don't think I'm going to bend for you guys." In contrast, I've listened to the women who are worried that they won't measure up with the right kind of social etiquette, or that they have health issues that are going to prevent them from doing what folks expect.

Whether a woman is high spirited and eager to be active in the congregation, or a woman is at the point in life when she is needed at home to raise a flock of little kids, the Office of the Holy Ministry does not belong to her. She may be able to enhance it. Finally, it's her husband's Call. Her calling is to keep a sound, harmonious home for him, enabling him to find rest and joy when he returns to it. Nothing anyone else can do for him will invigorate and encourage him as much as a happy wife and well behaved and happy children. It is enough to succeed as a good wife and mother. Finally, the success of the congregation is not all about YOU!

When I decided on the title for this book, I added "The Love Story of the Century" in my mind, because I hoped to show that through the hills and valleys of what married life in the parsonage is, in the end, it is Love that binds it all together. Love for God, Love for one's spouse and children, Love for the Family of God where you are. The deepest and most reliable Love of all is that love which our Lord so readily gives. That undeserved Love, when we are not lovable. That love that gives a reason to rise every morning to fill the endless needs of others. That love that overshadows the disappointments and restores our hope. That love that puts song into our hearts that allows us to love.

My hope for the reader is that each will recognize that the Master of the Universe knew, before each of us was born, where He wanted us to be in relation to His plans for His Kingdom. Nothing is so comforting as knowing that we are what God has made. We are where He has planted us, with those He wants us to serve. Sometimes, it is not some amazing deed that He wants me to do, but that I might enable someone else to do his/hers, giving God all the glory.

Things I Learned

Unless a woman has grown up in a parsonage, very likely there are many new experiences in store for anyone who marries a pastor. When I married my pastor/husband, my impression of being married to a clergyman was given me by my own pastor's wife, whom I watched all through my growing up years.

Mrs. Dorre had the most peaceful, beautiful countenance that it seemed to me as if she must have the most happy life. Sitting in the same pew every week, by herself, she generated a sweet joyfulness that prevented anyone from thinking badly of her. Mrs. Dorre was the second wife of our pastor. His first wife, and the mother of his two children, had died. She had never been able to have children herself, but took delight in mothering her new step children.

When, then, I married at twenty the pastor of a dual parish in Toowoomba, Queensland, Australia, it was with no idea of what it was really like to be a pastor's wife. When I retrace the history of our little family, it is with such gratitude to God, who walked with me and helped me learn the important things about being a wife, mother, friend.

I recall all the children He gave us to raise, including two foster sons, all the joint experiences we shared in the parish, the hundreds of people that wove themselves in and out of our lives. Maintaining a hospitable home for the family, as well as the many pilgrims who were always passing through, and lending stability to a home where the father was quite often missing, was a full time vocation.

I used to describe my life as being married to a streak of lightning. It became important that I always be dressed and be ready to leave the house, because if I wasn't, I found myself at home alone a lot. When I could go along on shut-in calls, or ride along to the hospital, I did. Sometimes we would grab the kids and head for a beer garden at one of the local pubs for lunch. There were isolated times when we could grab a few minutes together alone, and it was best to ready.

I discovered that one could throw a meal together for surprise visitors at the drop of a hat, that other peoples' needs rarely met with my convenience, that people were more important than money or anything else, that our children would feel about their vagabond father the same way I did, that they would love the church or hate the church according to how they perceived my attitude towards all the daily requirements of maintaining a working parsonage.

I learned that people change, that the book isn't over until it's over. I learned that sometimes when things go wrong, it's possibly my own fault, not the other person's, and that I should suspect that right away and get it over with. I learned that it's not necessary to always be right anyway.

I learned the wisdom of putting the past in the past, moving on, anticipating good, rather than bad. I learned that pastors are never "broke"; they just experience temporary inconvenience. I learned that there is nothing as precious as the soul of another, that every single person we meet will spend eternity in heaven or hell; that the work we are involved with is a life or death business. I learned that living in the parsonage is not like living in a fish bowl; rather, it is like living in the ocean with endless opportunities to meet and serve the needs of others. I learned that it doesn't matter that others know what we are doing if we are doing what we believe God wants us to do. If God and all the angels already know, what's the big secret?

I've learned that the best reply in time of controversy, the kind that doesn't matter in the long run, is, "I'm sure you must be right." I've learned that forgiveness is the dearest and best thing we can possess and freely give to one another.

The materials gathered in this book are meant primarily for women whose husbands are preparing for full time parish ministry, but also for those who are in the field. I have attempted to write for all Christian women, and I think anyone can enjoy some of the chapters. My prayer is that you will laugh, cry, learn, and rethink, as you read some of the stories and the information that follows. You may not agree with everything. That's ok.

Every pastor's wife is different. Every congregation is different. What works for one may not work for another. My hope is that you will find it easier to face the unknown after reading this, and that at the end of your road, you will be able to say with me that there are few vocations for women more intensely interesting and fulfilling than being a pastor's wife and living among God's people. May that be God's gift to you!

I
LIFE BEFORE KURT MARQUART

Mother – Daughter Relations

Regardless of our ultimate life pattern, it always begins with our parents. My story begins with memories of Margaret and William Martens. Margaret Mary, my Mother, lived from 1917 to 1989 (72 years). William Christoph, my Father, lived from 1910 to 1969 (59 years).

Following is a poem my Mother wrote when I was 13 (unbeknownst to me until after her death.)

THIRTEEN
"Hi Mom, what's new, get any mail today?
Did you get to go to town today?
Had a hard test, hope I didn't fail.
Boy, am I tired, walked all the way.
I'll iron a while, but first must rest.
That cake in there sure does look keen."
I listen quietly, she does the rest.
That's Barbara, she is thirteen.

"Did you get my blouse washed, is my skirt made yet?
I sure do need some new clothes.
The game is next week, so please don't forget.
I'll need money for that, heaven knows.
Don't polish my nails? Don't mascara my eyes?
Oh, Mother, I think you are mean.
I'm no longer a child, you must realize.
I'm now at the age of thirteen.

"I'll help with the dishes tomorrow, but now
I have lots of homework to get.
I'd probably be in your way anyhow.
Daddy will help you, I bet.
Did I make up my bed? Did I hang up my clothes?
My room—it just won't stay clean.
Perfection is out, the whole family knows.
After all, I'm only thirteen.

"I have to be leaving in ten minutes flat.
Hey Mom, does red go with green?
That cake that I ate, will it make me fat?
Does the back of my skirt have a sheen?"
She's busy, so busy, from morning till night.
Like a Mexican jumping bean.
God help me guide her in ways that are right.
God bless her, she's only thirteen.

M.M.M.

My Mother, Mama, gave color and purpose to so much of my childhood, that as my life played out as an adult, anything that developed in a negative sense could not be laid at her feet in any way. Any poor judgement or stupidity was all mine.

Mama was born into a Christian family, familiar with hard work and struggle. She, together with three older sisters and one younger one, shared the chores that fell to the women, while the single brother supported the father's tasks of farming the land.

In all our years together, she rarely talked about her childhood, except to say that the eldest sister, Bessie, was pretty much the surrogate mother of her younger sisters, while my grandmother maintained the homestead. Fern and Ruby were the middle children, and her baby sister was Lola. Most of my life, I was called Lola about as much as I was called Barbara. Lola and Mama were very close, right up until the time Mama died. I recall overhearing their final conversation on the phone that last time, when Mama told Lola, "I hope there's someone Up There to meet me, because I'm terrible with directions."

My parents met and were married when she was seventeen. I assume she finished high school. The only detail I know about her youth was that she played trumpet until she had to have all her teeth pulled. She developed St. Vitus Dance (a neurological condition caused by infection, also called Sydenham Chorea), and all her teeth turned black, resulting in her wearing dentures her entire life. She said they extracted the teeth all in one day, put the dentures in, and she never had a moment of trouble with them, wearing them until the day she died.

Mama's father was a devout man, better read than many farmers, and was the superintendent of the Sunday School of their church. I think Mama's family were members of the Congregational Church before she joined my Dad's Lutheran Church, after they were married. Mama adored her dad and was so proud of him. The fact that one of the school teachers mocked him and said nasty things about him behind his back really upset Mama. As she was nearing her death, she confessed to me that the teacher kept a pair of lovely little sewing scissors in his desk drawer. When she graduated, she stole them out of his desk and enjoyed using them the rest of her life. I was familiar with those scissors all the years I was growing up, and was amused to think she could have been brave enough to do that, in loving support of her father, and in retaliation against that mean teacher.

When my parents married, because my Dad was a pilot, they left Nebraska in search of work for him in the Southwest part of the country. My brother was born in Santa Fe, New Mexico, after which time, they moved to Albuquerque, where I was born. There were times during those early years when they were very poor, but there was never a time when my Dad didn't work at one job or another. He was very talented with anything mechanical, despite having left formal education after grade eight, and he always found a job, despite the depression and employment difficulties of the day.

When I was four or five, my family moved to Fort Worth, Texas. Living first in a duplex apartment on one end of town, we moved to a home of our own on the north side of town, in the Riverside area, right across the street from an elementary school. In that home, Mama lived until she died in 1989.

I don't recall Mama being a big reader. But she was extremely crafty and was always making very pretty things out of seemingly nothing with which to beautify her home. Every season brought out different colors and accents, ever so humble, to reflect the time of year. Christmas was the highlight of the year for her, with all manner of pretty things coming out of the closets to make a winter wonderland for us kids. I loved it—and it is a tradition I have carried out in my own home. Every mom needs to realize what lifelong memories kids have of these little efforts on our part, and how these acts enrich the lives of their own children and grandchildren. Someone has to continue just a tad of culture in this crazy world.

One amusing story she related, while I was her caregiver during those last weeks of her life, involved her methods of discipline. Apparently, and I have no memory of this, when my brother and I would fight, she would make us sit together out on the steps of the front porch until we could be civil again. She was tickled one day to have a neighbor from across the street tell her how sweet her little kids were, that they liked to sit on the step together like that!

I suppose my fondest memory of Mama was that while I attended elementary school, I could walk home every day. She was nearly always sitting on the front porch waiting for me, rocking in one of the two metal rockers that were there. We would sit together and watch the traffic for a while, when she would ask about my day. Eventually, we could go inside and she would reveal a fresh batch of German sour cream cookies! I wish so much I still had that recipe—I used it so often that the card disintegrated, and I didn't think to copy it until it was too late. They were the best dunking cookies ever.

While I was young, Mama was involved in my school as a room mother. But in those days, that simply meant providing goodies for parties, and doing favors for the teachers when asked. She never felt it her duty to hover, and she allowed me a lot of independence in that respect. Since we lived across the street, it was quite natural that our class Easter egg hunts would take place in our back yard. In the six years that I attended that school, she developed a beautiful garden, and I suspect making it pretty for those parties had something to do with that.

As well as being a den mother to my brother's scout group, she was also a troop leader for my little Blue Birds group, as well as my Girl Scout troop when I got older. Black and white snapshots document all the little girls who were always at our home during those years.

Once I entered Junior High, her activities at my school began to wane and she took on interests of her own at the church with the ladies there. That being said, she was responsible for teaching me to sew well enough that I began making all my own clothes by the time I was 14. She and I would pick patterns together, and she would go along to support my choice of materials for everything from aprons to formal gowns for school dances and banquets. Not only did I benefit from this, in that I had an original wardrobe for myself, but when I was in Australia, living on a very tight budget, I was able to make curtains and draperies, sew for my girls, and even upholster my vinyl kitchen chairs, thanks to the confidence I had gained on my little portable Singer sewing machine. By the way, my parents gave that machine to me as a graduation present, on the condition that I promised never to hock it!

She also entrusted the cutting and perming of her hair to me when I was twelve! I became very good at it, and sometimes her friends would invite me to their homes to do their hair as well.

Her gift to me was to convince me that I could do nearly anything I wanted to. Interestingly enough, I was under the delusion that all moms were like that, and that all girls knew how to do what I was doing. It took a long time for me to realize the special things Mama passed down to me.

From the time I could hold a pencil, I was writing stories. Mama told me a thousand times, "You could be an author someday." Perhaps that is the continuing motivation for my desire to do it today. She composed poetry herself, and as I have discovered, probably shared my impression that self-expression is an important part of feeling whole and coming to grips with one's thoughts and emotions.

At church, I was Margaret Martens' little girl all my life. Because she enjoyed the affection and respect of the other women, that admiration overflowed on to me all my years at home.

I witnessed my Mama cry once in my life. It was the occasion of a bouquet of flowers being delivered to the house from our pastor's wife. Mama had done something nice for her, and she sent her this small token of appreciation. My Mom was so touched, she wept.

During my teen years, like all young women, I was convinced Mama was the enemy, someone who could never really understand me, nor why I wanted to do certain things. My best friend would tell me that her mother loved her so much that were she to die, her mom would have her stuffed and stand her in the corner of the living room. I could never imagine such a fondness on behalf of my Mama. She sent me away to a big technical school across town, away from all my girlfriends. She presumably trusted me to do that. And yet, I was not allowed to date a boy alone until I was eighteen years old. I could double date with my brother and one of his friends from the time I was around sixteen years old, but never alone. I thought she hated me when she made me leave the school all my friends were going to, where I had to fend for myself among total strangers. But years later I came to appreciate that striking out on my own created a self confidence and courage that enabled me to do yet other challenging things in my adult life.

During my senior year, after I turned eighteen, I went out with a few guys now and again, and without fail, that porch light would go on the minute we pulled into the driveway. Nevertheless, she allowed me to attend the proms and Jr and Sr dances, as long as I doubled dated with friends. My social life was certainly not that of the cutsie cheerleaders nor the football sweethearts, who made the rounds to our classrooms with their fake smiles, soliciting votes for their elections. But I managed to have fun, primarily because I loved to dance. Any and all music went straight to my feet, and from a very young age, I could ball room dance, and was as good as they come at disco.

Boys my age? Well, what can I say? I found it hard to take them seriously. When I was a freshman, I had a crush on a senior who obviously didn't know I existed. There were always guys who rode the bus with me in the afternoons who seemed keen. But I was always looking for something different, someone special.

One time, one of the "bad boys" at school, probably on a dare, invited me to a party with some of the "popular" kids. Just for the heck of it, I went. They gathered at a pavilion at the park, and beer was being guzzled all around me. The guy who was my date tried to kiss me, and for the life of me, I could not help laughing. It was just too silly. Later, we all ended up at a club, where the guys knew they could score more beer, despite their youth. It was the most boring night of my life. After that, I was not pursued by anyone. I've thought so often since that time of that expression, "We always want what we can't have, and when we finally get it, we find it's not nearly as wonderful as we imagined." Because I was not allowed to date, it seemed the ultimate goal. But quite often, it seemed that the forbidden fruit was not at all what I expected.

My brother had warned me that guys will act as if they like you, and get you to do things you should not, and then brag about it in the locker room. It would have been amusing to hear what they had to say about me.

Oddly, Mama didn't make any waves when I started dating the young man (when I was a Junior in high school) who would become my first husband. She was not all that keen on the fact that he would come over and lounge around on her sofa. She did not, however, forbid me from seeing him, despite the fact that he was an airman and a bit older than I was. When we became engaged, I suppose she accepted the inevitable, and no doubt was disappointed that I had not done better for myself. Her relief was obvious when he was transferred to Indiana, and I'm sure she hoped that would be the end of him.

I know in my heart today, that if she had begged me to not marry this young man, I would not have done it. How often do we see people attach themselves to people we know are not right for them, and yet we say nothing? I've seen it so often. And those marriages rarely work out, just as my first marriage did not work out. It is a difficult time for parents—wanting to guide their children, but fearing losing them with "too much" guidance.

As I think about Mama today, when I am already several years older than she was at the time of her death, I have to ask myself what there was about me that she found so hard to deal with. I guess I must have been more rebellious than I realized at the time. I still find it interesting that this gentle, humble woman had led a city-wide corps of Lutheran women in the massive task of waiting tables at the Texas Hotel Ballroom for over ten years. These ladies took thousands of dollars in tips back to their respective congregations, with which even pipe organs were built. This quiet lady served the head table on the morning of President and Mrs. John Kennedy's final meal in Fort Worth, on that fateful date. And yet, this wise and long-suffering mother was seemingly intimidated by her daughter.

After her death, my sister-in-law uncovered some poems my Mama had written that I had never seen. Following is the one she wrote the night after I left Texas with my first husband.

SHE IS GONE
Funny fool that you are, why don't you cry?

You're hurting inside, why try to deny?
She left home today, to be at the side
Of the boy she loves, she now is his bride.

She said you're cold, hardhearted, without love
For her and for others, Dear Father above,
Don't she know that you tried so hard to do right
And have prayed for her so, both morning and night?
She was so extra special, so dear and so sweet.
You hoped for the stars to be laid at her feet.

Oh, fool that you are, why couldn't you show
Her your love and affection, so that she would know
How dear to your heart she was. Now it's too late
To prove that you love her, time just doesn't wait.
Only God knows how you're hurting inside,
But someday she'll know you were trying to guide
Her in paths that were rosy and best for her soul.
For her own little ones, she'll set a high goal,
Then all of a sudden, she'll see it so clear
That her own Mother's love was pure and sincere.
So, cry foolish one, let your soul be at rest
God gave her to you, and you did your best.
Cry on, silly fool, let the tears ease your heart.
She never was yours. She was God's from the start.

M.M.M
1959

Oh, how I wish we had enjoyed better communication between us. While I was no doubt making this choice to marry and leave home because I was so sure no one at home cared about me anyway, Mama was probably convinced that I was doing it to hurt her. So much pain could have been avoided. We will never know.

And when my Dad perished in a plane crash in 1969, my Mama authored the following:

FIRST LOVE AND HE

He was in love when I met him.
I could tell it upon his face.
Flying was truly his FIRST LOVE.
So, I settled for second place.
He was truthful and kind, this gentle man.
He thought the world just grand.
A stranger he had never met.
Just grinned and smiled, then shook their hand.

He tried to be a family man, and to the rules comply.
But FIRST LOVE was the only one
could put a twinkle in his eye.
They'd romp and play among the clouds,
happy, carefree as could be.
Oh, I was green with envy,
of FIRST LOVE AND HE.

FIRST LOVE always beaconed him,
"come let's sail off to the sky."
I shared him many, many times.
Many times, I said, "Goodbye."
One day, an Angel met them, romping through the sky so blue,
"Tell your FIRST and SECOND LOVE goodbye.
God has need of you."
He said, "I can't go just yet. FIRST LOVE and I have much to do."
The Angel took him by the hand, "Your Savior needs you, too."

"Life must go on." That's what they say.
"You must keep going day by day."
I turn my face up to the sky,
And can't but whisper, "Why?"
I know it was my Father's plan,
That FIRST LOVE take away my man.
Help me to understand why he
Chose FIRST LOVE instead of me.

I live now with my memories.
Yes, memories beyond compare.
I had many, many things, I guess,
that FIRST LOVE couldn't share.
So, no regrets. I'll carry on.
I know my Father has a plan.
I'm glad I rated second place,
back when it all began.

P.S. Someday, I'll go to meet him.
I'll greet him with a song.
I'll smile and say, "Don't worry, Dear.
I knew you brought FIRST LOVE along.
M.M.M (1969)

Good Shepherd Sunday

In 1989, on Good Shepherd Sunday, I sat in the church pew with those of our children still remaining at home. I was feeling more than just a little distracted. Back at the house, my bags were packed, and my one-way ticket was in the hand bag lying on my lap. In a few hours, I would leave Fort Wayne to fly to Fort Worth where I would be caretaker for Mama until she died. I was going alone. Three of the kids were out of the nest, one at college—living at home, and one was still in high school. Somehow, they and their Dad would have to manage on their own, taking care of each other, and none of us knew for how long.

Mama had been in chemo treatment for liver cancer for a year already, and her condition was deteriorating. My sister-in-law had done a mammoth job of taking her to her treatments and keeping the bills and insurance under control. But as home treatment was now needed, she was ready for me to come. They were both ready for me to come.

Mama nursed her mother when she was nearing her death, and I think she always assumed I would do the same for her. As it turned out, we returned from Australia in plenty of time for this to be possible.

Shortly after my arrival at Mama's it was determined that her veins were unable to tolerate any more chemotherapy, so it was discontinued. The time had come for taking care of her at home ... cooking nutritious meals and making sure she was comfortable. Mama was not taking pain medication, which was amazing, since I had been warned that liver cancer was one of the most painful there is.

Chemo had been so hard on Mama, that when it was stopped I think she actually began to feel better. Though there was not much she relished eating, we enjoyed our meals together in her bedroom, sitting at our TV trays in front of "Little House on the Prairie" and "Matlock". Before we retired each night, we would read the Bible for a while and have our evening prayers together.

Mama bathed and dressed every day and was always up, ready to face the day's challenges. While she did have to curb some of her normal activities, she didn't find the need to just lie around all day. After lunch, she would lie on the couch in the living room, and I would read aloud from one of her historical novels until she dozed off for her afternoon rest. She loved historical romances. I very much enjoyed spending that time with just her and me. I confess I had never read romantic historical novels until that time, and I suppose I enjoyed this time together even more than Mama did.

Some days, a friend would come by to visit and see how she was doing. She was always polite and tolerated company well, but inevitably, upon their leaving, she would say, "If only they could see what's in the bubble over my head." In other words, she was thinking, "Thank you for coming, but I'm so tired. Please, please go." She tired more and more easily as the days went by.

The next time we visited Mama's doctor, I made a point of telling the doctor just how things were at home, and how it was becoming more and more difficult for Mama to navigate to the bathroom and such. The doctor was stunned, because Mama had painted quite a different scenario for her. When the doctor realized this, she immediately ordered Hospice care. Within twenty-four hours, the equipment began arriving. I was surprised how many things they had to offer to make our home care easier for both of us.

It was very interesting to observe that this addition of the hospital bed and other items in the front bedroom seemed to signal to Mama that it was ok for her to let go. Her mind had been so sharp that one hardly knew she was ill. Once the intensity of the situation mounted, she became more and more confused, having fewer and fewer lucid moments. At one point, when I had pulled back the curtains on the side of the house, where one could see out the driveway side, for some reason, she was perturbed and said, "Well why don't you just put my bed out on the front porch and let nature take its course!" For this soft-spoken woman, this was pretty funny, but I don't think she meant it to be. I gently assured her that we just wanted to let some sunshine in and cheer her up.

Kurt and our youngest (15 years of age) had flown down for a short visit just during those last days. Mama was able to speak with them briefly and they were able to say their good-byes. They headed back to their airport hotel, and I was there alone again. At that point, Mama began slipping very quickly. Miraculously, I was able to catch Kurt and our son at the airport before they could leave for Fort Wayne. They were the only members of my family who were able to attend the funeral two days later.

Even though I called my brother to come, I was alone with Mama when she expired quite quickly. As her last breath was escaping, I was able to tell her I loved her and would always love her, words that had never been exchanged between us before this moment. I had heard that some cultures believe a person's spirit lingers as long as three days after death. I was counting on that, since it was important to me to know she heard my final declaration.

Mama, the eternal planner, had picked out the dress in which she wanted to be buried, along with the jewelry. She had exacted two promises from me. One was to check for chin hairs, and the other was to put woolen socks on her feet, as she had a horror of having cold feet under the ground. I did both for this now sainted woman. I've always been grateful that we could talk of death in such a way as allowed her to express what she really wanted.

When I went to the funeral home for the visitation time, she was wearing her glasses, so I put those away. Who sleeps with glasses? Who needs them in heaven? Also, I knew her hair was not to her liking, so I made the changes that made her look like herself.

My Mama had promised me that when she died, I could have her living room/dining room furniture. Though Kurt needed to return to Fort Wayne at that time, he soon returned with a 27' U Haul to drive Mama's things to our home in Indiana. What a labor of love, for him to do this. I have had many years of the joy of being surrounded by her lovely things. How nice that we shared such similar taste!

Those last weeks in the home where I grew up, spent with my Mama, in her last days, were a time I will always cherish. While I didn't really learn much more about her than I already knew, I hope she learned a few things about me that made her proud. Isn't it true that we always covet our parents' approval? I suppose we never really feel that we have "done it right". The generation gap makes many of us doubt ourselves, since ideas and behaviors in my parents' younger years were so different for me, and again, different for my own children. How thankful I am to have been given parents who took me to the Font, who led me in the way of Truth, through a church that remained faithful, despite the cultural changes.

Mama has been gone thirty years now, and I still miss her very much. I miss our phone calls, when I could make her laugh, when I could ask advice, when I tried to convince her I was a grown up, and that I had a measure of success at being a wife and mother. There was a big gap in our relationship. When I boarded that ship and went to the other side of the world, there was a great gulf created between us that neither of us could ever fill. She always said she just wanted her kids to be happy. I really hope she meant that, for indeed I have been happy.

I mentioned that Good Shepherd Sunday is the day I flew to Fort Worth to begin my last journey with Mama. Good Shepherd Sunday is one of my favorite days, partly because the hymns about the Good Shepherd are all so beautiful, and partly because of the memories it evokes from my past. I have found, through good and bad times, that the consistency of our Church's liturgical calendar, the hymns and readings assigned to specific Festivals keep my mind on those things which are important. Regardless of anything else that happens around me, those tried and true guidelines always reel me in and keep me grounded.

Mom and Dad in Dad's plane

Hang On, Little Peter!

Though I loved my Dad equally as well as I loved Mama, he was not as physically present in my life. Therefore, I have fewer happenings on which to base my memories of him. However, when he was present, we did extraordinary things together. He shared his love of flying with me, and we spent many hours in the heavens, following that horizon line.

Some of the hardest stories to tell are the best, I suppose. This one has taken a long time for me to deal with. Various versions of it floated around for a while, and I was not in the country to get the facts first hand at the time.

My Father was a consummate pilot, having taken to the air when he was a kid of 18. While he was gifted at many other things, flying was, as my Mother put it, his first love. You've been around people, I'm sure, who have such a passion for one thing that it is difficult for them to converse about anything else. That was my Dad about flying.

The thing I found exceptional and somewhat exciting about my Dad was that he didn't just know *how to fly*. He knew how airplanes were put together, where every part was, what made it all work, and what to do when something didn't work. This is how I knew that it was an unavoidable accident and not careless craftsmanship on the plane he died in. He had worked on planes, built planes, landed planes on highways, buzzed his local church as a young man, hired on as a stunt pilot at fairs, trained other pilots, tested new and renovated aircraft during the war. Nothing was more satisfying to him than standing around in a hanger on a Sunday afternoon with other pilots, exchanging stories, cigar hanging out of one corner of his mouth, wife and kids waiting in a smoldering hot car.

The final job my Dad had was as corporate pilot for the Coca Cola Bottling Company in Texas. His route was wherever the bosses were doing business, and his schedule was whenever it occurred to them to go. The company owned a little single engine Bonanza and a twin engine Beechcraft. They were hangered at an airport north of Fort Worth, and he personally maintained both of them.

In 1967, my Dad was diagnosed with chronic leukemia. He was about 57. I was no longer at home, so I'm not sure how this manifested itself in his daily life. I only have the memory of his saying, "I'm not going to worry. Worrying will kill you before anything else." Instead, he set about building a little airplane in his garage. He built it from a blueprint from Thorp. (Thorp was an aeronautical engineer who designed aircraft for Boeing.) This gave him something to think about and to do in his spare time.

As Dad's blood count rose and fell over the months, Mama would keep me informed, telling me that he was doing well and that as long as he didn't get an infection, he would be ok. They went through the whole carrot juicing treatment, and he was on meds, lost a lot of weight due to his illness, and carried on.

In order for him to be allowed to take passengers in his little plane, he first had to log fifty hours of flying—which he had worked really hard to accomplish before we returned home one Thanksgiving, so he could take us up. Our family and I had the joy of flying over Fort Worth (one family member at a time as the plane was a small two-seater) that last year. It was a legal necessity that Dad have a little plate which read "EXPERIMENTAL" below the window of the cockpit. This did not present alarm to anyone except Kurt, as we all knew Dad/Granddad was such a good pilot. Kurt had a strong aversion to small planes in general, but since he respected my dad's flying skills, he braved a short spin. I had shared the cockpit in many planes with Dad over the years, but this was the most exciting of them all. It was glorious, like flying on the back of a bird.

One Sunday in February, 1969, Dad decided he wanted to go out to do some touch and go's with the plane. He wanted Mama to go along, but she had other things to do. So he took Peter, the little miniature white poodle, and off they went to the air strip.

I have never seen an official report from the FAA, but the story goes that he was taking off and landing, circling, and then repeating the procedure. He received a radio alert that another pilot in trouble needed to make an emergency landing, and thus Dad needed to clear the runway. In the process of the sudden ascent, the wings snapped just near the body of the plane, and he plummeted to earth.

The owners at the airport, with whom he had been friends and in business for decades, got word of this accident immediately from Waco. They called my brother to tell him they were pretty sure it was Dad's plane. My brother jumped in the car to get over to Mama's. She had been listening to the radio and had heard about a crash in Waco, but she was sure it was someone else. On the way to Mama's house, my brother had to hear of his father's death by name on the news before anyone officially notified the family. It was a horrific experience for him. As an adult, he had developed a great friendship with Dad. They shared many interests and projects out in the garage, and had joined in the work of remodeling my parents' home over the years. This sudden blow was very difficult.

The plane had to be hauled back to the airport. My Dad was taken to the undertakers'. My brother and Mama had to make arrangements. It fell to my brother to call me in Australia to tell me that my Daddy was gone.

I remember the milk man coming to the door right after I got the call. I was crying and the poor man didn't know what to think. He was the first person I told. He nervously handed me the bottles, expressed his sorrow, and hastened off. It was not a nice time to be alone.

Since the children and I had been back to the States in November, just three months before, we could not afford for me to go back for the funeral. I felt so helpless, unable to help Mama through this dreadful time. She never saw her husband again. There was too much damage to his body for an open casket funeral. She never saw her little puppy, Peter, again either. I'm told his body was never recovered, even though they looked all over the area. No one knew what happened to him.

When Mama wrote to me about the funeral, she said the front of the church was banked with flowers, and there were hundreds of people there she didn't know. Dad never knew a stranger, and all his pilot friends from all over the country came to his funeral.

Someone has recently been interviewed for a new book he wrote about how to improve your life. He said there is a resume persona in each of us, a list of our talents and qualifications that make us good at our work. But there is also a eulogy persona in each of us, the characteristics that we have that make people remember us when we're gone, the things we do by which we help and improve the lives of others. My Dad had a short list of resume characteristics. The work on the farm required him to leave school early, and he didn't have plaques and framed citations hanging on the walls all over the house. But I have known few people who had more friends than my Dad.

Dad was honored to be a member of The Quiet Birds, an association of esteemed pilots around the country. A couple of weeks following Dad's funeral, a delegation of fellow members surprised Mama at home one day with a gift of a beautiful little black poodle. His name was QB. (QB for

Quiet Birds—a beautiful way for Mama to recall Dad whenever she used QB's name!)

From time to time I think back on those last moments of time for my Dad in that cockpit—and how God, even in the moment of death is still answering our prayers. For as many times as he said he wanted his death to occur in the sky, not in some depressing hospital, I wondered how he reacted when he knew he wasn't going to pull out of this one. It seemed the most natural thing in the world for him to have said, "Hang on, little Peter! Here we go!"

First Marriage

Growing Up — Growing Wise

How, then, did I arrive in a place where someone would whisper to me, "Love him for us"? Let me tell you.

On the very night of my high school graduation, in my youth and inexperience, I entered into one of the most confusing, disappointing, and emotionally torturous times of my life.

Barbara - High School Graduation, 1959

During the middle of my junior year of high school, I became engaged to an airman I had been going out with (double dating with other couples) since my sophomore year. My airman was a handsome fellow and I was crazy about him. When he was transferred from my home town to a base in another state, during the middle of my junior year, we had the understanding that we would be married as soon as I finished high school. He gave me an engagement ring, and it was official. When proms and end-of-year dances came up, I would go with my friends, some girls, some boys. One of my friends and I would double date with a couple of neat guys from our biology class, and we went Dutch to everything. However, it was quite universal, already in those years, that many of the kids in the senior class were either engaged or pregnant.

My airman and I left on good terms, and it seemed my future was set. But before long, he stopped writing, and it became clear that we were not going to survive a long-distance romance. With my mother's encouragement, I broke off the engagement and packed his ring up and returned it by post.

I should have known from experience that he was not the kind of guy who ever accepted "losing" at anything. Sure enough, almost immediately after receiving his ring back, he began pursuing me again. I was too young and naïve to "just say no", and we began a clandestine correspondence with him sending letters to me at my girlfriend's address. I knew Mama would not be happy about this renewed interest.

He was one of the most handsome boys I had ever met, and I did actually love him. While we were much the same age, he was much more street smart than I. Being with him made me feel very grown up. Before long, it was agreed that he would return to Texas and we would be married the night of my graduation. The fat was in the fire.

When he returned to Fort Worth, we had to go to the courthouse to get our marriage license. I was old enough to not require parental permission, but he was not. (I had met his parents only once, while he still lived in my home town. He was an only child, and his mother doted on him. That visit was the first time that I realized you could put more than one piece of bologna on a sandwich. His mother super-sized everything even way back then, and enjoyed spoiling him. His father was a sweet man who had grown comfortable saying "yes" to everything.)

In order to procure the license, he had to notify his parents that he planned to marry, and they had to send some kind of notarized form of permission to the courthouse, allowing us to go forward with our plans.

I was not comfortable going to the pastor at my own church (he being new), so we arranged to see a pastor at another local Lutheran church. There we received a short counseling session and that pastor's agreement to marry us. As I reflect on the whole thing, I cannot help but wonder how this pastor did not see that this was not a good idea. Though I was crazy about this young man, I still wasn't even dating alone; I had mail going to a friend's house so my mom wouldn't find out; and I was going to a pastor other than the one at my life-long church. He had to know, after giving us a superficial survey, that we had little in common that would make a good marriage, especially a Christian marriage. My airman had no interest in daily devotions, and nominal church attendance was about the most he would commit to—and that reluctantly. Rather than discouraging us or making us wait, especially since I was so young and still not graduated from high school, this pastor agreed to marry us.

My mother, poor thing, was so disappointed that I allowed this fellow back into my life. She had been so happy when he moved away, because she thought he was a little too sophisticated for her daughter. But she didn't show her displeasure enough to make me stop the process, and we spent time together, shopping for things a new bride should have.

So there we were. After my big high school graduation at a huge coliseum, we went to the chosen Lutheran church to be married. On the night of what should have been remembered as a time of good friends parting ways and celebrations of success all round, it became the night I gave away all vestiges of real freedom and happiness by joining myself to this man in marriage. I processed, along with hundreds of other seniors across the stage to receive my high school diploma, hugged all my friends good bye, and drove off to the church, where in the presence of two of my friends, two of my airman's friends, my parents and my brother, we gathered around the altar where we made vows and were married.

The ceremony was short and sweet, with a few photos taken afterward. If my memory serves me, we all went to a steakhouse for a celebration meal. (Oddly, I learned later that this pastor who performed our wedding was the brother of the pastor who had confirmed Kurt Marquart years earlier. What a small world.)

Once Mama knew of my plans, she and I had shopped for some pretty nighties. They were so elegant and beautiful in my eyes—and much more expensive than anything Mama had ever owned. They were as gorgeous as anything in the movies! She also purchased a necklace that was called "The Pearl of Wisdom" for a wedding gift.

I'm quite sure she didn't realize it at the time, but years earlier, as a very young teen, I had stumbled into the hallelujah psalms and when I came to Ps. 111:10, like a special seed, it became planted in my heart. *"The fear of the LORD is the beginning of wisdom; a good understanding have all those who do His commandments."* When, then, she gave the necklace to me, that pearl became a regular reminder to me of that Psalm. I wore the necklace nearly every day for several years. When we lived in Australia, however, the eldest daughter of one of our dear friends was being confirmed one year. She was a particularly devout young woman and we enjoyed a strong bond. I gave the necklace to her, so that in coming years of growing into maturity, both as a woman, and as a Christian, she, too, might draw on the strength of the same Psalm.

Entering into my first married night with my new husband, I was excited to have such lovely things to wear, gowns I thought would please him, too. It was very disappointing when he snarled at me that if I wanted to share the night with him, I needed to get rid of all that fluff and bother. Little-by-little, from that time on, all the lovely things that I thought women were supposed to do and receive were painfully peeled away like the bark from a tree. There was no consummation of the marriage that night.

The morning following the wedding, we returned to the home of my parents in order to collect my belongings. I remember being in the driveway, loading up, and Mama telling my husband, "Be good to her. She needs a lot of lovin'." This was the first time I ever left home, and one would expect there might have been some strong emotions. But Mama never cried, so there was a tearless farewell. While she never expressed her true feelings about my airman, she didn't express any enthusiasm either, and our leaving was under a cloud of doubt and disappointment. I never understood her when I was young. Only as I age myself do I get a glimpse of why she reacted the way she did sometimes. Many years later I was given a poem she wrote after I left. (The poem is included elsewhere in this book.)

We drove off into the sunset with high hopes—at least I had them. My husband had secured an apartment in a house, where we stayed for several months. Still our marriage had not been consummated. I *was* admittedly quite naïve, but not to the extent that I thought it was normal to never make love. The impression I had of the whole situation was that I was too unattractive, not sexy enough, not a good enough cook, too . . . well, —whatever. The development of any level of self-esteem is difficult when one is addressed as "Goody Two Shoes", which became his name for me. When we decided to move to a different apartment, I really thought this would be a fresh start and would mend our marriage and all would be well. Hope springs eternal in young women. However, even a new apartment did not change the state of my marriage.

The new apartment was kitty-corner from the pastor of the Lutheran church I attended. This pastor paid me a visit when I was home alone, and though I insisted that my husband was not at home, thus not a good time to visit, he put a foot in the door and took it upon himself to enter. The conversation had nothing to do with where we had come from, what we were doing in Indiana, or what our church background had been. Rather, the first, quite inappropriate question was, "How's your sex life?" It was a most uncomfortable visit, and I did not return to his church for a long time after that, going instead with the bookkeeper from work to her church. She was Presbyterian, and I didn't practice fellowship with her church body, but neither did I want to miss worship altogether. By then my husband was refusing to go to church, especially after the peculiar visit from the pastor. This was distressing since in my home town when we were engaged, he attended worship with me and had actually enrolled in the adult class in preparation to join the congregation. However, he was transferred to the new base prior to completing the class and prior to joining the church.

One weekend my parents paid us a short visit and we did go to the Lutheran church. As we were greeted at the end of the service, my parents were told, "Well, I guess the only way to get your daughter to church is for you to come to town." I thank God that he was not typical of the pastors of our Synod. I don't know what ever happened to him, but when I returned to my parents' home in Texas after the divorce, he would not give my new pastor transfer papers, and wrote that I was an unrepentant sinner and not a member in good standing.

As for my marriage, I am not capable of accurately describing the sad existence my husband and I lived. We married on May 28, 1959 and were divorced in February 1961—having lived in the same apartments together, but not as husband and wife.

The last time I saw him, he was distraught, frustrated, confused, twisted, but quite pleased to be rid of me. He filed for divorce, charging me with cruel and inhuman treatment, because I would not file for a divorce. (This requires no justification to anyone because he and I both know the truth, and that's the important thing.)

So it was, after coming home "damaged goods" to live with my parents, knowing nothing of what lay ahead, I found myself in limbo. The divorce would take some time to finalize, and truthfully, I didn't know if my husband would actually go through with it. It didn't really matter that I should not be seeing other men already, since in my mind at that time, Scripture dictated that I never remarry.

Since one hesitates to confess defeat, I told my parents little of my married life. On the one occasion that they came to visit, my husband really put on a show for them, and it was not possible for them to know how horrible things were between us. However, when I called to tell them that he had filed for divorce, I'm sure Mama was behind my Dad flying up the very next day to extricate me from that apartment.

While it was likely painful and embarrassing for them to have to receive this daughter back into their established tranquil lifestyle, they did. And in their own way, I'm sure my folks made it as pleasant as possible for me to start a new life.

In the most difficult times in our lives, we can look back and see that even then, the Lord is preparing us for our next steps. For me, this was in the job I procured while in this first marriage. I worked for about a year in the office of a factory. That along with having attended a technical high school, rather than the one all of my friends were attending, gave me the training and experience to obtain a job later in my life.

Shortly after arriving back at my parents' home, out of the blue, who should appear at our front door, but the pastor at the church I had grown up in. He just happened to pop in for a visit. His intention was to welcome me back to my home church. His ulterior motive was to ask me to be his private secretary.

Since the Pastor's arrival in Fort Worth, his wife had been serving as the secretary, but her mother had since come to live with them and required much of his wife's time. It had been determined that she should leave her job. It was perfect timing, since a week or so earlier I would not have been in town, and the job would have fallen to someone else.

With my training, as well as the experience I had gained at my job in Indiana, dealing with the public and supporting three executive bosses, I knew I could handle the work. It was a huge congregation, but there were volunteers to help with the printing. The pastor not only gave me gainful employment, but he validated me before the membership by hiring me as his personal secretary.

I had during high school been exposed to a guest preacher who made one remark, words from our Lord, that stuck with me, that I'd not heard before, and have not heard often enough since. It was from St. John 9. It read, *"As long as it is day, we must do the work of Him who sent me. Night is coming when no one can work."* It had a sense of urgency that I felt keenly, and believed that at some point, my life needed to be anchored in the service of the Lord. At one point in my high school years, a Vicar assigned to our church, encouraged me to attend Concordia Seward. By the time I was in a position to apply, they were no longer accepting applications. Recalling that encouragement, along with the St. John verse gave me the impetus in my second chance (after the divorce) to spend my time serving the Lord.

While my marriage had been a failure, and while it is a time in my life that I wish I could have avoided, I believe the experience prepared me to be a much better pastor's wife than I might have otherwise been. My husband didn't call me "Miss Goody Two Shoes" for nothing. Most things, for me, were either black or white. I had little tolerance for the gray area in people's behavior. They were either "good" or they were "bad". What happened to me taught me that, indeed, bad things do happen to good people. It taught me that sometimes people are trapped by their circumstances, or lack of wisdom, or whatever. One thing was sure: Not only can you not judge a book by its cover, but the book isn't over until it's over.

II
BARBARA & KURT

Voyage, Wedding, Honeymoon

The Courtship

Journal chapter
Ah, yes, there it was. It had followed me around the world, and had occupied my shelves for so long, it had become invisible. But there it sat among the "how to" books that I keep for research, wonderful little bits of helpful advice and wisdom that I like to quote in articles I write for other women, Christian women, many of whom are spouses to pastors of the Church.

Bound in faded blue denim, with burgundy tape protecting its corners, "RECORD" is stamped in black on the front, and an attractive black pattern decorates the edges. It is Account Book No. 50-300 from Herald Square, according to the inside cover, from the Stationary Department, F. W. Woolworth Co. Money Back Guarantee. In the top left corner is "$1.00".

At the very top of the front cover, in black ink, and about one inch tall is "1961". And in cursive below is *"Personal Account of My Job. . . Secretary to the Pastor"* with a black cross drawn below. On the inside page is written:

This is Personal and Confidential Material
Recorded by Barbara Ann Martens,
to be kept as personal and confidential.
This book is written for the
purpose of preserving interesting,
inspiring, and memorable incidents
which will follow my life,

*as I "write it", as a Pastoral Secretary.
Names of persons in some of the
following incidents will be omitted,
as they aren't important.
B. A. M.*

Gathered together and secured by a red rubber band that was growing weak with age, was a pile of letters. They were written on blue airletters, the kind that are triple-folded and sealed that would travel by Air Mail at a much cheaper rate than a sealed letter. Also, there were many letters some hand written, some typed, on fine onion skin. These were in the back of the blue Journal.

Taken together, the entries in the Journal, written by myself when I was twenty years old, and the correspondence attached to it, write a love story. It's not my love story. It's not "our love story". It's God's Love Story, and they are always the best.

There have been more than a few people, over the years, who have asked, with some incredulity, "How did you two ever end up together." It's a fair question, I suppose, given that Kurt Marquart was a highly cultured European, fluent in numerous languages, with impeccable manners, and known for his giant intellect. I, on the other hand, was a young, middle class, Texas cowgirl, educated in a local technical high school to be a secretary. In my own world, I held my own pretty well, but I was totally unfamiliar with his. "My Fair Lady" readily comes to mind.

Barbara on Ranch Day
(Texas Cowgirl)

When the questions came, therefore, one fumbled around, trying to make obvious the fact that neither of us had much to do with it at all. God knew what he had in mind, and despite the obstacles I kept putting in His way, finally His plan was put into place, and as Kurt wrote in his first letter to me, after I accepted his proposal, "The die is cast."

It was a happy rediscovery for me to recently uncover these writings. From the beginning, our courtship was recorded, and while it may have seemed rather unorthodox at the time, looking back, it is clear that God planted a deep affection in my heart for this man that enabled me to walk away from my life in this country and travel over 12,000 miles around the world to marry him. By the way, the theme song for our wedding was, "Around the World", sung by Nat King Cole.

In a little while, I'll tell you some of the background, much of which makes the outcome of our lives even more inconceivable, humanly speaking. At this point, I think it might be more fun for you to know as little as I did about Kurt Marquart, his background, even his age. For the first time ever, the Journal and excerpts from our letters will be published. You can ride the roller coaster of emotion that they describe. Shall we?

In the Journal – "To This Time"
(all in beautiful long hand, in ink)

Up to this date, Jan. 28, 1961, my life has been hectic, insecure, and undecided most of the time. I've gone through twelve years of school, made above average grades, graduated with a special diploma in Business Education, married, lived in Indiana, was divorced, moved to Texas, was accepted, and given a job.

As for my marriage, I am not capable of accurately describing the pitifully sad existence my husband and I lived. His name was Charles. He was stationed at Carswell A.F.B when we met in 1957. We were married May 28, 1959 and were divorced in Feb. of 1961. The last time I saw him, he was distraught, frustrated, confused, twisted, but quite pleased to be rid of me. He filed for divorce because I wouldn't, thus I was charged with cruel and inhuman treatment. This requires no justification to anyone because he and I both know the truth, and that's the important thing. So I left him in the service in Indiana and returned to my home in Texas.

Our culture during the time of these eventualities, not to mention the culture among Christians, frowned upon divorced women. I probably would have been among them, in the earlier years, when everything seemed to me to be black or white when it came to human behavior.

The climate, therefore, even among my immediate family members, was cool. My parents took me into their home, lock, stock and barrel, and I settled in for a period of recovery, and discovery. The embarrassment my Mother felt was evident. One could almost predict the comments coming from her friends, who until then had always considered me "Margaret Martens' little girl", a good kid, now ruined for life.

When I wasn't trying to be somewhat useful around the house to earn my keep, I attempted contact with former friends, girlfriends I went to school with, or with whom I had grown up with in church. I checked out a couple of boys with whom I had been friends for years, and was amazed at the response, "I've always loved you and am so happy you're back." Emotions rode a crazy roller coaster as I tried to establish for myself just who Barbara Martens was. (I took my maiden name back.)

One morning, my Mother and I were surprised by a knock at the front door. We were not expecting anyone, and Mother rarely had visitors. On the porch was this tall gentleman, dressed in black clerical garb, watching the busy traffic racing by the house.

"Good morning, ladies! I hope you don't mind my popping in like this. I thought I'd drop by to see how you're doing, Barbara." He came in and made himself at home. My Mother offered coffee, but he was not interested.

This was all just a tad embarrassing. This man was Pastor Edwin Pieplow, the pastor at my home congregation whom I had resisted when we needed pre-marital counseling. I had not particularly liked him when he came along to replace my childhood pastor, Walter E. Dorre, who had gone to South America to head up missions. Here he sat on my Mother's couch.

"Have you been able to find work?", he asked me. "Nothing yet."

"I have a proposition for you. My wife, Alma, has been serving St. Paul's as my secretary since we arrived last year. But now her mother has come to live with us, and Alma is required at home. I am looking for a private secretary who can also serve as office secretary for the congregation. I wondered if you might be interested."

As a graduate with a Special Diploma in Business, I had good training in shorthand, typing, printing, business math, telephone operations, etc. And I had a year's experience in the office of Moon Welding and Machine Corp. in Kokomo, Indiana.

"The fact that you grew up with the folks at St Paul would be very helpful to me. It's a big congregation, and I still can't make all the connections. What would you say about coming for a week to work with Alma, and see if you can handle it?"

I thought my Mother would fall out of her chair. It would be a feather in her maternal cap if her daughter could land a job like that at the church.

"I think that would be a good idea. That way, I could train on the job, and Alma could pass on all her secrets. When would you like me to start?"

"Tomorrow would be perfect!" His enthusiasm was contagious, and somehow I knew things were going to be all right from then on. His invitation validated me among the people of that congregation, and in no time at all, I was happily renewing old friendships with young and old alike.

Since, I've been given the position of secretary to the Pastor of St Paul Lutheran Church. I have been broken in and will be placed on full time pay Feb. 1. This is where my writings begin, with my new job.

Pastor Pieplow

Pastor Edwin E. Pieplow is definitely one of the most dynamic men I've ever met. His smile races all over his face, and his handshake, while just short of torture, truly lets you know what dwells within his heart. He allows love to flow freely . . . and it glows on his exterior. He is as tall as a mountain and possesses the same height in integrity. His messages "beller" out to the world soaking the air with the positive attitude that "everyone has the potential of being a saint". In fact, these were his very words when he illustrated the fact that he believes in people. Everyone deserves a chance, and mistakes are tolerated in his sight when repentance is apparent. He accepted me as he saw me, and without probing to any degree to discover the real causes of my unhappiness, invited me to share with him the joys and sorrows of God's eternal work by becoming his secretary. Again, exploding with confidence and completely assured that my presence was arranged by Heaven, he was "positive" that I was the one he needed and that he was the one I needed.... His only request is that I never cry.

And so it was, after coming back "damaged goods" to my parents' home, knowing nothing of what lay ahead, after being in limbo for a while, finally my life would begin to have direction again. The divorce would take some time to finalize. It didn't really matter that I shouldn't be seeing other men already, since in my mind at that time, Scripture dictated that I never remarry.

One important thing I didn't write about Pastor Pieplow was that he was an incurable romantic and match maker. Every time he ran on to a man he liked, he made sure to mention him to me, and more often than not, we ended up meeting. Since my divorce was not yet final, this tended to make things awkward for both me and any suitor. At the same time, it insured that I give any new relationship plenty of time.

The Journal notes that on February 2 ~ *The Reverend Kurt Marquart came by to see Pastor and 'chatted a bit'.* Suddenly, he was standing in the door of my office. I had not seen him come down the hill in his car. But there he was, in his black suit and clerical collar, very tall and poised. He had come to consult with Pastor Pieplow about taking over his parish after he left. I had never met him, nor had I heard of him before.

O, my goodness, what a beautiful accent! "I don't recall seeing you here before," he said. "Are you the new Mrs. Pieplow?" Well, he didn't mean that literally, of course. "I believe Pastor is expecting me." Pastor Pieplow must have overhead us and immediately popped his head out of his office. "Ah, Kurt! Good to see you. Come right in, won't you?" He gave me a great smile as he went by my desk.

"Barbara", Pastor said, when they came out of the study. "I'd like you to meet Pastor Kurt Marquart from Weatherford. He's off to Australia soon, and I'll be his vacancy pastor until a new man is Called." Ah, ha. "Pleased to meet yous" were exchanged, and then he left. Strangely, apart from his attractive accent, the thing I most noticed about him were his beautiful hands.

Suddenly, he stuck his head back into the office and said, "Know anyone who's looking to buy a car? Sadly, I can't take mine along to Australia." Being a prospective buyer, since I had been riding the bus to work, I told him I would ask my brother to come by and give it a bit of a test drive, since my Dad was out of town. It was a '57 Desoto 4 door, air conditioned, power everything, radio front and back, and in very good condition.

Upon a brief inspection, Brother Bill diplomatically said it was fine but would be hard to drive and maintain. (I presume because it was large, and no doubt a gas guzzler.) I could not restrain my excitement. My very first car, all my own. I didn't even have a license yet! I suppose it was not astute of me to make such a sudden decision, but because Pastor Marquart was leaving town on the 10th, he needed a commitment.

Feb. 2 ~ *I have a special feeling about this car. I feel as if it's just meant for me, just came about like everything else has. And it would please me to do him the favor of loving it as he did. He's off to Australia and has to do away with it.*

The good pastor most likely could have made a better deal, had he not been distracted with all the details of leaving the country. He was still packing up his library for shipping, unloading the lease on his apartment, and making final calls on all his members. The one remaining detail was the disposing of the car, complicated by the fact that he would have continued need of it until he left.

As people today are fond of saying, "long story short". . . The following day, I called Pastor Marquart to tell him that I had decided to purchase his car and that my parents had agreed to help me finance that. He was relieved at the news, but insisted that I should take it out on a test drive myself, just to be sure. He would have it washed and would come around to pick me up after work.

It was unusually beautiful that afternoon in February. We decided to take advantage of the nice weather and drive to Eagle Mountain Lake. It was the first time we had actually been alone together, and the drive allowed us to finally have a conversation. My status as a divorcee was mentioned, only because he threw out that famous line, "How come someone as pretty as you are is not married?" After a brief, unpleasant explanation of my disastrous and failed union, he commented that everyone he was ever inclined to like was either married or engaged. Apart from those rather noncommittal topics, we discussed philosophical matters more than anything to do with his background.

When we finally arrived back at the church, we agreed that I would purchase his car and that he could keep it until he had to leave town. He was going to New York and other points North to visit family and friends before leaving the country, and would not require it.

Feb. 3 ~ *I decided something else today. I decided I like Kurt very much. I feel a great personal loss because he's leaving – and I told him so. Each of us said how much we wished we had met sooner.*

Feb. 4 ~ All I could think about all day was Kurt. I finally decided that all this business about the car was meant to happen to give us an excuse to become better acquainted. . . and to stay in touch after he leaves. I believe someday he will come back for me.

Feb. 5 ~ Today, Trinity dedicated their new church. It's a lovely, reverent place. It was the first time I heard Kurt preach today. From such a quiet man, I never expected such a rich sermon. My heart and soul leap for joy as I admit to myself that I love him. I didn't want to when I learned he was leaving. But each day, I find myself drawn to him more and more. Every prayer contains pleas for God to guide me to what He has planned for me.

All right. Call it all the rambling daydreams of a young girl, if you will. Story book nonsense. But it's true that I was very awestruck by this man, and the fact shook me up a bit, after what I had been through with Charles. You see, I grew up with an older brother, who was four years my senior. He was such a gentleman and was my hero. When Charles didn't turn out to be like him, I discovered that most men were not like him. I rather lost any hope of every finding a "special" person again.

Overnight, we were thrown into this flurry of meetings in order to transfer the ownership of the Desoto. Because all the paperwork had to be done in Weatherford, we were required to spend some time together. We had lunch at one of his favorite Italian places, had the title transferred and attended to the insurance. He made sure I had a drivers' manual, since I didn't have a license yet. Naturally, we had much to talk about. He was excited to be going to Australia, and he related amusing exchanges with people who had asked him if he planned to drive there. Australia was not yet the tourist attraction it has become, and many people didn't even know if the people who lived there spoke English. I even had to look at a world atlas to see where it was!

I asked him how it came to pass that the Australians had extended a Call to him. He told me that he and some of his colleagues had attended the Synodical Convention in San Francisco, and while there, he had been impressed by the strong stance taken by the Australian delegation. He had an opportunity to speak with the Queensland District President, the Rev. F. W. Noack, who was scouting for a confessional man to fill a vacancy in Toowoomba, where the mother church was located. He was also interested in Australia, because one of his friends had received a Call there some time before, but had declined it. Now it was his turn to go "down under".

Feb. 7 ~ I let him keep the car until Friday. He will bring me home from work, then we will get a cab to the bus station. Then the car will be mine – but he will be gone. He insists that we write and said he hoped to be back in the States often. If I never see him again, I shall be thankful that I got to know him as well as I did. A finer man I shall find hard to find.

Returning to work the following day, after all the bulletins were printed, and we were able to pack it in for the day, Pastor Pieplow called me into his study to take some dictation. I told him I had purchased the car and would be taking Kurt to the bus station the next day. He asked me what I thought of him, and I told him I was pretty impressed with him. Pastor was strangely reluctant to toss all his support my way, saying, while Kurt was "head and shoulders above any theologian in Synod", I could do better. He said if he received an anticipated invitation to go to St Louis to teach an intensive, he would take me along, and we would scout out the seminary students. Nevertheless, if I felt strongly that I liked the man, I should write to him, and wait to see if God had future plans for us. He insisted that no matter who I married, he believed I would make a fine pastor's wife.

Feb 10 ~ *Today was one of the hardest, yet one of the nicest days, I've ever had. I worked hard at the office. I had trouble with the bulletin, so didn't get it finished until after noon. I finished typing Pastor's sermon and got the office in good order. Kurt was half an hour late, but was considerate enough to call me. We went to Harris Hospital for him to make a call on one of his members. Then we quickly ate a sandwich. We dashed home and grabbed a cab, and got to the bus station just in time. I had rehearsed all day what I would say, but didn't. I gave him my picture, which pleased him. He said he was going to get married soon, and the parsonage in Australia would hold a dozen children. He reminded me to write. I said he'd have to write first, and he assured me that he would. He said I'd done a great deal for him, when I told him he'd helped me so much. He said he was glad this wasn't a permanent good bye, to which I agreed. He will be back here for a few days in about six weeks. It's wonderful to have something to live for and to look forward to.*

Life goes on. . .

O.K. It's time to take a break from this steamy romance. Six weeks. That's an eternity to anyone who is walking an emotional tightwire. So let's fill in this little break with some background, so you will more ably understand the dynamics.

Please understand that the whole idea of becoming a pastor's wife was very secondary in this whole business. I knew nothing of that role, other than what I had witnessed in the public life of the pastor's wife in our congregation as I was growing up. She was a sweet and kind lady, obviously in love with her husband, happy, and adored by everyone. That was the picture I always had in my mind of the clergy family. No one ever breathed anything about how terrible it might be to be married to a pastor, that you couldn't cultivate your own career or have your own friends outside the parish. I had heard none of the horror stories about children being expected to be perfect or pastors' wives having to play the organ and sing in the choir, and teach Sunday School, preferably with one hand tied behind her back.

From the time I was a teenager, Eva Meyer, a spinster at our church, reminded me over and over again that I would make a great pastor's wife. I never gave her idea a two-minute thought. I assumed she thought it was her duty to tell all the kids they would make good pastors, teachers, or pastors' wives. She had been the self-appointed youth director for decades before we began having vicars who took over that position. It must have been a real slap in the face, after all her dedication to the youth of the church. I don't think she had a life outside her work with the teens at St Paul Lutheran Church, and goodness knows what she did with her time when it was all over.

Apart from that, I was in no way exceptional. In fact, I have an unpleasant memory of being so mouthy to my Dad, that my Mom threatened to ask the Pastor to come and make an intervention. No saintliness there. As well, my own Father once made the remark, "I feel sorry for whoever marries you."

One year, a Synodical college choir came to sing at our church. As one never fond of guest preachers, it was not the treat for me that I'm sure was intended. The preacher made one remark, however, words from our Lord, that stuck with me, that I'd not heard before, and I've not heard often enough since. It was from St John 9 and read, "As long as it is day, we must do the work of Him Who sent me. Night is coming when no one can work." It had a sense of urgency that I felt keenly, and believed that at some point, my life needed to be anchored in the service of the Lord.

Serious thought towards full time church work was finally given me by one of our Vicars, George Lange, who was eager for me to attend Concordia, Seward. By the time I was in a position to apply, they were no longer accepting applications and recommended that I go to a Junior College. But with that dream being shattered, it didn't make sense to pursue it further. Besides, my parents didn't have the money to send me to college.

Back to the Journal

Feb. 13 ~ I had an awful time keeping things going at work. It seemed like we had so many interruptions. Today was paper day, and we were busy all day. But my day of labor was rewarded by a card from Kurt. He wrote at 4:00 am from Tulsa. I was so excited, I could hardly contain myself. I had no one to tell or share my joy with. I read the few words he'd squeezed onto it over and over, reading between the lines and interpreting every way it could be. I'll be so glad when I have an address so I can write him.

Feb. 14 ~ What a day! Things were busy at work. I had to type Pastor's Lenten sermon in between everything else. I took my driving test today. The written test was pretty hard and I passed the driving test by a slight margin. But I passed, and can drive without feeling guilty now. I miss Kurt so much and keep thinking he will come driving up over the hill at any moment. I'll be so glad when I can write to him. He's on my mind all the time. I'm so afraid I'm in for disappointment. But even if things don't work out for us, at lest they have worked out for me and God.

Enter Officer Chandler

On Feb. 16 ~ *On my way home from a dinner with a girlfriend, I was stopped by a policeman on a motor bike. Good grief! I'd only had the car a few days and already in trouble with the law? At least I had a valid license to show him.*

"Good evening, ma'm". But his look said, "Hi, good lookin'. How are you tonight?" "Fine." "Just wanted to let you know that your left headlight is burned out." "Really? No, I just bought this car, and this is the first time I've driven at night. I'll get it fixed first thing." On my way home, I stopped at the first gas station I could and some kind man replaced my headlight.

Next day at work, I received a phone call from Officer Chandler. "Just wondered if you had gotten that light fixed?" How he knew where I worked, I couldn't say. But assured him it was taken care of. "Just thought if you hadn't, I'd be happy to take care of that for you."

There were several people in the office, and it was a tad bit awkward when he persisted by asking me out to lunch! Naturally, I turned him down and told him I was busy and hung up.

Feb. 21 ~ *Still no letter. Heard from June (Charles' mother) and she says that Charles went back to Indiana for the hearing.*

Feb. 24 ~ *Still no letter. We both worked so hard today. Pastor and I talked about Charles again. He just can't understand it all. He acts like I may not be telling him everything. He can't figure out why Charles would let me go. Sympathetic and wise, and yet he doesn't give me a chance to go around feeling sorry for myself.*

Feb. 26 ~ *I am anxious to hear from the courts in Indiana. Somehow, I feel Kurt is waiting until I am legally divorced before writing.*

Mar. 5 ~ *Officer Chandler continues to call. When I mentioned him to Pastor, he just said I was "destined to be a minister's wife, not a policeman's wife."*

Mar. 7 ~ *Still no letter. Grant me patience, Lord, to see Your will and do* *it to Your satisfaction. If it is to be that I go through life alone, please help me adjust to that life. In Thy Name. Amen.*

Mar. 9 ~ *Still haven't heard from Kurt. I still feel like he and I are destined to be together. But only time will tell. We both have a lot of decisions to make.*

Mar. 14 ~ *I finally went out with Don Chandler. We went on a double date with my friends to a movie and dinner. He's really a very nice guy.*

I did have a few dates with Don. He, like me, was divorced with two kids. I met them at his house one night for dinner, but they didn't like me. It became evident that he was really shopping for a mom for his kids, and I could understand that. While we saw each other a couple of times, we gradually drifted apart.

Mar. 24 ~ *I finally received a letter from Kurt. I might add, a lovely letter which brought me back to earth once again. He wants us to continue our correspondence, and hopes the future brings us together. He got into Dallas sometime today and goes to Tyler tomorrow. Then he will be in Weatherford Sunday and suggests we spend some time together that afternoon. I've been awfully sick with a cold, so don't know how we will arrange things yet. I'm exhausted. I'm down to 120 pounds now and look a little sickly.*

Over the weeks of waiting, many new developments had evolved. I had been asked to share an apartment with the new youth director who had been Called to St Paul's. I had been appointed to oversee the Junior Youth Group, and keep them busy. Both ends of my candle were being burned simultaneously.

At the same time, I was sensitive to the fact that this was my final chance, a time that would not likely return, a time for me to discover whether there was any spark of hope for the future with this amazing man. We had enjoyed just enough time together for me to know there was no one else in the world like him and once he was gone, the chance of his coming back to Texas was very unlikely, even though he had said he would. His attachment to the people in Weatherford was loving and strong, but not the sort of thing one cultivates long distance over a long period of time.

Mar. 26 ~ *I woke up at 5:45 this morning and got ready for church at Trinity. I got there a little early. But so did Kurt. We sat together and then afterwards he invited me to a picnic they were having. The gathering was a little uncomfortable because I felt a little obvious. But we didn't stay very long. We went out to the farm where he had lived while here, and then to Chandor Gardens. They're really quite lovely and I liked it very much, tho I* *felt he was a little bored. Then we drove to Azle and finally got some talking done. He didn't know quite where to begin, nor did I. But at long last he said he hated to leave with everything so indefinite, but he had little choice. I told him I wasn't in a position to expect any more than what he said in his letter, and not to worry. I gave him one of the book ends to take with him. (This is a bronze set, with an ancient prof sitting on a ladder in front of a bookshelf.) This he liked very much. We decided that it would be a reminder that one isn't much good without the other. So, once again we said our farewells, without tears. He doesn't know when he will be back, but <u>will</u> be. I expect all to go well now.*

Mar 3 *~ "Around the World" is on the radio. How it makes me miss him, so far away.*

It is important to realize that letters to and from Australia in those days took a long time to be delivered. It might take three or four weeks after sending one off to receive an answer back. Taking that into consideration, letters were few and far between for a while, during which time the young pastor settled into his new parish. During this time, my divorce had become final, and as there had been no formal proposal, I enjoyed the company of a few good men. I moved twice, having grown weary of being an afterthought of my parents, who, after all, had their own lives to live.

Since I was beginning to revisit the dating scene, the question of whether or not I could remarry, in light of Scripture, became a real and burning concern for me. I was sure I pestered Pastor Pieplow to death over this. He had given me assurances, saying that 1 Corinthians 7:15 could not be more clear than "if the non-believer depart, let him depart, and the believer is not bound."

* * *

Okay, Now Let's Hear His Side of the Story . . . Maybe!

It was dicey enough *that I had to walk away midstream in this new relationship. I know she is left hanging, but I don't really have an option. I have my own issues to work through, and I have a deadline.*

Receiving Call documents from Toowoomba out of the blue was the very last development I anticipated. I didn't even know where this place was. Sounded "African" to me, like Lamumba. One day, this strange telegram arrived from President Noack in Australia to say only, **"What is your age. Are you attached? Return reply prepaid."**

When the documents arrived and I realized that it was a genuine Call to a dual parish in Australia, I initiated communication with the secretary there. I established with him that I was not really at liberty to leave Weatherford for at least six months. I had two confirmation classes in progress and had just started a building program for a new sanctuary.

The parish in Australia consisted of the *mother church*, as well as a congregation of folks who had struck out to build a daughter congregation. They had been vacant for a year. The idea of another six months without a pastor would have been daunting had they not had three retired clergy as members who could manage to keep things going. Under these circumstances, and after quite some thoughtful prayer, he agreed to accept the Call and proceeded to wrap up things in Weatherford, where he had been for little more than a year.

There are unbelievable details involved in making such a move. International travel is one thing, but moving to the other side of the world permanently is not something one does lightly. My first concern is for the congregation I am presently serving. I've just gotten my footing with things, and it is really not a very nice thing to leave so abruptly. But in weighing the things pastors have to weigh, I know I made a God-pleasing decision to go to the land of the Southern Cross.

I must clear out my apartment. That won't be much of an issue since I've been living with my friends on a farm most of the time. My library has to be packed up to ship. That's about all I own, certainly the only valuable thing I own.

Obtaining passports and visas is never simple, nor inexpensive. Especially for a naturalized citizen. Keeping in touch with the saints in Toowoomba is important. I have plans to go North to visit my parents before I leave the country. When one's loved ones are aging and ill, the prospect of relocating so far afield is somewhat daunting, especially to the loved ones. I will spend a few weeks with them and attempt to assure myself and them that it is going to be all right. There is my friend, Herman, in New Haven, Missouri, too, that I need to see before leaving. We have shared too many battles to find ourselves separated, and it is important to forge a plan whereby we will continue to be in touch. After all, that kind of battle will never be over for us.

The Texas District has assigned Pastor Pieplow to be my Vacancy Pastor when I leave. There are details to wrap up with him, concerning a list of shut ins, members who are in hospital in Fort Worth, and other matters we need to share.

Then, what should happen, on one of his visits to Pastor Pieplow, but that he should run into this interesting young secretary?

She was not here the last time I visited. This could be worth investigating. But then, who has time to think of such things? Nevertheless, it's worth a try to mention the need to sell a car, right?

Bingo! She needs a car! How great, how convenient! Let us pursue that, by all means. She IS going to buy the car! That's perfect. Oh, dear, I'm not ready to give it up just yet. There is still so much to do. O good, she doesn't have her license yet. She says I can keep it until I leave town. God is good!

Come to think of it, she is rather nice. Maybe we could have lunch or something when we make the sale final. She certainly seems friendly enough. I really do enjoy being with her. O, dear Lord, why did we have to meet just now, at the most impossible time? Nothing can come of this. There is no time to cultivate even a friendly relationship. Dear Lord, what were you thinking?

Their farewell at the bus stop was brief, but poignant, with every sentence full of overtones and undertones. *Well, I will be back in six weeks. Maybe she will forget all about me. In any case, I will drop her a card to make sure, and if she is at all interested in me, she will know I have not blown her off.*

While on the Greyhound Bus, he got all the way to Tulsa, Oklahoma before he could stand it not one more mile. He grabbed a postcard from the rack in the stop-over joint and jotted a few words to her, and shoved it in the mail box near the shop door. *It occurred to me that such an effort might save my place in line, as it were. At any rate, I have many fish to fry and cannot get too emotionally bogged down right now. On the other hand. . . . .*

In six weeks, after no further communication with her, he headed back to Fort Worth for a final farewell party with his congregation. He was not too surprised that she had not written. After all, he did not give her an address where he might be reached. While staying with his parents, he had typed a two page letter to her, hoping that he had expressed enough interest that she would not completely discount him. He made a plea for time, *"time to see how the situation will develop. The future is open. God will direct it in a way best for both of us, that we know in advance. And I find myself hop-*

ing that the future will bring us together.... I believe Luther's dying words: "We are beggars, that is true." I have little to give; but what little is mine to give I am determined to give completely."

Once again, on the bus, as the miles flew by, he wrote another note to tell her he was on the way. *I'll give her a brief outline of my plans and just mention the picnic Trinity is having in my honor, suggesting that maybe she might join me for that, in order that we might have some time together. Who knows? Maybe she has completely forgotten me by now. What would be the point of her holding out any hopes, since she knows I'm leaving the country. But then, I did let slip that I was sorry we didn't meet sooner, and that I hoped to be returning to the States often.*

Sunday morning, he arrived early at the church, not knowing whether she would come with Pastor Pieplow or not. *But, look, there she is at the door. She is early, too. She is just as pretty as I remembered, and she is smiling and coming in my direction. Poor thing, she has a terrible cold, and it sure looks as if she has lost a lot of weight since I saw her six weeks ago. How nice to have someone other than sweet Widow Jones to sit with in church. My, what a nice singing voice she has, even with a cold!*

While the picnic afforded an opportunity to have a good lunch, and to go around seeing folks for one last time, it also sent signals to his little flock that there was perhaps something afoot here. *As soon as it was decent to leave, therefore, I suggested we do so, so that we could talk privately. This is my last chance to find out if there was any possibility at all that she might be interested in me. After all, she would never pick me out of a lineup. I'm tall and gawky, uncommonly thin. While I know I'm educated and civilized, why would she know that, since we haven't had a substantive conversation yet? She could have her pick of anyone she wants; she is so pretty. Ah, but the accent seems to sway the women. Let's make good use of that.*

Since it is common wisdom, and also seminary training in some institutions, that a young pastor is not at liberty to dangle women here and there, (It was even once thought that they should not date a woman unless they were pretty sure they intended to marry her.) it is not proper for me to proclaim any great undying love, nor to demand any from her, nor to even hint that I am looking for marriage. And so they spent the afternoon, strolling around parks and driving the car one last time.

I rehearsed lines all along the bus route of things I wanted to make clear to her. Uncharacteristically, I failed to retrieve them from my memory bank, resulting in a lot of small talk, which I normally despise. She is sweet and seems happy to be with me, but she apparently is going to force my hand and let me make all the first moves. As a result, the most I can say is that I hope we will stay in touch. She replies that I have to initiate that, which I promise to do as soon as I land in Australia. She tells me our friendship has meant so very much to her during a trying time in her life, with her recent unhappy marriage and divorce. I tell her she has been a blessing to me. I have nothing to leave with her, but the car, of course. But she has purchased a set of lovely bronze bookends, and wants to give me one of them, to remember her by. On them is an ancient gentleman sitting on a ladder, in front of a bookshelf, studying. While it is going to put my baggage overweight, I am so pleased to have it. In fact, I love it!

Flying to Australia in those days was a laborious task. One had to leave the country from one of the western airports, like Los Angeles or San Francisco. The next stop was Hawaii, then Fiji, then Sydney. The layovers were brief, but the trip still took many hours, and was exhausting. The only place that could take international flights in those times was the airport in Sydney. From there one then had to fly, or go by train, to Queensland, another day or two of travel. *By the time I get to Toowoomba, I am exhausted. But I love travel, and if I am tired, I'm never going to confess my fatigue to a soul.*

The parsonage is provided in Toowoomba. On my first visit to check it out, my sense is that it is a lonely place. Sparsely furnished through the good graces of Miss Krenske, a charter member, who has just moved into a rest home, it is adequate, but not conducive to spending much time in alone. Not having had an occupant for two years, its dreariness and musty smell motivates me to accept the warm hospitality of the Principal of the local Concordia College, another American, and his family. Since I will be chasing myself in circles, trying to get established with not one, but two congregations and their members, committees, organists, and ways of doing things, it is a distinct blessing to have one's meals prepared, and to have the added pleasure of a family with whom to enjoy them.

Many families were eager to have their new pastor in their homes, not to mention the mothers with marriageable daughters. *Nothing like checking out the possibilities, while there is yet time! Mmmm, wonder what Barbara is doing back in Fort Worth?*

As the dust began to settle, the time came to try to pick up the threads of his relationship with the girl back home. *Is she still waiting? Should I risk sticking my neck out? Maybe she has decided she likes the cop after all. What if she just blows me off? I'd better not tell anyone. If she rejects me, they would find out, and it would not be good.*

I need to get on the ball and get this thing going, if I'm ever going to do it. Too bad mail takes so long. Why do phone calls have to cost so much? It will be a month or more before I can hope for a response from her. Better cut to the chase right away. Better follow my instincts and just go the distance. I've prayed about it over and over. I've discussed it with my closest friend, Herman. Why take a chance that I might lose her?

Wait a minute! Wait just one minute! She really knows nothing about me. And just incidentally, I know little about her. She probably doesn't even realize I'm European. In my brief experience, Texans are not very cosmopolitan, and after all, she is so young. What I know about women would fit in a thimble that was already half full. What if she tries to change me? What if she decides I am foolish and boring? I don't even know if she wants a family, but I know I do. Yes, she works for a pastor, but that doesn't necessarily mean she loves our Lord enough to be ready and eager to give up everything to serve Him and His people. It's possible that she might be just too immature and silly to take it all to heart the way I do.

Okay, Cowboy! Maybe it's better if we try to initiate a long-distance courtship with a few letters. Maybe I can find out a bit more about her that way. Good. Yes, that's a better idea.

In the following weeks, he was to receive several letters to every one he managed to write. *She is a prolific writer. It seems as if she understands what my calling as a pastor really means. Yes, she thinks children would be nice, even though she has but one brother herself. She tends to be apologetic about her lack of education, siting that her parents had not been able to send neither her nor her brother to college. Yes, she knows pastors tend to be away from home a lot with their work but figures she could deal with it. To this I responded I have no intentions of being a house father, but want to fully participate in parenting my children.*

I won't try to explain Australia too much, and I'll be careful, when she asks about the parsonage, to say that it is lovely, and large enough for twelve children. When she asks me about what kinds of food the Australians eat, I will tell her they have seven meals a day: early morning tea, breakfast, morning tea, lunch, afternoon tea, tea, and supper. And as if it is pertinent information, I'll explain that if you want to make a lemon meringue pie, which I really love, first she would send me out back to pick a lemon. However, I hope soon, there would be children who would take over that task.

O dear, her letters are starting to talk about all the things she is doing. She is getting an apartment and will be living with the new youth director when she comes. She is signing on to be the counselor of the Junior Youth group. She is singing in the choir. She is taking on more and more responsibility in the office. Worst of all, she is starting to date other guys. Mmm.

Then came the letter asking pastoral advice. *Since she is embarking on a social life again, what if things get serious with someone? It troubles her that it might be advisable for her to just plan a life alone, since she believed, at the time of her divorce, that she was being forced into a position of never being able to remarry. She was miserable in her marriage, but she did not want to dissolve it. Hope eternal lived in her heart that Charles might someday grow into a caring, faithful husband. Now that he has destroyed their union, where does that leave her for a future with another husband. She will trust me completely to tell her the truth. What does Scripture say?*

While it is likely that her ex had committed adultery, that had not been the issue. The problem is simply that he didn't want to be married; he was not a husband to her in any way other than expecting her to cook, clean and launder his "whites" for work. He had made the appointment to see a divorce *lawyer without even consulting her, and then sued her for cruel and inhuman treatment, since she refused to divorce him.*

It is probably a good thing she has opened Pandora's Box, because if there is an issue with her previous marriage that would prevent me from marrying her, I need to know, and the sooner, the better. Well, it is time. I will answer her questions, and then, if she can satisfy me that she was the innocent party in the divorce, I will invite her to share my life of love and service to the Lord. Here goes!

* * *

May 13 ~ *Only this morning, after accepting a date with Steve, I received a letter from Kurt asking me to marry him. While I am thrilled and happy, I am not sure what to do about it. I have so many irons in the fire. There are so many matters to be cleared up, and I can't say I'm a very good cook and house keeper. (Kurt deserves the best, and unless I'm sure I can give him MY best, I dare not accept.) He seems pretty sure I'll say yes. And he's eager for an answer. I hope he knows what he's doing. I hate to think he's only lonesome. I'm sure the Lord will direct me in making the proper decision. I do so want to do His will.*

I had written Kurt a letter to ask him for specific Scripture verses that would state that in my situation, I would be able to remarry. While I felt confident that the 1 Cor. text applied to my case, I was concerned that maybe Kurt should not marry me because I was a divorcee. As a result of my specific questions, he wrote the following: (I add this because there were a couple of times during our marriage when he was attacked for marrying me.) Former students who sat at the feet of Prof. Marquart will appreciate his thoroughness.

. . . First, let us consider the immediate problems that concern you: whether it would be lawful for you to remarry. In the first place, I would refer to the MT. 19 passage, which you undoubtedly know well. I would call attention to the "except it be for adultery" clause. Notice that the text allows remarriage ("and shall marry another") in that case. Nor is actual adultery the only way in which a marriage may be dissolved. The marriage vow is actually broken by persistent refusal to fulfill it, i.e. desertion. In this case, give close attention to the logical structure of 1 Corinthians 7:10-15, Phillips translates in the last verse. . . "the Christian partner need not consider himself bound in such cases." The word for bound is really quite strong, and I believe it must refer to the marriage bond, which in this case, is recognized as having been dissolved by the deserting party. "Not bound" would mean that the innocent party is free to remarry. It certainly should not be taken to mean merely that a separation without remarriage is permissible, since that

point was already made in verse 11, and thus would be a useless redundancy here.

(next page) And now, without further preliminaries, let me surprise you a bit. Assuming that the questions of conscience can be settled for both of us, will you marry me? You would make me very, very happy if you could answer "yes!" On the other hand, if for some reason you find it necessary to refuse, then please keep this completely confidential, not for my sake, but for the Ministry's and the Church's. But I shall hope confidently that the answer will be in the affirmative. And, believe me, I shall await anxiously.

"As far as I am concerned, the question of conscience is easily resolved, if you will tell me that either (a) or (b) on the previous page were the case. (Pardon the legal sounding sentence.) Neither of us, as Christians and as servants of the Church, can nor wish to go against the express command of Scripture.

"Well, I must hasten to post this letter, and not to prolong the delay. I am confident that you are in possession of all the facts necessary for a responsible decision. Am anxiously and prayerfully awaiting same! Must send this off. Pardon the disjointed style. In haste, Kurt."

May 22 ~ *I did* receive a proposal from Kurt on Saturday, May 13, and although it did take me a little by surprise, I've known for weeks, for months, what the answer would be if ever he asked me. I knew the first day he came into our office. So I have written him back accepting and have begun spreading the glad tidings. Everyone is so happy about it, but no one as much as I! There are a million things to plan, but I don't know where to begin because I don't know where the wedding will be, or when. Pastor Pieplow is the most excited of all, totally assured that "it was all arranged in heaven!"

On the day I got Kurt's letter of proposal, I called my Mom to see if she had time for a visit, that I had something I wanted to talk over with her. The first words out of her mouth were, "I suppose you want to get married." I don't know whether she knew I was hoping for this proposal or not, but she must have, because she suddenly blurted out, "You can't marry a minister!"

O, no! What horrible skeleton do we have in the family closet now? The wind went out of my sails and I felt as if someone had dashed me with a bucket of cold water. "Why?" Calmly, she replied, "Well, silly. You can't cook!" I guess from a layman's point of view, being able to cook must have been the most important asset to have. Or, perhaps this was her subtle way of telling me that pastors don't marry divorcees. She exhibited restrained joy.

June 4 ~ *How can one be so completely happy? I'm so certain we were* *sent to each other by God. Only God could make such a perfect match. It will be difficult to leave home, but I've not admitted it to anyone. It will be easier for all of them if they don't think I'm having a hard time. I could never communicate my love for my family. Never could. . . and now, I doubt they would believe mere words. I hope my own family will be different.*

Many well-meaning people, having heard about our unorthodox courtship, have commented they didn't think it was very romantic. On the contrary. It was full of mystery, surprise, humor, anticipation, wonder and intense joy. The most amazing part of it is that God planted in the hearts of two of His children this affection, this unlikely attraction. No thinking person would ever have thought to match the two of us with any hope of success or permanence. And yet, His plan was perfect. The love would bloom and grow, bear fruit, and serve the Kingdom in ways no one but God could have foreseen. It's God's love story, and His love stories are always the best.

New Beginnings

Mom & Dad taking me to ship

Japanese aircraft ripped through the peaceful skies of the South Pacific, and blasted our American battleships out of the water in a surprise raid at Pearl Harbor. (1941) That marked the year of my entrance into this earthly life. The excitement, therefore, of my safe arrival, after three miscarriages by my Mother, was short lived, and the nation was engrossed in a bitter war that brought fear, deprivation and destruction to many.

At the time of my second arrival, (on the shores of Australia, 1961), the United States was entering into the Cuban Crisis; thus, as I embarked on my new life, fear once again was struck into the hearts of all Americans by the Bay of Pigs.

But there she sat, in the Long Beach slip, brilliant in the mid-day sun, proudly boasting her maiden voyage to the world. Even my pilot Dad was impressed with her massive sleek body, and almost as if going against his conscience, could not wait to board her and inspect the floating hotel that would become my home as I travelled to Australia.

Growing up, my Mother, a quiet, shy, unassuming woman, was rigorous in her efforts to impress upon me that I could do just about anything if I set my mind to it. As a result, the challenges and adventures into which I meandered would most likely never occur to most women my age or would have virtually terrified the rest. But youth and ignorance are bliss, and at twenty years of age, I was booked, alone, on *The Canberra*, a new flagship of the P & O Orient Line, headed for Australia to marry my future husband.

I was to become the youngest pastor's wife in the Queensland District of the Evangelical Lutheran Church of Australia. It's possible I was even the youngest pastor's wife in the whole country. As if I wasn't already a square peg in a round hole by virtue of my youth, I was an American. While our Yankee military was very revered during WWII, we no longer enjoyed popularity because of the irrational fear on the part of the Aussie that we were coming ashore to buy up their businesses. Little did they realize in those days that Americans went to Australia to relax and enjoy the beaches. Little did they suspect that in the next century, it would be the Japanese who would own the Gold Coast, not the Americans.

But I digress. My story really begins on the Pacific, traveling in a first class cabin with two very elderly ladies. One was a Scottish redhead, sporting blue tinted glasses, who was every bit of 80. She had made voyages around the world many times, and found it irresistible to land a novice to whom she could serve as travel mentor. She managed to comfort my parents to some extent, assuring them that she would look after me. The other cabin mate was a German lady who was equally old, and deaf in the mix. Because of her infirmity, as well as her lack of English, we didn't communicate much with her.

I believe I was the first member of my flying family to ever travel by ocean liner, and it was exciting in every way. My Daddy's parting words to me were, "There's a lot of folks on this trip who live a different life than you are used to. Be careful and remember who you are." This advice no doubt came as a result of his serving bosses who were quite wealthy and lived extravagantly. My Mom's difficult separation came out as, "You're marrying a minister! If it doesn't work this time it will be YOUR fault." The only way to understand such a remark is that everyone assumed my failed first marriage was due to my husband. In my new marriage, the idea that a minister would cause a marriage to falter was out of the question.

Despite these "cheery" good byes, I had a glorious time on my two-week long voyage. While many of the passengers were Americans, there were a number of British subjects. I was amused and surprised by the interesting way they held their cutlery. In no way did it appear advantageous to me,

Miss McClare (cabin mate) on "Canberra"

so I didn't attempt to master it. I did, however, seem to have an ear for the British accent, and had no trouble with some of the interesting terminology. It is harder than I imagined for a Texan to dispense with the drawl in favor of their amusing clip. How very grownup to be at dinner every night with wealthy couples, all dressed in their lovely gowns, and then dancing 'til dawn with handsome officers in the club, whose duties included dancing with the ladies...and I DID love to dance.

I had packed a few "Sunday, go to meeting" dresses. Assuming I would never need formals again, I had given my prom gowns to some of the young girls in the youth group. Realizing my deficiency, my Scottish friend turned into a fairy godmother. She had three big trunks in the hold, one exclusively for her furs. She would take me to pick out anything I wanted to wear for various occasions, and my favorite was a black ostrich feather wrap!

After a fun-filled stopover in beautiful Hawaii, and heading for New Zealand, we encountered a serious storm which prevented us from going into the harbor at Wellington, N.Z. We sailed up and down the coastline for three days, waiting for the weather to moderate enough for landing. Life on board was so difficult during the storm that many passengers were absent from the dining room. Many were violently sea sick. Those of us who weathered the turbulence, managed with boards across the edge of the tables to keep our dishes from sliding into our laps. Miraculously, I never got sick, therefore probably experiencing the reality of the storm even more than those poor souls down below who hunkered in their cots, waiting to die.

The crew members with whom I was friendly told me that one freak wave could have split the ship in half! There was much dispute among them concerning the captain's choice to head into the storm, rather than try to go north to avoid it. He had promised the mayor of Wellington a visit, and he was going to honor that promise, no matter what. The mountains of green water all around us were something I can conjure up in my mind to this day. The local newspaper that carried the story and featured a half page photo of the ship reported that there were but seven feet of clearance on either side of the *Canberra* when we finally followed the pilot boats through the heads. The incident resulted in a lot of local interest, and the shores were lined with Kiwis as we docked.

While in Wellington, which by the way was a beautiful, quaint, old world place in those days, I found myself deserted by the people that were usually my side kicks. My roommate, who never left my side, and with whom I walked the decks every morning to avoid being sea sick, was even distracted and nowhere to be found. When we made sail again, it became evident that they had all been out shopping for a bridal shower for me. (I still use the solid wood rolling pin they gave me!) Hosted by one of the couples from our meal sitting, it was a happy gathering of older passengers who had been following the drama of this young American, traveling alone, on her way to her wedding. That is to say, all but one Presbyterian elder, who wondered how I could ever be happy marrying a poor church mouse. He and his wife actually offered to pay my fare back home if I had changed my mind by the time we reached Sydney Harbor.

The party extended well past our dinner hour, and I felt awkward about arriving late. Finally, we began moving along to the lower deck for our dinner, no one seemingly bothered that we were behind schedule. I was always fastidiously punctual, and hated being late. Arriving at the big double doors, someone more or less shoved me inside. All the diners arose, and standing at their tables, lifted their wine glasses and sang "For She's a Jolly Fine Lassie". Our table was festooned with pink streamers and balloons, and our young Irish waiter stood behind my chair with a big grin on his face. The captain came by our table and said he was doing everything he could do to make up the lost time, since he knew there was someone waiting for me in Australia. In the club later, every other song the band played was "Get Me to the Church On Time".

Our table on the Canberra

The ship docked in Sydney. I was to be met by a step cousin of Kurt's and put on a flight north. Kurt's step aunt ended up in Australia, when everyone else in the family went to New York. Before she left Russia, while things were in total chaos, a woman with a little baby boy asked her if she would watch the child while she dashed off to take care of something, and promised she would be right back. She never returned. So the aunt adopted him and raised him as her own son.

This cousin, then put me on a flight to Oakey, Queensland, which was about twenty minutes from Toowoomba. Flying over all the terracotta tiles of the homes in Sydney was amazing. Every home had the same. Soon we were flying over beautiful mountains and made our way up the Eastern coastline to Queensland. There I was met by my husband-to-be.

Naturally this delay caused quite a stir on Australian shores as well. The wedding was scheduled for August 9. The bride was going to be late. Everyone involved in the wedding plans had to shift gears, changing the reception hall, informing all the guests, etc. I'll never know how they managed to pull it together. I had my wedding gown with me, and all that was required was to show up. The local paper reported over six hundred attended as guests and were "in the church yard to greet the happy couple." I'm glad I didn't know that at the time. Nor did I realize that it was just the beginning of life under public scrutiny. Newspapers all the way up the North Coast carried headlines like "STORMS KEPT THEM APART", "BRIDE LATE FOR WEDDING".

The Wedding Day

When I listen to young women talking about their wedding plans, I am always amused at the myriad of details on their "to do" lists. Chasing around to find reception halls seems to be the first requirement. Even before they check to see if their chosen minister is free on a given date, they have to find a hall. Then comes the photographer, the D.J., the printer for the invitations.

Many couples feel as if they have to include their entire gambit of friends and relatives in the wedding party. So it's off to the bridal shops to find something that looks decent on everyone, measuring, ordering, then dieting frantically for six months so they will not gain weight before the wedding. Groomsmen have to go to a tux rental establishment and inconvenience themselves with trying on and being fitted for cummerbunds, and uncomfortable shoes, etc. Oh, and don't forget the florist and the limo rental.

Diplomatic decisions are required for seating arrangements at family tables at the reception, since everyone knows this one is not talking to that one any more, or you know who probably won't show up anyway.

Given all these potentially explosive and exhausting scenarios, it was truly blissful to have others make all the arrangements for our wedding. Even before the proposal, I had imagined Kurt would come back to the States and that the wedding would take place in either my home congregation, or his former church in Weatherford. Then we would fly off into the sunset together.

But we were in a whirlwind at the time of his leaving Fort Worth. And technically, a decision had not been made for our futures. Once the proposal had been made and we had to begin discussions, almost immediately, the word "practical" came into our vocabulary. We might have to wait, said Kurt, until we could save enough money for a wedding, not to mention funds for getting me to Australia. The idea of waiting never occurred to me. I had hoped the waiting part was over. Being a woman of action, I had already planned in my mind how I would quit my job, start packing, and wrapping up loose ends to be ready to leave. Wait? Mmmmm.

To my relief, in a few days, after I accepted his proposal, a letter came saying that the parish had offered to cover the expenses involved in my coming to Australia, and that the wedding would be held at Redeemer, Toowoomba. This, of course, ruled out the possibility of either of our families being there. But we were soon to have a new family, and there seemed no other option. I suspect my Mom was relieved, since it alleviated a lot of stress for her.

It only made sense that Kurt set the date. I have no idea what rule of thumb he was using. But it didn't matter. He certainly had more boundaries and time limitations than I did. Perhaps it had to do with booking the reception hall!

Mrs. Johnston, who was making the arrangements, wrote and suggested that I might like to rent a bridal gown. It would be less expensive than buying one. I suppose that it may have been customary in some circles, but I had always made my own formals, and I had dreamt of making my wedding dress. I wrote Mrs. Johnston that whatever style she wished for herself would be fine, as she was to be my Matron of Honor, but that I would bring my gown along with me. As it turned out, another pastor's wife in Queensland had a street length lemon chiffon dress that served perfectly well for her. The flower girl's dress was made by her mother and was of tangerine chiffon. With the peach, white and coral Iceland poppies and white lilies in the chancel, they were perfect.

By the way, my Journal states that I made my wedding gown for under $25. My Mom and I picked out a pattern and found material. I think we purchased a crinoline petticoat, and the little pearl crown head piece on which a short veil was attached. The material was called "chrystaline" and glistened in the light. It was lighter than satin. Together with my Aunt Mae, who happened to be visiting at the time, I attached all the beads and pearls that made the floral design on the bodice. I think we had the covered buttons done by the lady down the street who ran a little tailoring business. It would have taken ages to do all 44 of them! It had a V-neckline in front and back, long sleeves coming to points at the wrist, with covered buttons on the cuffs, and the skirt was attached to a V-shaped waistline. It was quite lovely.

Rehearsal dinner? I think not. We met together at the church with Pastor Johnston (also an American) who would officiate at our wedding, and his wife, who would be my Matron of Honor. Another pastor in the district, a Canadian, had agreed to be Best Man. I remember being struck by him saying, "Well, this is one time the best man didn't win!" Two of the Johnston sons were in the wedding. One carried the icon, and the other was the ring bearer. (The ring bearer was to serve as his dad's Best Man at the wedding of his dad to me in 2008 – but I'm jumping ahead!)

The icon was painted by Kurt's step aunt. This aunt was the twin of Kurt's stepfather. Russian Orthodox couples always have an icon that follows them through their married life, and it is a part of the wedding ceremony. Just as the bride was three days late, so was the icon. You have to wonder if they were on the same ship.

It was a beautiful icon depicting the face of Christ, as St. Veronica is said to have captured it when wiping the face of our weary Savior as He was being forced up to Golgotha.

This special treasure has been in the room of every home where our family devotions have been held, reminding us of the love of this aunt, but more importantly, the unfailing love of Christ.

The morning of the wedding, therefore, was not spent in a beauty salon, together with the formal wedding participants, having our hair done, manicures and pedicures. If my memory serves me, I slept with my hair in rollers the previous night, which was my custom, combed my hair out next morning, and hit the road to shop that day for what else, but linoleum for the manse living room floor.

There was really nothing too special about buying linoleum for the living room, apart from the fact that it was our wedding day! And, maybe because I had never lived in a home where the living room did not have carpet. But the flooring that was there was ancient, brown, dingy, and even the trustees, men that they were, realized that an American might take exception to that. I'm just guessing. Truth be told, they had already laid out money for my passage, and someone must have paid for the reception. So it wasn't as if they had not shown generosity already.

It was touching to me that the gentleman who took us shopping for this seemed to understand that this was poor timing. Maybe his wife prompted him. But he was so kind, that the fact that I was getting this shiny, feathery, green floor covering, instead of a nice carpet square didn't really bother me. If I remember, it seems as if there was an implication that this would be somehow "temporary", that the goal was to build a new manse at some point.

We made two hospital calls on members, and we were together all day until it was time to dress for the wedding. I can't remember how I got to the church, but I dressed at the Johnstons', and my Matron of Honor and I arrived, together with the flower girl and the boys, at the church, just in time for the processional.

We were greeted by dozens of women, all wearing hats, and children, in their Sunday best, who were hanging on the picket fence that skirted the front lawn of the church. It was quite windy, and my veil was blowing everywhere. Inside the church, I was met by a sea of strange faces, all waiting to see the bride. The church was filled to capacity, with many standing. I recall most everyone in somber colors, all the ladies in felt hats to match their winter coats. It was pretty chilly in the sanctuary, as there was no heat.

The flower girl, a tiny little thing about four, very pretty, with auburn ringlets, and a headband to match her dress, led the way, smiling bravely, carrying her little wicker basket of petals that she scattered as she almost tiptoed down the aisle. Following her was the icon bearer, showing just an edge of shyness, yet determined to look confident, carrying the Wedding Icon. The Ring Bearer followed, somber and not too sure he wanted to be there, but was encouraged by his mom to get along, after which she lighted up the place with her lovely lemon dress, glistening in the afternoon sunshine pouring through the window over the altar. (These images are not only in my head, but were actually recorded on reel-to-reel tape.)

Being the only one left at the back of the church, it fell to me to proceed, half step by half step, as elegantly as I could manage, just as we had rehearsed. There was no turning back now. I went forward alone, totally focused on that tall young man waiting for me in the chancel. There was little point in being nervous or afraid at this point. I had prayed. God had answered. As Kurt had written when I accept his proposal, "The die is cast".

Practically everything about the service was strange to me. While I had spent the greater part of my life without a father in the house, due to his flying career, I suppose I had always imagined he would be beside me. No familiar faces of friends or family. The hymns that were selected were new to me, but the congregation sang them lustily. "Take Thou My Hand and Lead Me", and "O Perfect Love". The sermon text, however, was without any doubt in my mind, inspired by God Himself. Psalm 27 was the Scripture text I had chosen for myself as a teenager in Walther League some years before. No one, not even Kurt, knew that. But Pastor Johnston chose it without consulting us, and once again, I knew that this symphony was being written and conducted by my Father in Heaven.

"The LORD is my light and my salvation; Whom shall I fear?
The LORD is the defense of my life' Whom shall I dread?"

With some of our musicians having left town for holidays, we were fortunate that we had an organist. Since the organ at that time sat on the side wall near the front of the church, she was in her glory, playing for this big wedding. Grinning from ear to ear, she played on, enjoying her spot in the limelight. A member of a nearby congregation agreed to film as much of the service as possible for the benefit of our absent families.

Following the vows, the clergy and wedding party exited through a side door to the vestry where we and our witnesses had to sign the marriage certificate. After returning to the chancel, we were introduced as the Reverend and Mrs. Marquart, and together, we walked down the aisle for the first time as husband and wife. I was a bit concerned that Kurt seemed so somber, as we left arm in arm together. After years of watching clergy, I have realized solemnity accompanies anything they do in the sanctuary. Once we stood on the steps overlooking the crowd of well-wishers outside, he was smiling, at them, at me.

The wedding party gathered outside in front of the church for anyone with cameras to take photographs. As the congregants flowed out of the church onto the lawn, it very quickly seemed as if the entire city of Toowoomba was with us. Despite the warm reception, the wind was beginning to bite, as the sun trailed off behind the building. At long last, it was a relief to have said our greetings, when we could proceed by car to a local photo studio. Wedding photographs were taken in a studio, not in the church. These produced the one that met us in the newspapers in every little town up and down the Coast, as we traveled on our honeymoon.

The reception hall that had been booked for the clergy reception had to be cancelled because of the delay in my arrival. It was a miracle that the Picnic Point reception hall was available on such short notice, since it was a very coveted spot, and was heavily booked for weddings for folks all around the area. Picnic Point is called that because it sits right at the summit of the ridge that divides the Darling Downs from the towns and farms below the ridge. Through its big windows and from its meandering walks, one could see Mt. Tabletop and miles of range below.

There was a separate reception, consisting of all the circuit pastors and their wives, as well as the congregational officers of Redeemer and Good Shepherd. Some of those who would have attended had booked their holiday flats and because of the postponement, they could not wait for the wedding. There were still over a hundred people there. As the years went by, I never experienced an occasion where the clergy had their own reception again. I'm not sure why this was done, except that most of them were from out of town, and the hosts might have felt it nice to give them a meal before they had to head home. The parish reception was later in the evening and did not include a full meal.

The formal toast program followed by all Australian weddings began with a toast to the Queen, followed by the toast to the Bride and Groom. The Groom then responds. The Best Man then makes a toast to the Brides Maids, and in this case the Matron of Honor, as well as the attendants, namely the children. At that point, it would be customary for a toast to the Parents of the Bride and the Parents of the Groom. In our case, someone made a toast to Absent Loved Ones. Someone then read greetings and telegrams that had arrived from various entities and from people who had wanted to attend, but couldn't.

When it came time for the cutting of the cake, since I had not been warned that the cake was a fruit cake, and that its icing was an almond marzipan, it required a bit more determination to make that first cut. All Australian wedding and Christmas cakes are such. (My children made me promise, when they were young, that I would not make them have fruit cake for their weddings!) It was necessary to practice my first major act of diplomacy, so as to not offend the sweet lady who made the cake.

I had one request for the whole day. I wanted "Around The World" to be played with the dinner music. Nat King Cole favored us with his version during the cutting of the cake. After what I had been through on the voyage, the theme song turned out to be more appropriate than I imagined.

> *Around the world, I searched for you.*
> *I traveled on, when hope was gone, to keep a rendezvous.*
> *I knew somewhere, sometime, somehow,*
> *You'd look at me, and I would see the smile you're smiling now.*
> *It might have been in County Down, or in New York,*
> *In gay Paree, or even London Town.*
> *No more will I go around the world,*
> *For I have found my world in you.*

During the time that we were celebrating with the clergy, the members of the parish were busy getting Reception #2 ready at the church hall. When we could decently absent ourselves from Picnic Point, we made a mad dash for the manse for a bathroom stop, forgetting that said toilet was outside. So, in the dark, in a long white gown, I had my first experience with my wonderful outdoor plumbing. The hemline of my lovely dress was forever red with Queensland soil after that.

Around the walls of the fellowship hall were the brave members who had been waiting since the wedding to greet their pastor and his new wife.

It was quite a contrast to the party we had just left, but warm with genuine excitement, love and fond wishes for the new couple. After all, their plans had been changed in the middle of the river, as it were, when I was late. The ladies who had to decorate the church, those who worked to get the parsonage all fresh, as well as the many ladies who had prepared food for this supper.

Note: In Australia, "tea" is used for the main evening meal. "Supper" is used for the lovely time of the evening when people enjoy coffee/tea with a light treat. In a large public gathering as this was, one could count on hundreds of tasty tarts, piled high with whipped cream, piklets (which were not little fish, but small pancakes, topped with strawberry jam and a dollop of whipped cream), sponge cakes, fruit cake, biscuits (cookies), and all good things. All the stops come out, and the women compete for who can bring the loveliest and most delicious treat. What a delight!

There was great relief when we finally arrived and there was much joviality over the marriage of their beloved pastor.

On the gift table were a few pieces of crystal, some bowls and such. The Parish Chairman made a formal presentation of a chiming clock, as the parish gift.

Though the hour was already getting late, there were lots of children there as well. The little girls were excited to see the new bride with the long white dress. It was cute that they were impressed with my long fingernails. Women in Australia worked too hard in those days to keep long, manicured nails, and the girls were intrigued and excited to see hands like in "the magazines".

As I look back now, I believe most of the members of the congregation were happy to have someone in the parsonage who was a little different. I never sensed hostility or suspicion for being American, or for being so young. I was so impressed with the Australian wives and mothers that maybe that came through in my relationships with them. It was as if overnight, they all became our family, and it remained that way, on the whole, the fifteen years of living among them.

Our honeymoon plans included a road trip to Cairns in Northern Queensland. That is the home of the Great Barrier Reef. The farther north one goes in Queensland, the warmer it becomes as the Equator is approached. Sugar cane fields are everywhere. The coastline is always nearby. Periodically, we would stop to visit a beach and have a swim. There was no one for miles. Later, we learned that we had been in shark-infested waters. The saying in Australia is: "Never swim alone; give the sharks a choice!"

In those days, the only commercial tourist attraction on Mossman Island, where people went to sit in glass bottom boats to observe the beautiful coral, was a lemonade stand! It was pristine and quiet, with few people roaming around, the perfect place for newlyweds. Everywhere we stopped along our road trip, the Aussies would ask, "Aren't you the couple from Toowoomba that just got married?"

It's cold in Toowoomba in August, and we were dismayed to arrive in the evening to find that those who were charged with assembling a bed for us in the parsonage had not done so. Finally that was arranged, but we realized we had not procured hot water bottles, which everyone used to warm their toes at night! Fortunately, we discovered some tall beer bottles, filled them with hot water, put stoppers in them, and prayed they would not leak. That, then, was our introduction to our new walk together as Pastor and Mrs. Kurt Marquart of the Redeemer/Good Shepherd Lutheran Parish of Toowoomba, Queensland, Australia.

III
Life in the Parish Ministry – Stories of people and events during life in Australia – 1961 – 1975

Youngest Pastor's Wife in the District – Probably the Country!

How often have we women been held captive in the waiting room at a doctor's office, where we have been regaled with the rerun of someone's recent surgery? Or have you ever been part of a *"My labor was worse than yours"* pity party? Even on the social media, one can find blow by blow accounts of the latest delivery, and all the unexpected complications that were endured.

Well, if you attend many pastors' conferences, where the wives also have a meeting, you might run into the same kind of experience, where one woman will swear no one could possibly have a more disagreeable congregation, or a more pitiful excuse for a parsonage than hers.

Therefore, lest you think that because I have survived to the ripe old age of 79, and you see no visible battle scars, that all my years in the parish were paradisical, allow me to share some of the memories I have as the wife of the pastor of a dual parish in a foreign country. I'm prepared to bet none of you has done, or will ever do, half the stupid things I did, and still the people put up with me!

In another part of this book, I describe my voyage to Australia as a young twerp and our first years with the saints of the Redeemer/Good Shepherd Parish in Toowoomba. At that time, I was the youngest Lutheran pastor's wife in the country, therefore making me a bit of a novelty. When I recall those days, in an attempt to see myself through the eyes of the members, it occurs to me that some of them were most likely quite alarmed when I showed up. The previous pastors had been close to retirement age. It had been a long time since there had been children in the manse. I'm sure some of the more seasoned women, especially the widows of previous clergy who were members, most likely just held their breath.

The parish had been vacant for nearly two years before Kurt finally arrived. While there were a number of retired pastors who capably held things together during that time, everyone was happy to finally have the blessing of a pastor of their own, even if he was a bit young, and even if he was an American with European background, and even if he did have a strong and proper British accent. There was nothing typical about Pastor Marquart.

Clad nearly all the time, in public at least, in his black suit and clerical collar, he was quite thin and stood at 6' 4". Unlike his predecessors, he chanted the Liturgy. Resisting the inclination to wear the full liturgical vestments, he realized the people would accept the cassock and surplice before they would be comfortable with the alb, or ever more radical, the chasuble. With but three months to become familiar with their new shepherd, they had to then ready themselves to receive his new bride, and the lady of the manse.

Before my arrival, realizing that their manse was most likely below par, at least for a young American woman, the trustees decided they would at least try to cheer up the kitchen a bit with a fresh coat of paint. Their first mistake was to ask the pastor what colors he thought the bride would like. The result was a large room, with high ceilings, covered in Pepto Bismol pink on the walls and baby blue trim, all glossy finish. The floor covering was antiquated linoleum, dreary blue and faded gold squares. The counter tops were marbled forest green and cream linoleum with aluminum trim. The kitchen table, which would seat four, had the same green top, and its legs were gray, as were the wooden chairs.

Since most women in Australia in those days cooked on wood burning stoves, that was the center piece of the kitchen. It was old, and did not look as if food should be anywhere near it. But, alas, there was a second range, a tiny thing with three gas burners and an oven which lacked a thermostat. The fridge was quite small, maybe as high as I was tall, but had no freezer. The sink boasted three water taps, hot, town water and tank water. The sink was white porcelain and a nice window overlooked the back yard.

Since there was no central heating in the house, the kitchen was the heart of the home, and in wet seasons, or winter, we were happy to have the big wood burning stove. I even got accustomed to making fires in the thing after a while. Kurt's job was to keep the wood chips coming, and he prided himself on being able to chop the logs members gave us on the big stump out back.

So it was that I learned to cook in this kitchen. Kurt called on all his reserves to teach me all meals Italian. He had worked in a restaurant during his seminary days and had good skills to share. Rarely was a meal served in our home that didn't have onions or garlic! I don't recall ever eating out, since there really were no fast food joints at all, and we couldn't afford to eat at a hotel.

By the way, did you know that women were not allowed in the pubs? If a man brought his wife or lady friend to the pub, they had to sit in the beer garden. There were some pretty good meals in those gardens later on, and children were even allowed to accompany parents. It was one place one could get a decent meal at a reasonable price that included alcohol. Kurt's theory was that all civilized meals should include beer or wine.

As for the rest of the house, there was no need for a vacuum cleaner, since there was not one square inch of carpet. Except for the living room, all the floor coverings were dated, and cracking, and difficult to keep shiny. The day of our wedding, we accompanied one of the trustees to pick out and purchase some linoleum for the living room. It was at least shiny and required no waxing. Most Australian women used wax on their floors and owned electric buffers with which to keep them pretty. I question the idea of never using any water on a floor, though. Some of the floors were so old in the manse that a buffer would most likely cut them to shreds.

Since my new husband had been residing with another family before we were married, the parsonage had never been furnished. Thanks to one of the members who was closing up her home to retire into a nursing home, we had rudimentary items of furniture to start out with. As you can imagine, coming from the home of a spinster, the items, while good quality, were not family friendly. There were matching love seat and chair, upholstered in brocade with polished wood arms and legs. The table for the dining room was solid wood and in great shape, except that the cushions on the chairs were so thick, it was not possible to put your legs under the table.

The plus side of the dining room table was that it had a matching buffet, with a back panel of mirror. Very pretty.

A double bed, a wardrobe, and matching duchess (dresser) were in the front bedroom. Beds at that time did not have inner spring mattresses, but rather a chicken wire kind of spring base on which the mattress sagged. The study had a desk and two chairs, and fortunately, also some book shelves. On one wall was a pot belly stove, which we were afraid to use, as it looked as if it hadn't been serviced for some time.

Remember, I had been living at home, where I was accustomed to automatic washing machines and dryers. My mother had a dishwasher for a long time already, as well as a huge deep freeze that was stocked three times a year. The only time I had ever seen an outdoor toilet was when I visited the farm of an uncle decades before. Luckily, as a girl, I had learned the fine art of doing laundry with a wringer washing machine. That was an advantage since that was the next thing the trustee bought us, brand new!

Can you imagine how the trustee must have felt when he had to take us shopping for these things? I had just arrived, and the wedding was imminent. He had to know these embellishments were totally below the expectations of a young, modern bride. And yet, we had a grand time, and he ultimately was my favorite Elder and always made it his business to do whatever was needed to make sure the family was ok. It was he who determined that our fridge was too small after our third child was born.

The push out windows were all made of mottled glass, a white panel in the middle with green on top and bottom. In the minds of some, these windows eliminated the need for curtains, since you could not really see through them. There were no screens on any of the windows. No one had them, their reasoning being it somehow inhibited the air to circulate through the house. The hairy spiders and flies and mosquitoes did not seem to bother anyone. Each window in the dining room and living room was hung with a sheer, lacey kind of curtain that was donated by some kind person who had upgraded her own house.

Five clotheslines stretched across the width of the large back yard. In time, hundreds of nappies (diapers) would be hung there. The unattached garage was entered from the street that ran behind our yard, and there was no light anywhere to guide one coming in at night. There was no key to the back door, so when we returned home late at night, it was necessary to go around the house to the front door. Kurt used to laugh that he was the web sweeper, since being so tall, he would go ahead of us and knock down all the webs that had developed between the house and the fence.

The outdoor water closet had no light either, but that might be a good thing. One would not necessarily want to know what else was occupying that space at night. It was quite inconvenient to take young children outside at night to the toilet, so they had chamber pots in their room.

This, then, was said to be the norm for clergy in Queensland at that time. It was also about the middle range of the standard of living of our parishioners. It fell to us to make a home out of that space, which I think we managed pretty well. When it became evident that our colleagues in the district all had homes very much like ours, there was little to do but make it as pleasant as possible.

The manse was about a block away from the mother church, Redeemer, on Neil Street. The daughter church, Good Shepherd, was meeting at that time in a club, which smelled of stale beer and cigarettes on Sunday mornings. Eventually, that congregation managed to raise enough money to build a church of their own.

There was a mission church up in Harlexton that was attended largely by children from the area. It was a neighborhood of families who lived in government subsidy housing, and it was unusual to see the parents in attendance. At some point, those people were integrated into Redeemer whose faithful members drove out there to pick up those children to bring them to church. The mission was then closed.

Before the birth of our first baby, I attended all three services every week with Kurt. It was a good way to get to know the members. As we began our family, it seemed wise to concentrate on one congregation, so that the children would have a sense of a church home, with Sunday School. I attended ladies functions at Good Shepherd when they were doing something special, usually at Christmas. Redeemer was in easy walking distance.

After five years in that manse, when I came home after giving birth to our third child, we were told that the owners of the Lebanese shop on the corner had put in an offer to purchase the house, on the condition that we would vacate in three days. We were not even aware the house was on the market, and it was astounding, especially since I had experienced a bit of a relapse with my baby, to have to suddenly recruit volunteers who came in and tossed our belongings into barrels and boxes, mostly to go into storage, until a new manse was ready. As I sat on the bed, with my new baby, I instructed the ladies which things we had need for right away and which things to toss.

The worst of it was the men had no idea where to put us. Property had not been purchased, blueprints had not been drawn up, money was not even available for a new building. Finally, it was determined that we could live in one side of a duplex owned by one of our members. It had two bedrooms, a small kitchen, a smaller bathroom, and a sleepout (a closed in verandah). We would have to share the laundry facilities with the people next door.

Having had a rugged few weeks after the baby came, it was decided that one of the spinster ladies of the church, with whom we were friendly, would come and live with us to help with the children and cooking for a while. Our foster sons were already with us, too. So there were three adults, two teenagers, and three young ones staying in that duplex for six months until the new house was ready.

Today, as I sit and ponder the wretchedness of it all, and try to understand what our members were thinking when they did this to our family, it occurs to me that my husband must have had a special measure of grace and love for us all to have continued his work without complaint. The prospect of a new fresh house was the carrot that we kept dangling in front of ourselves. What a blessing to have Queens Park right across the street, where we spent many whole days with the children in fair weather. Our little kids learned to tell folks, "We're getting a blam blue house!"

Two main memories of that duplex still make me smile. One was the hilarious sound the bathroom sink made when it drained, and we actually entertained guests with it. When that wore thin, we would sit and wait for the little mouse that lived behind the tiny TV to peek out at us.

Kurt's childhood, spent largely in displaced persons camps or moving from country to country in search of freedom, was, I'm sure, part of the reason we were able to get through these rugged days without too much self pity. It was not a big deal for him to share a small space with many people, with nothing more than a blanket draped over a wire strung across the room to provide any privacy. In those days of deprivation, I doubt if his mother had the use of a washing machine either. The whole situation cannot have left any permanent damage to us, because we seem to recall only the humorous things that happened during that time.

The point of all this is simply that adaptation and flexibility is the name of the game. At twenty, it was all somewhat of an adventure. Had I a larger family, I would have met with different challenges and my attitude may have been different. At any rate, no matter what kind of housing our clergy families face, it's always possible to find someone who is worse off. Our missionary families continue today to live under very inferior conditions, and one hears stories of couples wrapping their sheds in plastic wrap to keep out the wind!

To some extent, it means we get to find out what we're really made of, what we think we must have to be happy, and how, as wives and mothers, we can teach our families to learn how to cope in all situations and thank God for the provisions we have, which in reality, we have no right to expect. When we complain in our hearts over the things we have and don't have, it's rather like saying to God, "I'm sorry, but I don't think you are cognizant of the fact that you are not doing your job of providing for me. I mean, I'm giving up my life to serve your Church. Are you stupid or something?"

Our Lord provides for us and protects us under his loving wings through the people we serve. Many times, the graciousness, or lack of it, result from cementing the love between clergy and members. Therein lies a good reason to establish social interaction with the members of your congregation. If they know we need something, often they will provide. Why would they even think about our needs if they are never in our home, or if we never interact with them?

The hospitality and affection that flows out of the parsonage are the beautiful décor that matters. The welcoming open door brings in folks that we will come to love the most, and who will offer us and our family support and defend us. They will be the ones who will babysit at the drop of a hat if we need to go to the doctor. They will keep us company when we miss our families. They will remind us and our husbands of all the needs of the ordinary folk who are the sheep of the flock we are there to care for. All we need is love. Not from them, but FOR them. Genuine affection for God's children that they will recognize and respect.

At the same time, if our housing is provided and is in need of some help to make it livable, our husband is the one who will get the best results. Let him deal with the trustees, until one of them asks us our advice. Yes, he's busy. No, he doesn't want to do it. Yes, he should. Especially if the need is something that would normally be found in every home. It's not too smart to go in with demands for color change unless asked, or appliance replacements when their previous beloved pastor's wife never complained. We take our time, and find out what we can work with, and what doesn't work. There's a difference.

It's helpful to keep in mind that we are not the family of the new boss moving into a company. We are moving into a family that is established, and while our husband is the shepherd, the sheep have been there a while before us. We treat these dear folks as a family with whom we will be living and working, being careful to avoid offending any efforts they may have made for us. If we move into a house that we purchase ourselves, we try to live by medium standards of the folks in our church and avoid a posh palace that will make them imagine that we are wasting God's provisions. I used to wonder what our poor seminary students thought when they were, for the most part, living in tiny apartments or "affordable housing" and would be invited to the homes of their professors, some of whom lived in virtual castles. Somehow, we don't visualize the servants of the Church preaching humility and charity when they are going home to five bedroom mansions, possibly with a pool, unless that is the norm for the local area.

I would be remiss if I neglected to say that the pastors' wives I knew in Australia never complained about their housing, nor their members.

Toowoomba ~ Garden City of Australia

At this point, it might be fun to talk about Toowoomba, since it was where we made our home the first fifteen years of our marriage.

Most Americans have heard of Brisbane, Sydney, Melbourne, Adelaide and Perth. Sitting on the Great Dividing Range in Queensland is one of the loveliest cities in the country. The name "Toowoomba" is derived from

Aboriginal for "swamp", and the town lies on the edge of the Darling Downs, a region so fertile that farmers yield two crops most years. The city itself inhabits the hollows of an extinct volcano, and the soil lends itself to beautiful gardens and parks. Thus, it's name: "Garden City of Australia".

Kurt was excited that we had arrived in our new town just in time for the Carnival of Flowers, for which the city is famous world-wide. An annual parade of floats and bands is only the beginning of the week of tours through neighborhoods, chartered buses loaded with eager passengers who make the rounds to all the private garden entries all over the city.

Citizens may enter their gardens in the competition, in several categories depending on size, and also by blocks. In other words, if a street of neighbors wish to compete as a group, the entire block would be open to hoards of garden lovers walking through every day to see what lovely things owners had done. The bigger gardens were usually whole property entries, front and back, and it could take an hour to visit each one. Clever folks would set up stands with home-baked goodies to sell, as well as cups of tea and water. It was a very great honor to place as a winner in this competition, and some families went to a great deal of expense and labor to put on a good show.

As a result of this annual enthusiasm for gardening, many people who live in Toowoomba are somehow compelled to keep lovely yards out of habit, or out of consideration for their neighbors. Poinsettia bushes, six feet tall, live throughout the year in front yards there, as well as flowering Jacaranda trees and Birds of Paradise. It is a perfect climate for decorative gardens as well as those for home-grown fruits and vegetables. While the old parsonage had little to offer in that regard, we did have a banana tree in the back yard, the very existence of which amused Kurt no end, even though it never gave a harvest.

When we tell folks we lived in Australia, more often than not, they conjure up a mental picture of "the bush", miles and miles of nothing but dusty red sheep (because the soil is red) and prickly pear, with kangaroos hopping around. Until recently, people in other parts of the world did not realize that major cities in Australia are large and sprawling, much like Los Angeles, and for the most part, the standard of living is equally as high, if not more so. In fact, when we were living there in the 60's and 70's, slums were non-existent, and no one knew what "the inner city" meant.

That being said, housing in the older parts of town was mostly pre-war, or approximately forty years old. The average home was a single-story wooden building, up on stilts of varying heights, with a verandah, sometimes wrapping all around the front, and inevitably, a corrugated iron roof. The first heavy rain we had was quite a revelation!

The impression of outward prosperity may be derived from the "dole system", where it is possible to live off the government pretty well, if you know how to use the system. Emancipated young people, who are allowed to leave school at sixteen, may join forces and live on the beach, sharing expenses, and never work a day in their lives. At least, that was the way it was when we lived there. Socialized medicine and child endowment allowed otherwise quite poor people to all live pretty much equally well.

For instance, when a couple had a child, the government allocated an amount, first for the birth, and then a regular amount each month that went directly into the bank account of the mother. This may have been improvised to encourage population growth, but as far as I know, it continues and goes a long way to allow mothers who wish to stay out of the work force to remain at home to raise their families. Naturally, all these things necessitated high taxes.

Toowoomba had several very prominent private schools. Families who lived on the land either sent their children into the cities to these schools or provided radio school for them at home. (I'm sure by now they have progressed to an internet education in the outback.) The Church of England, the Lutheran Church, the Roman Catholic Church, and most likely the Presbyterians had large private schools of this kind, and they provided excellent education, as well as great intramural sports programs for their students.

The Lutheran school was Concordia College. The student body consisted of both boarders and day students who lived in town and attended local congregations. There were always half a dozen young people there from the Aboriginal mission station up North, two or three boys and two or three girls.

The Redeemer/Good Shepherd parish, of which Kurt was sole pastor, also built and supported an elementary school. It was the first Lutheran day school in Queensland at the time we were married, and classes met in an army barracks on the campus of Concordia College. The headmaster was Viv Kuhl, a young male teacher, who was responsible for spearheading the building of the new primary school when it moved across the road to its own property.

After its infant years under Mr. Kuhl and a variety of other teachers, Mr. Schiller came on as headmaster, and under his leadership, there were modern brick classrooms and an apartment for the teachers erected. At the time of our leaving, there were over two hundred students and at least eight full time faculty. A second primary school was under construction in another neighborhood and now operates as well.

Also, a kindergarten was born and housed in a brand new facility on the corner of the block of land owned by the school. It was called "Nalkari", Aboriginal for "Star", and was operated under the theme of THE Star which would guide children to God. The school board asked me to paint a large picture which would hang in the entrance which would depict little children coming to sit with Jesus in the light of The Star. It was lovely, with Christ sitting in the midst of children from all nations, and the Star shining down out of a deep blue sky.

Redeemer congregation met on a property right down town, about a block away from the first parsonage we lived in. As well as the sanctuary, which was a delightful pink stucco building, there was a large red brick fellowship hall with a stage, and a kitchen and place for dining downstairs. Membership numbered about six hundred at that time. The toilet facilities were in a little metal shed outside with two toilets for the men and two for the women. There were rarely toilets in church or school buildings. They were considered unhygienic. When attending a conference in a country church, it was advisable to take along your own T.P.

While the toilets at Redeemer were indeed flushing ones, the facilities at the initial school buildings were not. The container that caught the waste was picked up weekly by the "dunnie man", who drove a truck with a large tank on the back. Our kids found it quite amusing to talk about the "dunnie man". Parents of enrolled children took turns at cleaning those facilities, and the smell of phenol still reminds me of that unique experience.

Redeemer operated a large Sunday School, which Alex and Rose Klibbe were superintendents. Devoted to the Christian education of all children two and up, they were the surrogate parents of our little ones, teaching them prayers, hymns and the Creed in their home when they babysat for us. As our children turned two, someone in the neighborhood would pick them up and take them to Sunday School, while I finished getting the others ready to be gathered by their Dad when he made his way from Good Shepherd to Redeemer.

All the years we were there, Kurt never conducted an adult Bible study on Sundays at either congregation. He led studies with his Board of Elders, consisting of an hour each month in the Book of Concord. He led various studies with the women's and men's groups, as well as the Youth Group. Even students at the College were required to receive Confirmation instruction under him if they were members of his parish, despite having it at school as well. If adults wished to be instructed, he normally went to their homes if the scheduled time for the class was not convenient for them.

The daughter congregation, Good Shepherd originally met in a little club. The members had originally been members of Redeemer, but at a certain point, decided to build a second church in another part of town. That congregation grew rapidly and also supported the elementary school, as well as the College.

Toowoomba had a lovely theater where operettas, plays and concerts were regularly offered to the public. Because of the city's cultural inclination, there were many musical opportunities for singers, instrumentalists, choirs, and the school participated in many of them, thanks to some very talented individuals who gave endless time to teaching the children. An annual Eisteddfod was conducted, drawing hundreds of individuals and schools from all around the area. Our little school enjoyed the reputation of being winners of those contests many consecutive years.

The Darling Downs was primarily farming country, and many retiring landowners came to Toowoomba to live out their old age. The population was balanced, with young families, spreading their wings, along with mature, established Christian folk who provided a lot of stability, both by their having achieved their own goals, as well as their on-going support for those coming along. There were many new shops and small industries established while we were there, providing employment and productivity.

Not being an industrial city as such, there was, however, a big bacon factory for which Toowoomba was known, as well as one or two other big manufacturers, Western Transport, a large trucking company, a number of junior colleges, two major hospitals and a couple of private ones. A large mental hospital that employed many medical people, as well as an epileptic home, both on the outskirts of town. With all the markets and shops in downtown, and growing suburban offerings, the population of approximately 112,000 was served well. The nearest aerodrome was in Oakey, about twenty miles from Toowoomba.

There were three political parties in Australia in those days. The Liberals were the conservatives, the Labor Party were the liberals, and the Country Party was the moderate party that furnished the swing vote and kept things sane.

While we occupied the old manse for at least five years, we were not close to our neighbors socially. On one side of us lived elderly sisters, one of whom operated a hair dressing business out of her home. Every morning, their clicking heels could be heard on the front walk as they made their way to their Roman Catholic Church for early mass. I can't recall ever waving across the fence, since the shrubs were too high. But I have the distinct memory of the smell of burnt hair, which seemed to come every time I hung out my laundry. If I dried my diapers outside, they absorbed that stench. If I dried them inside around the wood-burning stove, they smelled of that. So much for fresh out-of-doors laundry.

The young couple on the other side had two little boys. I seem to recall her name was Beverly, and she was very kind to let our foster sons stay with her when we had to go out of town, since she was cognizant of the fact that the State paid for their support and she would benefit from some of that.

Since there was no carpet in our house, it was a matter of mopping everything. Since the soil was red, it was a matter of mopping, especially the kitchen, with water and powdered Ajax. Or sometimes I would just use bleach and water. In any case, its near to impossible to look on your floors with any sort of pride afterward, with the exception of the flooring in the living room, which had its own shine.

Rain water was collected off the slanting iron roofs of homes, and town water, being at a premium, was sparingly used for gardens and lawns. Most Australians used tank water for drinking, making tea, cooking and laundry. It would not occur to them to wash their hair in town water, as it was considered too hard. Yet the thought of a dead toad or worse in the tank, rotting away, didn't ruffle their qualms. When we built the new manse, it had running water and no tank was attached.

Kurt & Bob Johnston & sons in Toowoomba

Kevin, Kurt and Colin
- Toowoomba

Kurt with his first child
- Toowoomba

Peter Boesch, Viv Kuhl & Kurt
getting ready for VBS

Sylvia

Scarcely having regained my land legs, following two weeks on the Pacific Ocean, and then a flight from Sydney to Oakey, and then a drive to Toowoomba, I was to meet the hosts where I would stay two days before the wedding. They were a charming family, with four handsome little boys, and everyone ran out of the house to meet us as we arrived together for the first time.

Afternoon tea was on the table, and all was going well. Then, suddenly, there was a word of caution! "Stay away from Sylvia. She's bad news."

Why was she bad news? And goodness, how was I to manage to stay away from her, since our first social obligation was a visit that very afternoon at their home! Sylvia's husband was the chairman of one of our congregations, and it was most natural that they would assume the role of welcoming me.

Arriving at their home, we were surrounded by four charming children. Susie was a diminutive toddler, and though winter was already on the way, she was still sporting her Australian tan. Jill, with a sunny smile and bleached blond hair from the beach, and Greg, a handsome young teen, very adept at conversing with adult strangers had also joined us, after which Robin, the eldest, tall and lanky, a clone of her father, with his sad, slanting eyebrows and wistful smile.

"Mum's coming in a minute," Robin announced in her wonderful accent, when indeed she entered. The mysterious lady, the bad news kid. This lovely lady, clad in a flowing floral shift, right from the islands, rushed over to me and gathered me into her large bosom, with such genuine affection, that she literally took my breath away. Her speech was engaging, sweet, cheerful, and as soprano as if she were singing to us.

As we sat around the "spread" of wonderful tarts and sponge cakes, tea in China cups all arranged on a linen cloth, the first concern was for **our** well-being, **our** settling in, **our** wedding plan, the terrible experience at sea, and "is everything all right now?" O, what a horrible woman! If she had a plot, I was ready to fall into it, and fall into it I did. A plot that grew into a wonderful friendship that lasted through our fifteen years in Toowoomba, and until the day she died many years later.

Having no blood relatives anywhere in the entire continent, it was necessary to let down one's guard and have at least one "go to" person. Sylvia became mine. She monitored my first pregnancy, walked me around the neighborhood when it was time for delivery, and was there for the second, third, fourth and fifth baby with equal enthusiasm. She respected and liked Kurt, too, so she was able to counsel and comfort the young wife through many domestic upheavals, always with the reassurance that "these things happen".

That then sets the scene for my story. To understand the dynamics, one has to know all the characters. Enter Kevin 13 and Colin 12, foster sons who came to live with us when Danny was one month old. Local boys from a family of five children, they had been removed from their home due to parental alcoholism and physical neglect. Unable to keep all five children together, the State of Queensland had at least kept the brothers together by putting them in the Salvation Army Home for Boys in Brisbane. How we were made aware of them is of no consequence, but once we had met them, we could not leave them with the indifference that is the rule in any institution for children.

Kevin was a malleable fellow and tried hard to please and make us like him. He was glad to get out of the regimented home and closer to where he grew up. Colin, on the other hand, could not overcome his grief and anger, and despite efforts, he worked as hard at being obnoxious as Kevin did at being likable. I believe he thought if he was bad enough, we would send him back.

Add Kurt's childhood history with a militaristic sadist of a stepfather, and nothing normal was likely to happen under our roof. Every attempt I made at making them feel special, like providing a tube of tooth paste for each of them, was taken as an affront by Kurt. He wanted them to feel as if they were part of the family, and that meant they were to use our toothpaste! If they misbehaved, he would not punish them if I could not bring proof to the table. It didn't take long for the boys to realize they could manipulate the situation, and a season of extreme stress dawned on our home for at least five years.

The stage is set, then, for a night of frustration, offense, and about which Sylvia said, "Some day you will laugh about this!"

The parsonage was furnished with bits and pieces of furniture, most of which had been in the home of a dear spinster member who was moving into a retirement home. It was tapestry, it was silk, it was high varnished, and everything that teenage boys should never touch. On this particular evening, following dinner, the boys and Kurt were wrestling on the beautiful sofa. Not only was this likely to make the springs pop through the fabric, the noise was most assuredly going to wake Baby Danny who had just gone to his crib.

Attempts on my part to break up this horseplay were met with total disregard, and if anything, only egged them on. Finally, when I could stand it not one more instant, I stomped to the kitchen and slammed the door hard, which brought down a clock which had, until then, resided over that door. Its ceramic splinters flew everywhere, and my heart was smashed along with it, since it had been a wedding gift from special friends.

Undone by the whole episode, there was nothing to do but storm out of the house, get into the car, and drive in fury to Sylvia's. Where else can an exasperated pastor's wife go where there is some hope that the whole story would not be all over the parish the next day? Thank goodness, Sylvia was not entertaining, and Harold was out in the hatchery, since by the time I arrived, I was a mess.

"Have a cup of tea, Dearie." In Australia, cups of tea solve all problems. Patiently, she sat and listened to my tale of woes. This was not the first time we had bemoaned the fact that a young and new wife had this extraordinary tight wire to walk. We both understood that there was supposedly some act of kindness intended by providing a home for these boys, but as I learned later, many in the parish were disconcerted that this young American novice, with a new baby yet, was being put into this untenable position.

Having a sympathetic ear was helpful and settling, but eventually, it was necessary for me to take my leave, since Danny was, after all at home with these cretins. As she loaded me into my car, she put a big double tray of fresh eggs in the back seat to take home. She never sent me away without some gesture of kindness. "Someday, you'll laugh about this," she said as she slammed the car door shut.

There was no way I was going to sleep in that house, I decided. Kurt would just have to take care of his baby son, if he was going to be so unsupportive of his wife. Smoke was still coming out of my ears, then, when another driver out late failed to honor a stop sign, and it was necessary for me to throw out the anchor, or in other words, stomp on the brakes and screech to a halt. You guessed it. The eggs all flew onto the floor in the back seat! "Well, I guess I won't be sleeping in the car tonight."

Another option was to sleep in the nursery on the floor. There was no way I was going to share that bed with Kurt. I was angry before. . .now I was furious! I think the guys must have been in the study, as I didn't encounter them as I slipped in the back door. I went to Danny's little sleep out, made a bit of a mat on the floor, and in my clothes, curled up to try to sleep.

Before long, as I lay looking out the window at the lovely Australian stars, I noticed with no small alarm that a huge fuzzy spider was making his way over the window sill, and coming into the room. O my goodness! What do you do first?

There was nothing for it but to grab Danny and retreat to the dreaded marital bed! My final thoughts as I drifted off were, "Someday, you're going to laugh about this." Sure I will!

Every time I recall that awful night, I also recall dear Sylvia, for she was right about so many things, and how I've missed her. I think I figured out why some of the people in our parish were unkind to her. Virtually everyone was a cousin of a cousin there. Sylvia had one sister, who had a TV Cooking Show out of Brisbane, another sister who married a doctor, and a brother who was a pastor. She married a man who prospered and was able to back much of the building and progress of their congregation. Their eldest daughter married one of the young men in the parish, and everything he touched turned to gold, and they were very well off on the Gold Coast. Greg was a pharmacist and did very well. Jill partnered with another artist in crafting some of the most significant stained-glass windows in Northern Queensland. Susie married a pro-golfer and lived very well in a suburb in Brisbane.

Harold and Sylvia sold their hatchery after we left Toowoomba. They moved to a unit on the Gold Coast and became very active in a Lutheran congregation there. They were instrumental in spearheading one of the best retirement centers in Queensland, unique in having a school as part of their campus. Sylvia was a leader in providing crafts and activities for the residents of the center, and Harold was on the Board of Directors.

I feel sorry for the cousins and others who missed out on knowing the real Sylvia. They were so invested in their jealousy of her outward happiness that they could not love her for what she was. They were not able, either, to console her when she lost her much-wanted infant in a miscarriage, when her son was involved in a serious auto accident on the Range one night, when she was longing for family connections and had to reach out to foreigners to have them. I feel so blessed to have known her, and I have to smile every time I think of her and recall our times together.

It Must Have Flowers

He was supposed to be a passenger on the same ship, the P. & O. Liner, "Canberra", on which I sailed to Australia in 1961. His name was Pastor F. W. Noack, and he was the President of the Queensland District. He would remain so for a total of forty years. He was the person responsible for my husband being Called to Redeemer/Good Shepherd Lutheran Parish in Toowoomba, and the hope was that he would be at our wedding.

Well, he wasn't on the ship. I don't know why. He wasn't at our wedding. I don't know why. He just didn't arrive when everyone thought he would. So it was that I didn't meet him until we returned from our Northern Queensland honeymoon.

Mrs. Noack was still living at that time, but she was not well. She and her nomadic husband lived in a beautiful traditional Queensland home, wrapped by a verandah, lost in country gardens, front and back. The first time I was a guest there, we had a cup of tea at a long, majestic table in the dining room that was covered with a heavy red velvet tablecloth. The massive table had, in years past, seated numerous children and family members as they came along, and was the heart of the home.

We were together in semi-darkness, as traditionally, in Queensland summers, blinds were pulled, and the blistering sunshine was thwarted in every possible way, to keep the indoor temperature bearable. Even without the comfort of central air, the older generation was commonly found to wear long sleeves and even their straw hats inside the home, since great attention was given to keeping the equatorial sun rays from causing skin cancer. Their days were filled with going in and out, attending to the garden or chooks, so they just kept themselves covered.

Pastor Noack was the epitome of a patriarch. Father of four grown children, he had been and continued to be very strict and resisted all attempts at moving into the new world. Four of his grandchildren lived under his roof, together with their mother, who had divorced their father, and Grandfather's rules were many and fierce. Magazines that found their way into his house were scrutinized for pictures and articles that he might find offensive before anyone in the family was allowed to see them. The dress code was severe, and the behavior of the grandchildren was very rigid.

Pastor Noack was rather a law unto himself, in retrospect. Many of the decisions that he made in the capacity as President of the District were made unilaterally, and complications and misunderstandings were not unusual. Having met people in other parts of the world that he considered appropriate for positions in Australia, he would just announce that they were to be Called. It would not matter that the local boards and committees had other plans for those positions. It seemed as if he felt he had direct communication from the Lord, and that he was incapable of making a bad decision.

Whether from fear of the man, or fear of his God, no one seemed to try to control the old gentleman. There was never any question of anyone competing with him for his office, and time just kind of went on, with the church and her schools mercifully growing and succeeding, for no apparent reason.

Pastor Noack never learned to drive. He was not a person who was in any way mechanically gifted. It required, therefore, others to transport him to various and many places he needed to go. It was not unusual for a local pastor or layman to receive an early morning call from him, when he would put the question, "Are you going to Warwick today?", or "Are you going to Brisbane today?" This meant that, yes, you were going to this place and you were picking Pastor Noack up on the way. Nor was it his custom to share expenses. It would be considered your privilege to serve the Church by serving him!

Just as it was not his custom to drive himself anywhere, it was not his custom to spend nights in hotels. He had ways of finding families along his route with whom he could stay, and he did not hesitate to make use of the convenience, or inconvenience in some cases. Ladies have reported his showing up unannounced late at night, expecting a bed. His morning routine included jumping over a broomstick a dozen times, to get his heart going.

When travelling in the United States, he assumed his tactics would work also among the people in the Lutheran Church. More than once, he took great offense when advised by a local pastor where he could find a YMCA.

Pastor Noack always wore the African hard hat everywhere he went. His black suit and clerical collar were his standard attire. I never saw him in anything else. He made sure he always carried a big white handkerchief. In Australia, he used it to shoo away the bush flies. Otherwise, it came in handy to put it on metal folding chairs before sitting down to prevent the seat of his pants from getting shiny, since he had but one suit.

Yes, our District President was very legalistic, but demanded no more or less from others than he imposed upon himself. He was not very popular among the younger set, as they were ready to dance and wear pretty clothes and make-up. It is said that at one convention where the delegates were debating the addition of folk dancing to the youth programs, he got so animated against the trends of our church that he shouted out, at the podium, "We have not yet given the square light to green dancing!"

The students at the boarding college called Pastor Noack "Old Fred". When he got wind of this, he was very upset and offended. Finally, he was appeased when my husband assured him that it was merely a term of endearment!

This, then, was the old gentleman who surprised me one day with a telephone call to say that he wanted to meet me at Palmer's Fabric Store to pick out some material for me to make a dress! The pattern choice was mine to make. The only requirement was that the material must have flowers. We met out front of the store on the appointed day. He in his black suit, walrus mustache, and sly grin.

The material I picked was a beautiful white organza with teal flowers and green leaves. The pattern was for a dress with a lovely ruffle around the V neck, three quarter length sleeves and a full, gathered skirt. It was truly lovely, though a tad low in the front, requiring a safety pin to make it a bit more modest. I think he liked it, although we never mentioned it again. I was very close to one of his daughters, but she didn't know he had made this arrangement, and we never discussed it. His motives remain a mystery to this day.

As Pastor Noack walked everywhere locally, one would frequently see him down town, doing his shopping, or just getting some exercise. It was not too surprising, then, when we got word that he had been struck by a train. He had been working on a sermon while walking along the tracks, and apparently never heard the train coming. I suppose it was miraculous that he had never been struck by a car in all his walk about trips. His hearing was not very good, and he was always deep in thought.

To say that Pastor Noack was a remarkable man would be an understatement. The years that he served the Church were many, and the changes that came during his tenure were as well. It is safe to say that he was very much an influence in the retaining of the truth and purity of the Scriptures in Queensland during those years and was very much an instrument of God. He regaled us with stories of how Lutherans were persecuted during the war because of their German background. He told us how he had rode horseback through the bush in the early years, hacking down prickly pear to make a path, visiting all the congregations that were then scattered throughout Queensland. Deprivation had been his constant companion in life, first by necessity, and then by preference. But he was a strong man, and I believe from his firm leadership followed a strength in the district which was never quite the same following his death. Realizing his deep devotion to God, I found it a little amusing to discover he had a little streak of vanity. I discovered he kept a little jar of cream handy to put on his hands to avoid age spots!

Mrs Margate

As a new pastor's wife, it's sometimes difficult to integrate the well-established women's world in a congregation. That sphere consists of mostly older, competent, experienced leaders, usually women who have owned the reins for a very long time. I found to my dismay an awkward unwillingness to entertain any thoughts from the new kid on the block, even though she was the pastor's wife.

Naturally, then, I retain vivid memories of that first meeting with the Redeemer Ladies Guild. It was a Fall meeting, when everyone was appointed to a sub-committee, each with its own assignment. Our committee was to field ideas for service projects for the upcoming year. Our little group was perched outside on the fellowship hall steps in the Queensland sunshine. Someone said, "Let's try to do something different this year. Any ideas?" Ladies associations are notorious for repeating the same monthly events, and someone must have finally gotten bored.

My Mother had been active in her ladies' organization in the States, and one of the service committees on which she served planned meals for families suffering a bereavement. Bravely, I proposed this program, explaining that it had been successful for years and provided an opportunity for useful service to fellow members in a stressful time. The idea was met with silence.

Finally, after an embarrassingly long time, one of the women said, "Well, we've never done that before. We take care of our own when there is trouble."

That was the last time I offered a suggestion.

However, as it happened, Toowoomba had a huge mental hospital (Willowburn), and a separate, rather large home for epileptics. The mental hospital had been established in a beautifully wooded area on the outskirts of town. It was housed in stately old buildings from the last century, from the look of them, but well maintained and deceitfully inviting. There were several big blocks of gray stone buildings, each housing a different category of patient.

One of the buildings was strictly for people with minor mental disorders, such as depression, or short-term nervous breakdowns, etc. Those were the patients we were allowed to visit as a ladies group, and the Redeemer ladies' guild had enjoyed a long-standing relationship with the hospital, most likely because it gave the staff a break. We were highly anticipated, since we always brought lots of food!

No one, however, had ever done anything with the residents of the epileptic home. That's what it was called: The Epileptic Home. It sat across the valley from Willowburn, on a bit of a rise. It was not impressive in the same way that the other hospital was. One got the feeling that it was rather more "matter of fact" in its layout, sprawling, low, white timber buildings, with verandahs out front, pretty gardens, and surrounded by beautiful, old eucalyptus trees which were full of squawking kookaburras and magpies. A long, winding drive separated it from the main road. But there was no fence around the property, nor even a gate with a guard. It could easily have been assumed to be a private home, albeit a large one. I suppose the fact that families never visited the patients, there was a less intense need for appearances.

The people who lived there were lifelong residents. No one ever *got better* and went home. The patients were of all ages, but mostly from about thirty years old and older. The main population consisted of people who were diagnosed as epileptics as children, whose parents could not cope with them, or for whom the stigma was too great. They had been admitted to this home and made wards of the State years before. Nobody visited them, as far as I could tell. They had only one another.

Coincidentally, one of the women of our congregation who lived just down the street from us, and who adored looking after our children, was the matron of the Epileptic Home. Visiting with her one day, I asked her if the people in her care were capable of enjoying entertainment, participating in games, making crafts, and such. She told us that everyone there was medicated and functional on a different level. The main problem, as she put it, was that they were bright enough to be bored from inactivity, and then they would fight among themselves.

The State provided no funds for extracurricular activities. Her dream was that someone would undertake to provide some very basic training in simple skills to help keep them occupied, as this would enhance their mental state, as well as be a welcome relief for the staff. The ideal situation would be if activities could include men and women, because they associated well, and even had their girlfriends and boyfriends.

Keep in mind that at this time, I had three small children and two foster sons at home. There was nothing in my history to indicate that I had any ideas about hospitals and sick people, with the exception of a year or two as a candy striper at a children's hospital as a teenager, when I was entrusted with the serious business of cleaning the bird cages!

To my surprise, I managed to seduce about eight ladies to become part of that program. I can't recall the names of all the women any more, with the exception of perhaps two. But I can see their faces as clearly as if it was yesterday. There was no hesitation from them at all, even though we didn't really know what we were going to do.

To my credit, I did have experience in arts and crafts. That got the ball rolling. As we went along, the ladies would introduce little crafts that they thought of, and often started leading the people in singing along while we worked. They always brought mountains of homemade scones and pikeletts for the patients. (Pikeletts, by the way, are not little pikes, but small pancakes with butter and jam.)

Twice a month, then, we set out in car pools from the church to the home, where we were always met by a gathering of happy faces and hugs from anxious patients, excited for us to arrive.

"My name's Don!" one man would say, over and over, as we walked into the hall together. After the first five minutes, we all knew which one was "Don". On our very first encounter, I became "Mrs. Margate", because they couldn't wrap their tongues around "Marquart". After that, my husband, who sometimes joined us for special programs, became Pastor Margate!

Everyone would gather around the tables, eager to see what we had brought and those who could still speak had a flood of questions for us. They didn't want so much to know what we were going to do, but they asked about our children. The hunger for contact with the outside world was palpable. In consequent years, some of us took our children out to meet them, and it was a high delight indeed. They loved the children and babies!

As time went by, we became more and more comfortable with their problems. Sometimes, one of them would have a seizure, suddenly collapsing onto the floor. Their friends knew how to deal with that, and after a few minutes, when it was over, we would proceed. Sometimes a nurse would come and take the patient to the sleeping dorm, but more often than not, they didn't want to leave.

Since most of the patients had been sick for many years and had suffered multiple falls, resulting in injuries, some of them wore helmets. But the larger handicap was that the illness had caused their fingers to shrink in and become claw-like, making simple tasks very difficult for them. Their determination to make the crafts was gratifying, and with the help of our ladies, the results were pleasantly surprising.

One year, for Easter, we made a beautiful big picture of a sunrise behind a silhouette of the three crosses on Golgotha. Laboriously, all different colors and kinds of seeds were glued to a big board. It took weeks to finish, and it was really quite splendid. Everyone had a hand in it, and the idea was to use it as a backdrop for our "altar" for the Easter service. When it came time to get it out one last time to make sure it was ready, we were shocked to find that the mice had eaten off all the seeds! Some of the patients cried. Some laughed!

This mutually enjoyable project was sustained for several years. It morphed into all kinds of fun activities, like fashion shows, cosmetic demonstrations, Easter egg hunts, Christmas pageants. They, without exception, loved putting on costumes and acting out simple plays. In time, this fragile community became so much a part of our lives, that we would not consider missing a visit. I believe we were the only visitors they ever had, and we were an extension of their unique family.

We watched big changes take place in some of the younger patients, as they met bigger challenges socially and physically. The older patients knew they were there to stay until they died. A quiet calm replaced a nervous anxiety in our company. But most of all, it was gratifying to watch the women of our congregation genuinely learn to love these people, learn their names, their favorite cookies, the songs they liked to sing. When I think about it, perhaps it was because these not so simple people loved unconditionally. They enjoyed spontaneous, uncomplicated fun, and they soaked up every drop of affection.

The ladies' organization of our two congregations led two parties every year for the patients at the mental hospital, as well. One was at the hospital itself, and was held in a large auditorium that had a stage. We took a small choir of ladies to lead singing carols, and there was always someone who could play the piano. The medications kept the patients perpetually hungry, so we took lots of yummy treats, as well as small gifts, like personal hygiene items. Some years, the ladies would make a pretty sachet pouch, or a lovely corsage for each lady. (There were always at least fifty patients there.)

Some of the people just sat. Some sat and ate! But most of them joined in and had a great uninhibited time with their hosts. Since the male patients were included in these parties, some of our husbands came along with us. I always suspect they thought there were going along to protect us, but in the end, they had as much fun as we did.

The second party was at the church hall. It was a special treat to get out of the hospital for a few hours, and the patients were always very excited when they hopped off the bus. There were no gentlemen at this party. Our ladies made hundreds of little sandwiches, cupcakes, and tarts for this party. There were always at least fifty patients, along with their nurse. Everyone went home with a little gift.

One year, the ladies were playing musical balloons, where everyone sat in a large circle. While music blared from the stage, a balloon was passed from person to person, which was a sight in itself. When the music stopped, the lucky person holding it, had to sit on it to make it burst. It was a hilarious time. My husband, the only male at the gathering, sat in the circle along with the ladies and was surprised and amused to have one of them look up at him and swoon, "Blessed are thou among women!"

After about ten years, the hospital changed some of its policies and we were no longer allowed to have our parties. We missed those dear folks, and the interaction we had shared. We tried taking little Christmas gifts out to them for a few years, but somehow the establishment cut more and more from the programs, and we finally had to stop.

Typically, activities like these result in blessings greater for the givers than the recipients. We, who thought we had such problems in our daily walk with husbands, children and homes to take care of, without exception, were given much more than we gave. Not only were we given the opportunity to take the Gospel to forgotten people, but every time we drove back to town, it was with thankful hearts for good health, loving families, and the freedom to come and go at will. I often wonder if The Epileptic Home still stands. With all the advances that have been made in treating that illness, maybe everyone has finally gone Home. I just know I miss being Mrs. Margate!

Second Hand Children

On two occasions during our life in Australia, Kurt was called upon to "take care of my child if something happens to me."

He was ministering to a woman, in the middle years of her life, who for some reason or another had been given the care of an infant Aboriginal boy. I don't think we ever knew the full story of where this child came from, or why she had custody of him. The woman's life was no doubt in disarray, to the extent that she felt it wise to designate someone to take him, should she perish for some reason or another.

This little boy, whose name was Ricky, was not yet three. He was a beautiful child, but had suffered inhuman abuse at the hands of someone in his life, leaving him with undisciplined behavior and virtually no manners, humanly speaking. He had been confined in locked, darkened rooms, and had no toilet training nor interest in hygiene. In other words, he was not much more than a little savage.

The woman with whom Kurt was meeting regularly, instructing her for membership in the church, asked him whether he would promise her that if she should die, he would take Ricky and make sure he was raised properly. Of course, said he.

It was impossible to guess that within two days, the woman would faint, fall into a tub of laundry water and electrocute herself to death. She must have left something in writing with regard to Ricky, because the authorities found us, and Ricky would be delivered to us in a day or so.

At this point in our lives, we had two children of our own, Danny and Cindy, and two foster sons, Kevin and Colin. The thought of dealing with a special needs child was way above my pay grade, and it threatened to drive me over the edge of an emotional cliff.

We were good friend with Pastor Peter and Coral Boesch. (Peter had been the Best Man at our wedding, and Coral was a very dear friend of mine.) They had one little boy by then, Andrew. They reached the decision very quickly that they would take Ricky to live in their home, since it was obvious to them that I was not going to be able to manage. It was such a Godsend, since there was really no other escape for me. Kurt would have just brought in another bed, and Ricky would have become a Marquart.

As it turned out, Ricky was a handful even for Coral. She confessed that she learned a great deal about herself, working out how to deal with this willful little boy. Ricky lived with Boeshes until he was a young adult and married in South Australia.

The second time Kurt was asked the same question was from a member of our congregation, with whom we were friends. Huey Cass and his wife Del, had three boys, Marshall, Russel and Phillip. They were wild little things, the kind of children who would wake before their parents, to be seen by neighbors scaling the roof of the house on a lark. Fearless and funny.

Phil was the youngest, and because the other boys were already working he was left to his own resources a lot. He was confirmation age, and he and Kurt became good friends. We spent a lot of time with the family over the years, and Del and I were very good friends.

Huey was a projectionist who worked in a local movie theater. He was diagnosed with glaucoma. At one point, he took a job in a theater in a nearby little town, which necessitated his coming home only a couple days a week. As his sight deteriorated more and more, he knew that his job was short-lived and that soon he would be blind, and maybe worse.

One day, when he and Kurt were sitting around the bar-b-que pit on their own, he told Kurt of his fears and asked him to promise that should anything happen to him, Kurt would see to Phil, and make sure he grew up all right and kept close to the Church. Once again, Kurt agreed.

Within a month, we received news that Huey, in his depressed state, had taken a revolver and shot himself to death. It was a terrible time for everyone. The members of the congregation were very supportive of Del and the boys, but it was a terrible tragedy for us all.

After the dust settled and everyone started to get back into the swing of things, little by little, Phil became more and more a part of our lives and all the decisions we made. Just as it had been with the foster sons, decisions about holidays, family outings, etc. were made on the basis of how it would fit into Phil's life. If we had to go away, the first thing Kurt did when we got back to town was to drive to Phil's house to make sure he was all right. Once again, the Messianic complex kicked in, and the wishes and needs of someone else were primary.

Minnie Bradhurst, Ugly Duckling

In the early days of my life in Australia, I believe shortly after our first child was born, so probably in early 1963, it was determined that I would join an adult oil painting class which was held at a local college. The college was downtown on Margaret Street. It sat on a corner across the street from Ernie Noack's pharmacy, and cattycornered from Queen's Park, where we would spend many hours over the years with the family.

The structure was a beautiful old Queensland sandstone, with ornate bannisters under the windows on the second and third stories. Small community classes now replaced previous hoards of boisterous youngsters running through the halls. Empty trophy cases lined the walls. It was a constant effort to find uses for this stately old establishment, but the city tried.

It doesn't seem possible that I would have been bored enough to go to such extremes so early in my married life. New husband, new baby, new lodgings, new parish. Why DOES one take a class while saddled with all that responsibility? Perhaps it was because the house did not afford much opportunity for creativity with regard to furnishing or decorating. Or maybe it was because our salary was hardly adequate to even think about replacing the basics that had been provided. What offense would there be if one disposed of a tapestry couch, or worse, the solid wood dining room table, despite the fact that it was such that no one, no matter how small, could sit with their legs under the thing, and replace any of that with furniture that was family friendly! After all, a lovely lady gave those nice things to the church, especially for the new pastor, because she was moving into a nursing home.

Since I was not let off the leash very often to do things by myself, I remain mystified as to how it came to pass that I would have enrolled in this class. I don't even remember how I discovered it. At any rate, somehow, I mustered the courage to enter this unknown world and walked into a classroom of total strangers, who uniformly turned and stared. Each had art supplies already spread out on their desks, so I figured I had found the right room.

Loneliness creates strange bedfellows. It was hard to tell Minnie's actual age, because her body was ravaged by arthritis, and so she was bent and somewhat withered. But I'm guessing she was well into her seventies, tiny and disfigured, crooked back, obviously weak, but spirited, with beady little eyes darting around behind her blue tinted spectacles, scouting out who among us would be her next painting buddy.

Our very first assignment was the study of light and shade, and the work was to be done in sepia initially, and then in color, with matching tonal qualities. My painting was of an English cathedral on a lake front that was lined with trees, whose branches were over the water. This was my first exposure to painting with oils, and it was exciting and satisfying to discover that I could actually produce something recognizable.

Minnie and I became, as they say, fast friends. It didn't take her long to realize I was from the States, and that I didn't have a lot of women friends. As a couple, Kurt and I were surrounded by "acquaintances", but there were few women with whom I was close. Before long, I was invited to her home for afternoon tea.

Minnie's palatial home was built on a double block of land, not all that far from our home. Toowoomba was called the Garden City of Australia for a reason, and her property was a good illustration of the passion the citizens had for creating park-like gardens. Half of Minnie's land was a garden which she had designed and cultivated, for the most part, by herself. Coming in from the hot Queensland sun, one was immediately swallowed by its refreshing shade, provided by beautiful flowering fruit trees. There were various perennials, and many ferns and vines clinging to the sides of the house and verandah. Benches scattered throughout, were strategically placed next to active fountains, splashing into pools which attracted the smaller birds. It occurred to me that the Garden of Eden may well have been very similar to Minnie's garden.

"Sit down right here, and I'll get the tray. No, no. I can do it. You rest." Magically, she would come tripling down the path with a tray heavy with a tea pot covered with a cozy, two cups and milk, and of course, biscuits. She always acted as Mother and poured for us both, insisting that I eat more than one biscuit (cookie), since they were freshly baked that very morning.

Minnie was a spinster. She and one sibling, a sister, lived with parents who owned a sizable station called "Tara" out in the bush beyond Dalby. While the family had astonishing assets, the girls were taught frugality, and Minnie was not a stranger to deprivation from years when the draught would strike and belts had to be tightened. Her childhood was blighted by psychological pain more than hunger. I was to hear reruns of the same sad story, lamenting her having overheard her parents talking together in their bed, just on the other side of the bedroom wall. As a little girl, she was to hear them repeatedly bemoaning, "Mary is so beautiful She will marry well and have a wonderful life. Minnie is so ugly. She will never amount to anything."

When her parents died, pocketing her inheritance, she moved into the city of Toowoomba, and it had become important to her to acquire everything beautiful and to attract as much acceptance and esteem as she could. Unfortunately, as often happens, for her to attain the desired status, she felt she had to allow herself to be exploited by theater groups and art circles who loved her money and the fact that she would give huge cocktail parties for them and their cronies.

The furnishings in Minnie's home were one of a kind. Finding antique furniture here and there, she would refinish them and reupholster them. Every color coordinated with every other color, and walking into her formal rooms was to enter into a world of enchantment. She had not only painted all the beautiful pictures, but had mounted and framed them all herself. Each item was perfect and placed in the perfect place. She said often, "If you scan a room and see one thing that catches your eye, it is out of place." Thus, her haven was a palate of balance and harmony, where we sat for hours discussing art, culture, music, Australia and world history. My friendship was all that it cost for me to become a part of this paradisiacal landscape.

A life-long member of the Church of England, Minnie was quite disenchanted with the institution of the church. Working with nature as she did, she could not deny the Creator, but she never confessed the Redemptive Act of Christ on the Cross. Turned off by the neglect of the clergy, and the methodical visits by her priest, who came only at Christmas time to collect her customary annual gift to the church, she was convinced that the whole thing was all about money to be engaged in for mere social advantage. She hated what she believed to be the hypocrisy of it all.

Naturally, then, the fact that Kurt was a pastor was distasteful to her. But she tolerated him because I did. She did not hide her dislike of the foster sons with whom we shared our home and life, quoting frequently, "You cannot make a silk purse out of a sow's ear." Her resentment of their intrusion into such a young marriage revealed itself in her attitude towards them when she would visit our home.

One day, she called out of the blue and said, "Pack a bag for yourself and Danny. I've booked a flat on the coast, and we will go there to paint." And so we did. We took picnic lunches out to the edge of a cliff, where there was a bit of shade and a view of the pounding surf, and we would spend the entire day there. Knocked out by the intoxicating sea air, Danny would doze in his little basket. Truthfully, I think Minnie and I did a bit of snoozing as well. It was my first exposure to painting on site, and especially learning how to capture moving water, and I'll never forget it.

Often when I would visit Minnie's home, I would sit in her sun room and soak in the place where she spent most of her time alone. She would tell me how she watched her ivy traveling across the beams, waiting for each new leaf to open, year after year. She had the TV on all the time, but just for the sound of someone else in the house, she said. I would imagine what it would be like for me when I grew old and would be alone. How would I fill my time? How would I deal with isolation and cope with debilitating health problems? Would my highest elation come from an ivy leaf opening? How does a woman with so much finally have so little? How does that happen?

Our relationship continued for several of the fifteen years that our family lived in Australia. Never having had good health in the first place, her body let her down more and more, causing her to be bed-ridden for days at a time. She would resurface, go strong for a while, and then down she would spiral once more until she didn't enjoy much outside her beautiful haven any longer. Once she could no longer drive, she was limited to her own company and enjoyed the occasional visit, which obviously was very tiring.

I don't know when Minnie finally died. It was after we returned to the States. Since I never really knew her actual age, I'm not sure how old she would have been. I had hoped her family would let me know, but they never did. Since she had no children, it had been her wish that her Bible be sent to me, along with a favorite painting of hers. But it's ok. Finally, she gave me the ultimate gift of love. It was an element of my life that was sorely lacking at that time, and she could feel it.

Young brides, far from family and home, have many minor bumps in the road of a young marriage. I was no exception. Since failure was not the sort of thing one talked about to church members, hers was the door I found when my heart was broken. Hers was the number I called when I was crushed by disappointment. Hers was the legacy, the lesson that one can amount to something, when no one else thinks it possible. She amounted to a great deal to me. She was not a part of my family life, nor my church life, but she filled a void no one else did. She WAS ugly, stooped, and frail. The casual observer might even regard her as self-serving and using a younger person to boost her own vanity. These critics would be sadly characterized as not grasping the possibility of honest friendship, of two women who were totally different still being cut from the same cloth in matters philosophical. These critics are to be pitied.

For while we were very alike in some ways, Minnie was educated, I was not. She was wise, I was not. She had suffered, I had not. She was strong, I was not. I like to believe she saw her young self in me, working through my problems, encouraging me to believe in survival. But most of all, she loved beauty, she created beauty, she recognized beauty, and in the end was no longer jealous of it.

Underserved Adversaries

Sometimes a pastor's wife will encounter a person in the congregation who seems determined, from the outset, to be an adversary. It's normally another woman, but it doesn't have to be. There was a gentleman in our parish who could not say a civil thing to me, and I couldn't think why. Years after he died, someone told me that he had a difficult time in the military that seemed to make him think he could bark at everyone.

It could be someone who was best friends with your predecessor. Sometimes, couples who have enjoyed an intimate relationship with the previous pastor and his family will take time to warm up to the new situation, where they are suddenly on a level playing field with the rest of the members.

Ah, yes. Human nature is so incomprehensible sometimes. Some situations and issues are the result of a mere misunderstanding, and it may be wise to initially assume that, should you encounter conflict. Yet others may be the fruit of an action that you will never even know about, an offshoot of a problem in someone's life that has caused her/him to react in an unexpectedly unkind manner to everything. No matter what you do or say, the reaction might be different from anything you anticipated. The issues are present in all walks of life, in every business. Clergy are not particularly targeted for abuse. It just seems as if Christians should behave kinder to one another, and since clergy are in the middle of parish life, I suppose we have more visibility and therefore more reasons for people to lash out, when they might not get away with it among other people in society.

In my personal experience, and through listening to other clergy couples, it seems to me that often the most uncomfortable kind of animosity flows from women. Perhaps a person who likes your husband very much, but at the same time derives pleasure from tormenting you in some way. My gut feeling tells me that this kind of personality is drawn to authority figures, and if she realizes it is not right for her to have certain feelings, her guilty conscience will bring about irrational behavior towards you. In other words, she has nothing against you personally, but if she is nice to you, then she must clean up her intentions with your husband. And she may not want to do that.

I have no training in psychology. So please do not assume all these examples have any scientific basis. Simply a study of human nature, and being around long enough to see the drama of life situations play out tends to give us insight into reasons others do what they do. After all, we react to situations the way we do because of previous experiences, or because we have a wise husband who has advised against cat fighting on church property! One of the most important things I have learned, however, is that these things rarely are the result of anything YOU have done.

When I married Kurt and became the youngest pastor's wife in the district, there was one woman, right off the bat, who didn't like me. Even though she had been involved in our wedding plans and was all smiles at the wedding, it seemed that every chance she got, she made a crack about what I was wearing, or she would make fun of something I said. Sometimes she omitted putting me on her guest list if she had a party, when she knew I would find out.

A friend of mine had passed along a hat she no longer had use for. She attended a different church, so it wasn't likely anyone would recognize it. The first time I wore it, this lady, grinned at me and said, "Well, I like Sylvia's hat on you. I'll have to dig around and see if I can find some old thing to give you, too."

She never came to our house. However, she was best friends with the only other American pastor's wife that we knew, and so it was difficult to avoid her. One late afternoon, I was sitting out on the back steps of the parsonage, just enjoying the peace and quiet, when someone was at the front door. I had not turned on any lights yet, so the house was unlit. I was totally astounded to find her at my door, and as she strode in, uninvited, the first words out of her mouth were, "Why are you sitting here in the darkness? Whatever are you doing in here?" She had a high penetrating voice that sounded as if she was about to laugh, but she never did.

I stepped aside, as if Cruella Deville herself had entered, with her long furs training behind her. I had been sewing all day and had left it all out to work on the following day. The dining room, therefore, looked a bit like a Chinese workshop. We had two foster sons at that point, besides our baby boy, and while the house was generally tidy, it never attained the perfection that her cleaning lady achieved.

When I apologized for the mess, she had the nerve to remark that my house was always in chaos, wasn't it? (It was the first time she had been there.) I explained that I had a policy with the boys, that I would leave their stuff sit out for two days, after which I would toss it. She turned around slowly as she took in the room and said, "Looks as if you've been doing that a long time." She was the kind of person that if you turned your back, she would take her gloved hand and run it along the chair railings to check for dust!

To this day, I don't know why she came. Maybe she thought I had a lover stuffed under one of the beds in the absence of my husband, who had taken some kids camping. There had to be some calculated reason, because that was just the way she was. After you discover that someone has gone to the trouble to go to the courthouse to check your marriage license in order to see if your foster children were the byproduct of a former marriage, you never really feel the same about them. (I calculated that it would have been necessary for me to be nine years old to have made that work. But boy, it sure would have been a feather in her cap to discover such a thing!)

Now that I'm old and almost forty years and ten thousand miles away from that woman, I sometimes think about her and I think I've figured out why she was the way she was, with me, anyway. Maybe. First of all, everyone in the parish was related to everyone else. Her parents were wealthy, she was an only child, thoroughly spoiled, married well, and had two adopted children. Her house was very flash, and she could buy anything she wanted.

Her mother was an unpleasant person. She was mean-spirited, waspish, critical. After church, she would not mingle, but rather go out and sit in her car in the parking lot and hold court for those other older members who might wish to greet her. Her husband was a sweet old hen-pecked man. So, it was not hard to imagine the daughter's upbringing.

This woman was not a particularly attractive person, tall, lanky, long British nose, goofy laugh that could be fun. She was connected. That is to say, she grew up in that parish, knew everyone, and everything, about everyone. Somehow, she had managed to become best friends with the other American pastor's wife, and by the time I arrived, she had already established herself with my husband as well.

I may be totally mistaken, but looking back, I think she must have felt somehow threatened by my arrival. I was young, attractive, and American. The local papers had made a big fuss over our wedding, and everyone in the parish was very excited about my coming to marry their pastor. All the attention was going to someone other than herself for once.

My husband and I spent a lot of time in the home of her best friend, and it must have been very vexing to her, wondering if I would steal her friend away from her. She and my friend enjoyed numerous shopping and lunch dates together, and I suspect she was very generous. She sucked up every spare minute my friend had, in order to keep her to herself.

This woman and I never had a real confrontation during the fifteen years I was there. Her cutting remarks continued to cause me pain, and it was hard to be in her company, and impossible to avoid her. She left her mark, even on my new kitchen floor, by grinding her spiked heel into the soft floor covering. "O! Did I do that?" It was a lasting dig to remind me of her lack of respect for the home of her pastor.

Had I been more mature, I would have perceived the source of her antagonism. The fact that my husband tended to defend her actions didn't go down well either. He never understood why I allowed her to upset me. He would say, "Why is she such a threat to you?" That's a fair enough question under most circumstances, and during the many years of interactions with parishioners, I have stopped and asked myself that question about many people. In actual fact, most people are not a real threat, only a perceived one, to us. The old saying "They can't hurt you unless you allow them to" is a good one to remember and keep handy. Rather than continuing to ruminate over offenses, we are asked to forgive and forget. It really does make us more attractive, more interesting to be with, and no one has to feel sorry for us, if we don't feel sorry for ourselves.

After the birth of our second child, I developed pleurisy. I was in so much pain, I could not even lift my newborn, much less go to the doctor's office. He actually came to the house. Danny was about eighteen months old, so he was quite mobile. The foster sons were helpful to a point. Kurt, in his infinite wisdom, decided it would be helpful to me, if he took the boys off camping. I suppose he figured with them out of the house, at least I wouldn't have to do any cooking. I don't know. The fact is, he was not very good around sick people, never quite knowing how to comfort or take up the slack. To his way of thinking, getting out of the house was most likely the most he could offer.

So, there I was, bedridden, with an infant and a toddler. Dishes stacked in the sink and laundry accumulating in piles. You know what I mean. In the midst of this chaos, the woman I thought was a good friend appeared, along with her husband yet, to visit. Most likely she wanted to see the baby, since she was a real cutie. They didn't stay long. They looked around, and I guess they decided they wouldn't stay. As she left the bedroom, she turned and said, "Too bad your friend, Sylvia is out of town. She is always so good to you."

This probably would not have been quite so offensive to me except that when this person, who had four kids at home, was in hospital, giving birth to her fifth son, I cooked and cleaned for her family every day until she returned home. I was sick before they arrived. I was devastated when they left.

Since we were so close with the family, and spent a lot of time together, it was thereafter a somewhat strained relationship. I couldn't really say anything to them, nor anyone else for that matter, about how hurt I felt. I think it was the first experience I had when I realized that someone I thought was a good friend, really wasn't there for me when I was desperate for help.

After years of pondering over this unfortunate situation, it occurred to me that this woman may well have had a grudge against Sylvia, for always "being so good to me". She was, after all, the one who warned me against Sylvia when I first arrived in Australia. Women can be very vindictive, and it does not have to be anything you have done wrong.

Perhaps the one woman who was kindest to me in the world was the one I didn't really realize until long after I left Australia. There was a family that lived behind us. A man, his wife, and a daughter. She was the only other Barbara I met the entire fifteen years, and there she was in my back yard!

Barbara was the kind of neighbor who would lean over the fence and visit, she would come in for coffee and chat while I ironed. Her husband was not an easy man to live with, and we would offer consolation to one another nearly every day. She sewed maternity clothes for me. She cleaned for me once a week, when I went to work. For pay, of course. She was a good friend outside the church, and good to my kids. Sometimes these are the connections God sends us to help us get through the daily trials of homemaking, people who do no harm to us when we reveal our pain or disappointments. People whose expectations of us are so different from the members of the church.

I've discussed before in one of my lectures the most hateful person in my life was another pastor's wife. While everyone was a target for this woman's vindictiveness, it became apparent that she had her hooks out for me. When we first met, it appeared we would enjoy a good relationship. But one day, this lady discovered that I had endured an unhappy marriage before I married Kurt, and in her mind, it was a vile sin for a pastor to marry a divorcee.

Immediately, this woman launched a character assassination on me, telling everyone who would listen what a terrible person I was. She even called the Sunday School Superintendent and asked her, "How can you let a woman like that near the children?" She proceeded to lay traps for me and poisoned her own children and husband against me.

When I discussed this with Kurt, his advice was simply to go about as if nothing happened. He said that if I acted normally others would soon assume the pastor's wife was lying. Besides, that kind of gossip can be kept alive for only so long.

While working as a teacher's aide for a preschool at one of our churches, after a year of perfect harmony with the teacher, she suddenly became hostile and wanted me to leave. She told the pastor that when she heard me coming in the front door, she wanted to run out the back! No one could get her to say specifically what she didn't like about me, but it was clear that, while we had in fact worked like hand in glove the previous year, she was not going to remain if I did. I was blown away to realize how she was literally seething inside about it all.

It broke my heart. I loved working with the kids and maintained good relationships with the parents. Maybe, once again, she saw me as some kind of threat. It is very easy, I have found, when we are good at something, that some women are either jealous or frightened by us. Prepare to pare back your gifts and talents a bit if you sense that you are shining too brightly. It is natural for us to do the best we can to advance the work of the congregation in a suitable capacity. Perhaps, if we are too good at what we do, we bring on this irrational fear of us. We need to be very sensitive to the impression others may have of our successes, and if necessary, reel them in sometimes.

In the situation I described, the teacher was a frustrated person who had married outside her faith. She had been through our Synodical schools and liked to name drop, recalling student friends who had become pastors. I believe she really had longed to marry a pastor, and perhaps when we discussed my situation as having been the wife of a pastor in Australia, it may have grated on her. We shared frustrations over home and family issues. But suddenly, something snapped, and even though we even had reconciliation meetings with the pastor at the church, she never specified to me exactly what was wrong. When I told her I had decided to leave, all she said was, "I was hoping that's what you would do."

We never spoke again. Years later, she had a serious stroke. I went to the hospital to visit her, but she became so agitated that I could stay only a few seconds. There was some deep struggle within her that was never settled. How very sad, for both of us.

Pastor Perry Mason

There lived in Toowoomba a wonderful family of Challenors. I'm not certain any longer how many children there were, but I remember four of the sons — Lindsay, Barry, and then twin boys, whose names I can't remember

The father of this family was Kurt's first funeral. This meant that Mrs. Challenor was left to care for this growing family on her own for a goodly number of years. She was beloved by everyone. Her boys were admired and became active in the congregation, as one by one, they grew up, married and began their own families.

As Barry grew into manhood, he found a wonderful woman, Kay, to be his wife. They were both devout Lutherans, caring for any and all of those in need. I believe it was the first child, a lovely little boy, who was born with some learning difficulties. It seems to me as if he was also mostly deaf. It was such a heart-breaking thing for this wonderful couple, to find that there was little they could do for him at home. Finally, it became necessary to admit him to a facility in Brisbane for children with physical and mental deficiencies. It was the hardest decision of their lives, but they were convinced the school would help him learn in ways they could not manage at home.

After their son had been in Brisbane for a while, they received a call to tell them that he had been killed in an accident in the dorm. The very place where they believed he would be the safest turned out to be his death sentence. Immediately, they experienced not just grief, but guilt. If only they had kept him at home, etc. It was tragic on every level.

After the funeral, it was determined that the facility where he had been living was at fault and that they were within their rights to go to court for some kind of satisfaction. The little boy lived in a dormitory with a number of older children. Apparently, during a wild scuffle, a bunk bed was overturned, and the metal bar at the head of it fell across his throat, choking him to death and breaking his neck.

It just made sense that there had to be serious negligence by the staff for this to have been allowed to happen.

There was no one else in Barry and Kay's corner. They could afford no legal advice, and so their pastor stepped in. Kurt went to the facility in Brisbane, interviewed the staff, looked over the evidence and the room in which the children slept. He gathered evidence that showed that the child actually died a wrongful death, and that the facility should give the Challenors some kind of compensation.

They had a court hearing. The local newspaper had photographs of Kurt entering the court with Barry and Kay, and the big headline was "PASTOR PERRY MASON". The article told the entire story about these people from the Downs who came for justice. They characterized Kurt as looking like a TV detective! In full clergy regalia, mind you. The entire case was summarized in the article, and anyone with a brain would conclude that negligence on part of the facility was the cause of the death. The court decided against the parents anyway. And they had to go home, not only without their little boy, but with no comfort in the form of payment from the place where he died.

Kurt was very good with details. His second choice, had he not become a pastor, was to be a lawyer. His brain processed information in a way that most people in a state of anxiety, fear or guilt could not. He went to court over the years with several of his members, with various measures of success.

Aboriginal Relations

Perhaps because he himself was an "outsider", Kurt gravitated to those who were in one way or another displaced, or lived outside the walls of normal society.

Having come to the States as a teenager, around fifteen years old, he was sensitive to feeling "different", to being seen by others as a foreigner. I don't believe there was anywhere, or in any company, that he didn't feel this way, until he began going to Haiti. The people in Haiti's streets didn't know the name "Marquart". They had no idea of his background, or his status in the academic world or that of the Church. They most likely were initially attracted to his money, since he fed them when he was in town. But after they got to know him a little bit more, they enjoyed just going to the beach, or hanging out around the pool with him. They had no expectations of him to produce anything amazing. He was just one of their friends. It was in their company, with their simple expectations from life, that he could totally relax and be himself.

I have no recollection of how we were introduced to the small world of the Australian Aboriginal. They didn't come to our church in the beginning. But before long, the few that lived in Toowoomba had our phone number and didn't hesitate to call when they were in need.

The family name was Anderson. In true Aboriginal fashion, they lived generationally, usually with an older parental leader, and the younger married couples lived with them, all endeavoring to scrape up enough money to keep the clan fed and housed.

It was nearly impossible for any young couple to strike out on their own to make a go of it in civilized society. Tradition required that when family came along, they stayed with you, and you were obligated to feed and house them as long as resources continued. When things ran out, the visitors moved on. As a result, no one ever had anything they could call their own. There was no such thing as a single couple saving anything for themselves or their immediate family. Communal property was the name of the game.

Kurt made regular trips to the home of the young couple that he knew best. There were always extras staying, along with many children, and there was always need for groceries. While I didn't mind the charity of it, it was a nuisance to have one's dinner interrupted with an urgent call for groceries. With one Easter coming up, I decided to preempt them by getting a big box of nice things together for Kurt to take to their home on Saturday. I hoped this would allow us to enjoy our day without our Dad having to drive off in the middle of the meal to save someone!

Honestly, Kurt had been back in the house five minutes when the phone rang, and the very people he took food to were desperate for food, since family had come to town. It was then that I fully understood what he meant when he said, "Other people's needs rarely meet our convenience."

During those years, however, Kurt did marry one young couple, and confirm them. We were in touch by mail after we moved back to the States, and the last we heard, they were still going to church and were employed. The members of our congregation never entered into any form of support for the natives in their midst. It was not a racist thing so much as a cultural thing. Aboriginals that moved away from their villages had a difficult time, and even those among them who managed to become educated had trouble cutting through the wall of discrimination.

It is possible that in later years, the number of Aboriginal people may have grown so that they would have succeeded in finding their place in society. Perhaps in the larger cities, there was more opportunities for them. One tends to think that those who stayed up in the North with their "own kind" may have been more content.

The college that our Synod supported, a boarding high school, sponsored four children from our Aboriginal mission field up North. Two boys and two girls. They came and lived in the dorms and were educated, the theory being that they would go back to their tribes and share their wonderful knowledge with the people, thus improving their life. Kurt used to snort with laughter at such a silly idea, saying, "Don't they realize that in that culture, it's not the teenagers who dictate policy for the tribe? It's the elders." He felt that these students would go back to a place where they no longer belonged, nor were able to ever be content again.

The Tropic of Capricorn

Did you know that 23.5 degrees north of the Equator runs an invisible line around the world called the Tropic of Cancer? 23.5 degrees south of the Equator, a similar line encircles the world which is called the Tropic of Capricorn. The area bounded by these two imaginary lines is called "the tropics". It is a part of the world in which the seasons never change because the sun is always high.

As a twenty-year-old kid from Texas, I never knew that simple fact until I ended up in Australia! I think the first I knew of it was when Kurt commented on it as we drove past the little marker in Rockhampton, on our honeymoon, way back in 1961. But its significance apparently did not impress me enough to leave much of a mark.

However, in 1973, I had another opportunity to drive through the tropics. The events that surrounded this trip were quite a bit more memorable than my honeymoon, not necessarily in a good way, and now when I hear that term, Tropic of Capricorn, I'm taken back to a journey that one could not have planned on purpose. The events just kept unfolding all by themselves.

From the beginning, then: In earlier stories, I have written about the two brothers who lived with us from the time our first baby was one month old. The younger, Colin, moved to Northern Queensland when he left school, and worked changing tires in an auto shop. He had purchased a couple of motor bikes, one of which was a nice big BMW. The other was a racing motor bike. On weekends, he would compete in the circuit races and had succeeded in becoming the champion in his class.

At one point, Colin had suffered an accident on the race course which resulted in the toes of one foot being jammed into his foot. When he was finally recovered from that, he decided to race one more time and then retire from the game. We had never watched him race before, and he pleaded with us to come up to the big finals.

Kurt had a previous meeting scheduled that would take him to Adelaide for a week, and therefore could not make it. However, there was a family from the local college who had relatives up North who were going to make the trip about the same time to visit them. They said I could go along with them. Honestly, I have no memory of what I did with the children, of which there were four. But they all had friends in the parish with whom they stayed occasionally.

It was a 650 mile drive up the coast road to Townsville, and it required an early departure. There were four of us, and two of us took turns driving. We had a great time, just Lorelle Matthews, her big brother, her little sister, and I.

There are few places in the world as scenic and untouched as the north of Australia in those days. No super highways cluttered the beautiful outback. Quiet inland roads allowed you to meander from one quiet holiday cove to another, passing through the occasional industrial spots where sugar cane was being processed or pineapple groves were in full swing.

Australia is described by some as looking as if it survived the great flood, with its few mountains and hills being worn down and non-threatening. Unlike the jadedness of the landscape in much of our continent, there was a smoothness about the countryside as it rose and fell before the traveler.

Arriving at a prearranged location, we met up with Colin when we reached Townsville. The kids found their relatives, and they ran off to get something to eat. The races had begun earlier in the evening, and there was no time to find anything for me to eat. Colin didn't want to eat before he raced anyway, saying it would mess with his stomach. We headed for the grandstands, where Colin planted me where he would be able to find me again. He had to go make sure he was registered and make a final check on his bike, in case anyone might have tampered with it while he was gone.

Any kind of motor racing is noisy, and dusty, and pretty exciting. This being a final contest, the riders were merciless and somewhat careless in their determination to grab the trophy. Anyone with a friend, or skin, in the game was just a little tense, praying that no rider got too messed up on his last race.

Finally, Colin's class came up, and off he went. I love speed. I love the way a jet rips the sky open with its sound waves. The sound of motors all pitting against one another, and the skill it takes to stay on track is pretty exciting for me to watch. I had attempted to ride a motor bike a couple of times. Once when Kurt was driving and I was passenger, we both hit the dust with no harm done. Again, when the boys were attempting to teach me to ride alone in our back yard, I did fine until it came time to stop. No one told me that part, and I pretty much rode right up the chain link fence. Therefore, I had a great appreciation for those who could ride well under pressure.

But I digress. Colin won the race, and the cash that came with it. I was pretty excited to stroll around the crowd with a champion, and he would, depending on who it was, introduce me as his "mum" or his "Sheila"! What a different crowd from my usual Sunday morning friends.

We spent a couple of hours of good byes from Colin to his racing mates. He also had to sell his racing bike before he could head back to Toowoomba with us. Being the winning bike didn't hurt his chances of getting a good price. At long last, he made his final farewells to the whole thing, and we returned to the home where he lived with a local family, where we were able to sleep a few hours before heading South.

The Matthews kids were right on time and met us at the designated departure place. Colin was going to ride his BMW and follow us home. Lorelle said, "Wouldn't it be fun if we took turns riding with Colin?" Naturally, the kids were keen. They insisted, however, that I go first. Then I could do the tail end of driving the car when we got to Brisbane, where I knew the road.

The idea, then, was that I would ride with Colin to the spot in Rockhampton where the Tropic of Capricorn marker was along the highway. We had passed it on the way and knew where it was. At that point, the second pillion passenger would take over. Colin and I unloaded all our surplus clothing, my handbag, our money, ID's, everything into the car. He didn't want to take his prize cash on his person, so we left it all in the car. I donned his leather jacket and his spare skid lid, and off we went.

Being a pillion passenger on a big bike is very comfortable. They purr along nicely, and the wind fording itself into your nostrils gives you energy you didn't know you had. It was purely exhilarating to me, and the miles slipped away in the gentle morning sunshine.

When we arrived at the marker, we were happy to slip off the bike and stroll around, stretching our legs and relaxing a bit. We had not gotten there much before the appointed time, and after half an hour or so, it became worrisome that the others were not arriving on schedule. While it was still daylight, we knew it would be dusk before we reached the next check point, where Colin would go on alone. We gave them another half hour, and when they did not come, we decided to backtrack, thinking they might have misunderstood where we were to meet.

Going fairly slowly, so that we could check oncoming cars, we went for some time to no avail. Cell phones did not exist in those days. There was no way to even call Toowoomba to see if Lorelle's parents had heard from them, because all our cash was in the car. Our main concern was that something unfortunate might have happened to them and they were in trouble.

Suddenly, with no warning whatsoever, the back tire on the bike blew! The bike fishtailed, and Colin was able to bring it down without it smashing into anything. But not before I was thrown off the back. I tried to remember that relaxed persons have fewer injuries, and as I watched the moon go by half a dozen times, as I rolled, I was very thankful to have had a helmet on. When I finally came to a stop, Colin rushed to see if I was all right. I had some pretty nasty scrapes on my knuckles and my backside was sanded off pretty well on one side. But otherwise, the bike was of greater concern.

We walked the bike to a nearby motel, where we suffered great humility with a clerk who was not buying our story of being left behind with no means of support. After several attempts at trying to explain how we happened to be stranded, I gave him the name of Lorelle's father and asked him to call him and verify our story and get some assurances that we had good intentions.

It was all very embarrassing. But he finally gave us a room, and while I lay down, Colin went to procure bandages for my wounds with what change he had in his pocket. Then he took the bike to a garage and fixed the tire himself, since that was, after all, what he did for a living. The owner of the motel brought us some sandwiches and put himself at our disposal. But after a few hours of sleep, we got back on the bike and headed South.

As we reached the top of the mountain we had to climb to get on our way, the view of the valley behind us was so beautiful that I had to paint a picture of it when I reached home. As I look at these watercolor paintings today, I can't help but chuckle at the memory of my famous ride. I would never have trusted another person to take me on such a long trip on a bike. I literally put my life in Colin's hands, and as a result, he gave me the ride of a lifetime!

First Years of Marriage

Kurt, after being away on our honeymoon, had to hit the ground running when we returned to Toowoomba. The never-ending research and decisions for his next sermon, (He never wrote out a sermon. At most, he took a few notes to the pulpit.) members in the hospital to visit, shut-in Communion calls to make, board meetings to attend, were all waiting for his return.

There was no office at the church, only a vestry, with no shelving, and a small table for a desk. This required him to do all his work at home. There was a study at the house, and while it was not very cozy, there were at least bookshelves and a useful desk. It also had a separate exterior door, but we found members continued to come to the back, simply out of habit.

This reminds me of the two monetary allowances he was given, in addition to his basic salary. Of course, his existing library filled the shelves of the study from the first day he moved in. But for additional books relating to his Office as pastor, the congregation allocated him five pounds a year. (Five pounds in those days amounted to about $10.) If you have ever seen his library, you would readily realize that the allowance, while kindly meant, didn't even buy the paper on which he typed. As well, the budget allowed him to receive ten pounds a year towards entertainment/hospitality. ($20). Occasionally, I get questions from women who ask how they can entertain their members without going bankrupt. Toast and Vegemite worked in Australia!

Kurt never had the service of a church secretary the whole time we lived in Toowoomba. He did all his own typing and printing, including bulletins and newsletters. An old duplicating machine requiring stencils occupied a shelf in the closet off the spare room at the back of the house. I offered many times to type the bulletin for him, but he had his own ways of doing things, and preferred to do them himself. Personally, I think procrastination was part of it! Late at night, he would walk over to the church, a block away, and put a pile of unfolded bulletins on the vestry table for the ushers to find and fold the following morning. Many times, he said he had to shoo a sleeping drunk away from snoozing on the church steps.

+

Having enjoyed so much undivided attention from Kurt during our long road trip, I had difficulty for a while being on my own. While he was home a lot during the day, he was always reading, studying, writing, or he would be out making calls. It didn't take long for me to realize that if I wanted to spend time with him, I had to be groomed early in the day and be prepared to hop in the car at any given moment so that I could accompany him on his calls. At least we would have time together in the car.

Most of the time, I could go into the hospital with him to visit someone. Otherwise, I simply waited in the car, sometimes with a book. My own motto in those days was that "I lived with a streak of lightning". There was little time to consider whether or not I wanted to go with him.

During those first days, it fell to me to unpack my trunks of household items that I had brought with me, and decide where and how to use them. While it doesn't take long to unload two trunks, there was also the matter of finding closet space for my things.

If you have ever tried to get an organizational task done, you know how distracting it can be to have constant interruptions. In my case, it was the kind people who unexpectedly appeared at the back door, laden with piles of produce, eggs, or freshly baked goodies. The "open door" policy was established right from the beginning, which meant if anyone arrived around ten in the morning or three in the afternoon, they were invited in to join us for a cuppa. (Cup of tea) It was not unusual for us to invite visitors to tea (dinner) whose visits had slipped into the time when meal preparations were begun. Whatever we were having would just be stretched a bit, and maybe some fresh bread and butter added. The aim was to always be flexible without adding unnecessary stress to things.

While many people would find this way of life intrusive, it was a Godsend for me, because it allowed me to get to know people on my own terms. It was one thing to appear in public once a week, greeting perfect strangers and smiling for no particular reason. It was another for me to get to know each one on a personal level. Looking back, I believe this was an important part of why I enjoyed a good relationship with the parish.

When people accepted my invitation to come in and sit down for a cup of tea, they could see that we were living just like they were, in meager comfort, with little more to offer than our friendship. If I did not have biscuits (cookies) on hand, I made toast and Vegamite, since everyone loved that. They could see at a glance that their pastor was in good hands.

Maybe some were just curious to see what this young American was going to do with the interior of the manse. Since its two previous occupants had been elderly clergy couples, what would this young thing do with it all? In many cases, I'm sure it was the first time some of them had ever had a personal conversation with their pastor over the kitchen table. For whatever reason, it was obvious this Grand Central Station atmosphere was going to be our lifestyle, and fortunately for me, I thrived on it.

In my youth and inexperience, I had not yet heard the term "fishbowl existence". The clergy couples that we knew never talked about their lives in this way. Possibly, extended members of one's family might find such public exposure extraordinary. For Kurt and me, however, it was a foreign concept. As I look back now, I know that it was these extemporaneous visits that convinced me that the clergy family was not some kind of special species that folks were anxious to gawk at. Rather, we were living in the ocean of humanity, an ocean rich in opportunity to meet, love, and encourage people who would most likely have never entered our lives otherwise. We all swam together. We all met the same threats and challenges of life. We all enjoyed God's blessings, and we all felt pain when loss came. So very often, Kurt expressed his theory that more is accomplished over a meal and a glass of beer than nearly anywhere else. It fell to me, then, to facilitate that as often as I could.

It stands to reason, that in most cases, if someone came to the manse to see the Pastor, it was not just a social call. Often, the real reason did not even surface for a while. If, however, they found themselves in a relaxed setting, having a cup of tea with him and his wife, and sometimes a youngster, their guard was dropped and the thing that was troubling them would finally come out. In a non-threatening atmosphere, they were able to talk freely about what was troubling them, and their defenses were down so that they were also able to receive positive suggestions for solutions.

I am convinced that this acceptance of our members in our home, no matter how otherwise inconvenient it may have been, was one of the main reasons the pastor was loved and trusted by the people. One of our elders, who was working on lowering his blood pressure by running after dinner, began dropping in to have a beer with Kurt, when he knew he was home. His concerns were such that he would never have addressed them in a formal meeting of his fellow elders. This connection not only allowed him the support of his pastor/friend, it gave Kurt an ear into areas he otherwise would not have known about. It allowed him to prevent, or head off, troubles before they grew too big to handle.

It is hard to imagine this kind of pastor/member relationship in our city congregations today. I recall one night at a students' wives' class, where another professor's wife and I took over the evening because the prof had to be out of town. The subject arose about entertaining members in the manse. I said that in our time in the ministry, we were either preparing for someone to come, or there was someone there, or someone was leaving all the time. We had teachers boarding with us from time to time. We had international visitors sleeping in our home as they journeyed through the country. We sometimes invited members home from church for lunch. The professor's wife was very quiet throughout, until she said, "My husband is so burned out from dealing with people all day that he doesn't like to have anyone around at night when he comes home."

While there may have been truth in that, it could also be the case that hubby knew better than to entertain the thought, because he knew she would not be willing to host anyone spontaneously. I grew up believing in "angels unaware". I know people are put in our path for a reason, and to reject those opportunities leaves us just that much less blessed.

Actually, I received much more than I gave through this "kitchen ministry". When my babies were sick, or the ironing was piling up, or I was sad about something, these wonderful people managed to soothe and encourage me, too. Many times, if it was a female parishioner, she would put a pile of ironing in a basket and haul it off to her home where she would do it. No one ever minded if I put the ironing board up and continued to iron while we visited. I was adopted as their daughter/sister in the Faith, and there seemed nothing too monumental for them to do to come to the aid of their pastor's family. God provided so many blessings through those wonderful people.

Since we had no other obligations, while we were awaiting our first baby, we made a point of trying to make home visits to every member during those months. Families in the evening, and the elderly during the day. Without exception, nearly every elderly couple we visited provided a full-blown morning or afternoon tea, with linens and China, and wonderful pastries. More often than not, they had a basket or parcel of something nice for us to take home with us. I was amused, and somewhat embarrassed that nearly everywhere we went, we were asked if we had a baby on the way yet. Since then, I have been equally amused to hear clergy wives asked by folks, "What, not another one?"

Back to the trunks! While I found it strange that Kurt had so few articles of clothing it was a good thing, since there was scarcely any storage space in the manse. There were no closets, only one wardrobe and one duchess (dresser) in our bedroom. Fortunately, the "sleepout", that later became the nursery, had built-in cupboards with shelves, so we had somewhere to put linens and towels, etc.

Kurt's wardrobe was very utilitarian, and I liked to divide it into two categories: his dress clothes and his play clothes. His dress clothes consisted of his single black suit, two black clerical shirts, one clerical collar, one pair of cheap Walmart black shoes, four pairs of black socks and four white T-shirts. His play clothes consisted of one pair of khaki pants, one khaki long sleeved shirt, one pair of flip flops (thongs in those days), and a white tropical hard hat. Oh, yes, and four white handkerchiefs. You may ask if he had work clothes. The answer would be, no, since he didn't do any work. In later years, when he mowed the lawn to darken his tan, he could be seen wearing his swim togs, together with his tennis shoes and black socks. Otherwise, because there was no earthly interest in any sports or gardening, he could rarely be seen in anything other than his "uniform", as he called his clerical garb.

In packing things for me to take to my new life, my Mother insisted that I have lots of underwear. She recalled her early life when it was the last thing a wife and mother did for herself: buying new panties, bras and slips. Years after we left Australia, and on one of our return trips, I was visiting with the widow of one of our original elders. She related how one day her husband came home from a visit to our home. Naturally, he had come in through the back, and I had just hung out all the laundry for the day. There was almost an entire line devoted to panties. When he came through the kitchen door, he exclaimed, "I've never seen so many gussies in my life!"

Among my things were four new dresses, for honeymoon and church. Two pairs of heels, white and black, a portable Singer sewing machine that I had been given by my parents for graduation, on the agreement that I would never hock it in time of need. Perhaps four towels and two sets of sheets, tea towels, a setting of six Corellware plastic dishes, and some cutlery. I had a few pieces of cookware, and I must have taken at least a skillet and some saucepans. We were given a six place setting of Noritaki China as a wedding gift from the Johnstons.

It didn't, therefore, take long for me to unpack two trunks and two suitcases!

+

The setting up of the household thus begun, I soon realized there would be a lot of improvising necessary. From the beginning, as I examined each new room, a myriad of ideas flew through my head as to how I would make it work. I saw a lot of potential for it, for the most part, but it had not yet occurred to me that we would have little or no cash to pay for my creativity.

Fortunately, I liked painting. The interior looked as if it had been painted decades before, and was all the same dreary shade of aging linen throughout. Did I mention it was glossy finish? All walls were board to board and were one board thick, with a cross board on the side of the wall that was considered less important. You know? You've seen old Westerns, where the cabin walls are primarily to hold up the roof, and not to create privacy or make anything pretty.

For the years that we occupied that manse, every time I got pregnant, I painted another room. So, there were three rooms with a fresh look when we moved out!

The hot water heater in the manse was in a closet next to the big wood-burning stove in the kitchen. The luxury of warm or hot water depended upon keeping that stove stoked and going, and the water was only for the kitchen. Being out on calls so much of the time, this proved to be impossible, and eventually, the trustees managed to connect the water heater to electricity, and behold....hot water! While I never attempted to cook on the big stove, it remained quite useful for heating the kitchen in the colder months, and especially for drying diapers during rainy days.

You might ask, if there was no hot water to the bathroom, how did you take baths? Well, attached to the wall, and overhanging the tub was a small water heater. So, before you could take a bath, you would unearth the box of matches, turn on the gas, light the thing, and let the water heat while you did something else. It was not very big, so as our numbers increased, we found ourselves making use of that water for more than one person's bath.

While it wasn't the happiest of arrangements, after visiting friends in South Australia where the little water heater had to be started with wood chips, I felt quite grateful to have the little gas one that we did.

One of the saintly members of our parish used to come once in a while, with her little tin of black paste, to polish the big stove in the kitchen. She said she always did it for the former pastor's family, and she liked doing it for ours. It didn't occur to me before then that the ugly big thing could look nice. But she took great pride in making it ash-free, so that if one wanted to actually cook on it, it would work.

The stove I had to learn to cook on was a tiny gas range, with three burners, and an oven that was free of a thermostat. Kurt's survival skills from years of batching came into play as he patiently taught me how to prepare all things Italian. He had worked in a pizza joint while putting himself through seminary, and had all kinds of useful talents. Therefore, nothing was ever cooked that didn't have lots of onions and garlic included!

My first kitchen, then, was a large room with high ceilings, painted glossy pink and blue, a sink, over which hung three faucets for hot, tank, and town water, and a nice window overlooking the back yard. (There was a big tank in the back yard that caught rain water. Most Australians would not think of drinking town water!) The countertops were marbled forest green and cream linoleum, trimmed with aluminum, and the fridge was almost as tall as I was (about 5'4") with no freezer. The table shared the same green and cream topping, and its legs were painted gray. The floor was dingy blue and gold squares on linoleum that had seen better days.

There was a huge walk-in pantry in the kitchen with many built-in shelves. One single dim light bulb hung from a cord from the ceiling. It was the perfect place to hide all despicable items that we didn't want anyone to see, including mounds of spoiling veggies that had been left on our door step that we had not succeeded in using.

Australian homes never had a toilet in the bathroom. It was considered unhygienic, even in new homes, and the toilet was always in a little room off the bathroom with a separate entrance. It was actually quite convenient when our family began to grow, to have a chance to go to the bathroom in the middle of a long line of baths. At least in more recent times, they were in the house, while many of the older homes still had the plumbing outside, as did the old manse.

If, therefore, you were visiting in another person's home, and you needed to go to the bathroom, you could not get away with saying, "I need to wash my hands." You had to ask outright, "Where is your toilet?" As the mother of little ones, it was a terrible nuisance to have to leave them alone to run outside to the bathroom. The smaller children always had chamber pots, since night visits to the toilet outside were not practical.

In those days, and even when we had been there for fifteen years, few people had window screens. Something to do with the idea that having them would cut back on the flow of air though the house. It didn't seem to bother them that all creatures great and small had access to our home, and we were on a constant watch for the big furry friendly spiders that like to crawl over the edge of the windows into our domain.

Oh, yes, I almost forgot to share that our laundry was also outside. There was no light in the W. C. (water closet), which was probably a good thing, since we didn't have to see the critters that were also occupying that space with us. The wringer washer was brand new, purchased just for us, and shared the laundry room with two big wash tubs and a "copper". A copper was a big tub with about the same capacity as the washing machine, that was wired to heat water. Fortunately for me, hot water came directly to the laundry from the kitchen, so I never had to employ its services.

As a child, I had learned to operate a wringer washing machine. Before we got our first automatic washer and dryer, it was one of my tasks. I recall it being very time-consuming. But that was my first new appliance when I arrived in Toowoomba. When I started washing diapers, laundry day was long. Washing, rinsing, wringing and rinsing and wringing again, and then hanging. But it was a mindless job that allowed me to think of other things while doing it, and it rarely occurred to me that it was a hardship to hang all those cloth diapers every other day.

In fact, after a while, I employed the time it took me to hang out the laundry as my prayer time. It was one of the few times I could be assured of privacy, and the Queensland sun kept the out-of-doors an inviting place to be most of the year. It was there that I began the habit, if you will, of praying for the members of my family back home, my new little family, and the members of our congregation. It was there that I prayed for grace to love some of those members, who might not have been so lovable. It was there that I enjoyed memories from home, and it seemed to be a magnet for recollections of events and people that I had thought I had forgotten. It happened more than a few times, that when someone came to mind about whom I had not thought for ages, within a week, I would receive a letter from that person! It became my own private telegraph station!

The Australian women used terry cloth diapers. (They were called nappies.) It seemed to me as if they were so bulky that they were likely the cause for so many bowlegged toddlers. My Mother agreed to send me cloth diapers from America. They were the long gauze ones that were double thickness that had to be folded in threes and then in half. The present model was not invented yet. Disposable diapers were not even heard of yet.

When our second baby was born, I was in the laundry one day, and in a moment of distraction, ran my left hand and arm through the wringers, right up to the elbow. It was quite a shock. But instead of hitting the emergency release bar, I turned the handle and ran that arm right back out again! Thankfully nothing was broken, since the following day was to be the baptism of that new baby.

+

Down the end of our block and around the corner was a butcher shop. It was owned by a man and his son-in-law, who was a member of our parish. We were able to get nice meat there, despite the confusion that initially came when I would ask for "half a leg of mutton", and he would hear me say, "I'll have a leg of mutton."

Meat and fish were not sold in the grocery stores, but were found only in butcher shops, and bread was sold only at the bakers'. One could have milk and bread delivered to the home. I recall hearing, "Bakah!" outside the window, and one would pay on the spot for fresh unsliced bread. In the beginning, unpasteurized milk was delivered to your saucepan left on the front steps. Eventually, bottles took over. I recall selling milk bottles to be able to afford postage to write home on more than one occasion.

Around the corner of the other end of the block was a little mom and pop shop, where small necessities could be procured in a pinch. The owner was also a member of our church. Sometimes it seemed as if the whole town was Lutheran.

The first few nights we slept at the manse, we would wake to a shrill sound that sounded like elephants calling one another. We couldn't think how it was possible to have large animals in the heart of town. In time, we worked out that the noise came from the big trucks starting their engines, just down a few houses from us at Western Transport! They could be heard shifting gears as they inched their way down the Range road on their way to Brisbane and points East, in the small hours of the morning.

+

Nearly everyone was older than Kurt and me. The young families who invited us to their homes had at least ten years on us. Apart from our regular association with the Johnstons, we went to another family's house once a week to watch "Bonanza", since they were among the few with TV sets. Kurt would take his Russian Orthodox Liturgy record along, and we would sit before their fireplace, listening to the haunting chants.

As in every congregations, there were families who did things together, and we were frequently included in their cookouts, swimming parties, etc. Down the Range from us was a natural spring resort called "The Helidan Spa". It had two big pools and because the water was always warmer down there than at the local pool, it became one of our favorite diversions.

We often included the Johnston boys on those getaways, as well as kids whose dads rarely, if ever, did anything fun with them. Naturally, some of those activities had to be adjusted once I became pregnant with our first baby.

Strangely, I have little memory of our first Christmas together. I know it was hot, and that Christmas Eve found the sanctuary busy with Christmas Beetles, as they were called there. I think we called them June Bugs in the States. They buzzed and bombed worshippers all through the service. The beautiful turquois sky shown behind the silhouette of the palm trees in the front yard of the church.

There was nothing about the whole thing that was in the least similar to "home". No one had Christmas trees, as we know them, as in the December heat, they were considered fire hazards. Those which decorated their homes would cut a decent branch off a bush, stick it in a tub of sand, and hang ornaments on it. Many escaped to the Coast during that holiday period, so didn't even bother to decorate at home.

There most likely was a tree in the chancel at church, but I do know it would have been a real tree, since there were no artificial trees yet. The Sunday School children put on their annual Christmas Eve service, with beautiful costumes and music. Instead of the children having parts, they formed a tableau for each Scripture reading in the chancel, with an adult reading the story about the birth of Jesus, followed by carols. It was touching to hear the little people singing, "They look-ed up and sar a stah." What a lovely accent.

Towards the end of the evening, when everyone would hurry to their cars to rush home in anticipation of Santa having visited, we would greet families in the parking lot, where they loaded us with bottles of wine, fruit cake, bath towels, and other kind gifts to take home. As far as I can recall, it was about getting home for sermon preparation. Nothing was going to replace being with family, and once we had celebrated together with the congregation, that was the end of that. In following years, having our own children would change all that.

Despite the seeming lack of excitement over Christmas, it was a time when each of us recalled families and shared our childhood memories. Little by little, I began to realize how differently the Russian culture approached some things in their families. My own family was so small, and most of our celebrations involved just the four of us. It was very telling to learn that I had lived a very cloistered life and didn't know it.

It was an on-going learning/growing experience, discovering how everything would forever revolve around its spiritual meaning and foundation. The secular was slowly peeled away from activities, from the books I would read, the music I would listen to, the movies I would watch. For a person having grown up in the church, believing that all things religious were important, I slowly realized that they were not just important, they were not just beautiful, they were central. All these values were critically important to Kurt as he passed them along to me, and through us to our family.

The British world puts great importance in having reached one's majority, resulting in a nice party of friends for my twenty-first birthday. Many of them were surprised to discover in this way how young I was!

When it was discovered that we were expecting our first baby, somehow it seemed as if I was finally "one of the girls", and the women were happily helping me anticipate this addition to our family. Many of them set about, crocheting dresses (yes, even baby boys wore long white dresses) and jackets for the newcomer. I felt as if I belonged at last.

The fact that we had foster children so soon after our first baby was born makes it hard to think of us as parents of a newborn. We had him but a month before the boys came to live with us. Kurt was forever calm, and was very good about rocking little Danny to sleep while I cooked dinner, etc. His calm firmness allowed babies to relax and give in to sleeping, while I was probably always pressed for time, rushing to get something done. In any case, having a baby did not prohibit our making calls and visiting friends. The baby was carried around in a big basket and because it was winter, he was smothered in blankets and rushed from the cold car to the fireside of people who wanted to see him.

From the moment of his birth, there were always ladies who were happy to share advice. Mostly, they were worried that if I didn't dress warmly enough, while going in and out to the laundry, I would get "milk sickness". I was always instructed to cover up for even the shortest trip outside. August was the coldest month of the Australian year, and the Easterly winds could be brutal.

While it would have been wonderful to share these early days with my Mom, I don't recall feeling homesick during this time. It would have made me very happy to have both my parents there for the Baptism. But it was a constant reminder to me of how many years my own Mom was away from her family during her early marriage. I don't think her mother was ever there to help her with her babies either. Kurt and I decided from the very beginning that we would be building our own family unit, that we would create our own traditions, that we would very likely never be with extended family again. As a result, I was never homesick. There was a strong sense that while we loved our families back home, it was very likely that our decisions might not always meet with their way of thinking. It was important, therefore, that the planning was carefully thought through, and we knew if we remained strong in our conviction, we would always feel secure together.

This resulted in several positive developments. For one thing, we didn't have grandparents spoiling our children, or competing with our disciplinary decisions. If "the nuclear family" means anything, I guess we were one. We had our husband/father as our leader, our mother as the nurturer, and the children, who respected our authority. Because most of our member families lived by a similar financial standard as we, none of us ever felt strange, or that we didn't belong. The kids were embraced by a number of families who literally competed to babysit them, and if we wanted to travel together, there was always someone who was happy to keep the kids. They did well in school, had friends, and loved their church.

It was such a joy to raise children in what then was a time of sanity in Australia. School children were polite to their elders, and if they talked back to their parents, they didn't do it twice. It was an unfortunate disappointment for our kids to return to the States where chaos was so typical in the classroom, and where children thought nothing of being rude to teachers and other adults. There were actually times when we felt we had done them a disservice, bringing them back.

The Petition

It might be inconceivable for those who knew Kurt Marquart on a professional level to imagine for a moment that, at any point, people might have such a distaste for him that they would actually sponsor a petition to get rid of him.

Because he was such a gentleman in his dealings with virtually everyone, friend or foe, even those who were not keen on his methods tended to be reluctant to take a stand against him or his followers.

Nevertheless, Satan can not stand it when one of God's servants is actually succeeding in teaching and leading people to the Gospel, and he will use any way he can to disrupt his work. In the Toowoomba parish, there had been a history of intimidation and dictatorship by a small group of families who were all interrelated. They had the numbers and the money, and when they liked something done a certain way, it was done in a certain way. When they wanted something stopped, it was stopped. Sound familiar?

While this core group of people were considered good solid Lutherans, they were, all the same, limited in their indoctrination... but didn't know it until Pastor Marquart came along. The "great white fathers" of the clan thought they were God's specially appointed overseers of the rest, and when the preacher began teaching things they had never heard of before, they took grave exception.

You know how it works. It begins with a discussion over the Sunday lunch table, with just a few. Then those few carry the germ to the next table, and before you know it, there is a buzz in the parish, an unpleasant, yet irresistible undercurrent that spreads into even the circles of those who admire and trust their pastor with their spiritual lives. One man described Pastor Marquart as "an after-dinner speaker, not a preacher", on the basis that he was actually interesting to listen to, and God forbid, people were beginning to understand the Faith they had followed all their lives, by faith.

Sadly, the previous pastor, who had moved on to Ipswich, had been a cousin of the mob, and during his tenure had been pressured to leave, because he would not dance to their preferred tune. But Kurt Marquart was not related to anyone, and they could not control him in this manner.

The great white fathers set about to distribute a petition to have their pastor removed. I don't know that I ever read it, so I don't know what reasons they set forth. I only know that there were only twelve names on it, which apparently qualified for the circuit counselor to be drawn into a parish meeting to try to sort things out.

Whether or not Kurt knew it, I didn't, this is the same group that had gotten wind of my previous marriage. We had told no one but the pastor who married us and his wife. While I thought it might be wise to tell the District President, Kurt felt that we could let the people get to know me before putting anything into their minds that might prevent them from accepting me. I have my suspicions, but don't really know, who it was, but someone actually went to the court house to check our marriage license, in order to verify the horrible truth that the pastor had married a divorcee! She was only too happy to share this juicy tidbit with those who were promoting Kurt's dismissal. Before the date of the parish meeting, it was even rumored that the two boys we had living in our home as foster children were my own by my previous marriage. I figured I would have had to be 9 and 11 to manage that.

I did not attend the meeting. I've never attended voters' meetings of my husband's congregations. But my friend, Sylvia, did, as she wanted to hear for herself how the men comported themselves, and to make sure at least her husband had the courage to stand up for his pastor in the face of this mob.

When she returned home, she gave us a report, which in summary was that the men could prove no false doctrine nor improper behavior on the part of their pastor. She said that at the end of the meeting, Kurt stood and with a brief explanation of my divorce, announced, "I don't deserve the wonderful woman who married me."

Interestingly, over the following year, all but one of the twelve men who signed the petition died unexpectedly. Some had health issues that had not preexisted the meeting, a couple had dreadful accidents, some just died in their sleep. The twelfth man, Rufus Ubergang, repented his part in the campaign and became a dear friend and supporter of his pastor.

Sanctity of Life

Almost equal to my ignorance about the evils of Communism at the time of my marriage to Kurt Marquart was my total lack of knowledge about the Pro Life Movement. In fact, I don't think I even knew what an abortion was. It only became legal in the United States in 1973. The battle continues in Australia today, with each state deciding its own laws on it.

Almost immediately after we began our life together, Kurt was connecting with others throughout the community in an attempt to stop the practice from becoming legal. I don't recall the details of the evolution of its importance in our family, but it didn't take long before Kurt became the Pro Life spokesman on many occasions. He not only had an awareness of it, but had done much study in the area of "when life begins", and was competent to give sound argument against the practice. Over the years, his library of resources in opposition to abortion grew astronomically.

Kurt said from the beginning that while Christians were naturally appalled by the practice, it was also a matter of civil rights. He was convinced that the general public would identify with that reasoning where they might not be attracted to the news that abortion was a dreadful sin. If it was morally wrong to take the life of a year-old child, or a ninety year old grandmother, why was it not equally a breech of everything civil to end the life of a helpless baby in the womb?

Dozens of Letters to the Editor were written to our local newspapers, and an equal number of appeals prepared and sent to members of local and national government. These acts resulted in his entrance into segments of our population that would have otherwise probably not been a part of his life as a pastor. People in many walks of life became familiar with the name, Pastor Marquart, Toowoomba, and before too long it was an annual event to have a Walk for Life, with first a smattering of citizens, and then larger and larger gatherings. Many times, he was the keynote speaker at the climax of those marches.

As to the question of whether the church is to be vocal in things civic or political, he believed that while the congregation was not in that business, he as an individual could and should have a public stand.

When we returned to United States in 1975, abortion had recently become legal across the country. With the outrage in some quarters came active movements in Fort Wayne to attempt to stem the numbers of babies lost. I'm not certain, but I think the Allen Country Right to Life was already active, and it didn't take long for him to become involved with those dear people. Together with faithful Roman Catholic Pro Lifers, public meetings were held, materials were published, Letters to the Editor were written once again. It seems to me as if they asked him to be their leader at some point, but because of his commitments, he could not give enough time to do that well, but agreed to be their spokesman when they needed anything published.

Before long, Lutherans for Life became active on the national scale, and a local branch was created in Fort Wayne as well. We thank God that there continue to be men and women who faithfully give of their time and means to keep that group vibrant even today.

A few years following the death of our articulate and courageous champion of the unborn, the Allen Country Right to Life presented the Telemachus Award in his memory. For those of us who did not know who Telemachus was, this is what we learned:

Telemachus, a fourth-century monk who lived in a monastery, felt God calling him to Rome. He couldn't figure out why God would want him in Rome, but he felt the pressure to go. When he got to Rome, people were running about the city in great confusion hurrying to the amphitheater. He had arrived on a day when the gladiators were going to fight other gladiators and animals. Telemachus thought this must be why God had called him to Rome. He walked into the amphitheater. He sat down among 80,000 people who cheered as the gladiators came out. The little monk thought to himself, "Here we are, four centuries after Christ, in a civilized nation, and people are killing one another for the entertainment of the crowd. This isn't Christian!"

Telemachus got up out of his seat, ran down the steps, climbed over the wall, walked out to the center of the amphitheater, and stood between two large gladiators. Putting his hands up, he meekly cried out, "In the name of Christ, stop!" The crowd laughed and jeered. One of the gladiators slapped Telemachus in the stomach with his sword and sent him spinning off into the dust.

Telemachus got up and again stood between the two huge gladiators. He repeated, "In the name of Christ, Stop!"

This time, the crowd chanted, "Run him through!" One of the gladiators took his sword and ran it through Telemachus' stomach. He fell into the dust and the sand turned red as blood ran out of him.

One last time, Telemachus weakly cried out, "In the name of Christ, stop." He died on the amphitheater floor. The crowd grew silent, and within minutes they emptied out of the amphitheater.

History records that, thanks to Telemachus, this was the last gladiatorial contest in the history of the Roman Empire.

When we were advised that this award was to be presented at the banquet that year, it was decided that my eldest son, Danny, would receive it on behalf of the family. Following is his speech:

Senator Long, Congressman Pence, Congressman Sauder, Ms. Skillman, Ms Dannenfelser, Mrs Humbarger, Joe Hilger, Ladies and Gentlemen:

First of all, on behalf of the family of Kurt Marquart, my sainted

Father, thank you for inviting us as guests tonight. As far back as my memory allows, the pro-life movement has been at the center of our lives. Our Dad believed that one of a father's most important tasks in life was to pass on to his children his own values. The moral and civil rights issue of the protection of those who cannot protect themselves was one of the most important parts of his work, both professionally and privately.

There were many January mornings, when at the last minute, we children would be painting and putting poles on banners and posters to take along to the March for Life that was always held on the coldest Saturday of the year. While a lover of the tropics himself, he faithfully pulled on layers of clothing to brace himself against the bitter winds and joined those citizens of Ft Wayne and outlying areas as we trudged through slush and ice in defense of the unborn.

We, the Marquart Family, thank you for this significant honor. We would also like to remind you of the others who were there at the beginning of what has, under God, resulted in a successful and significant organization in Allen County. As a young man, I vividly recall Donnelly and Anne McDonald, Frank and Phyllis Avilla, and Phyllis Morken. Mrs. McDonald and Mrs. Avilla were Nurses for Life, and long before the beautiful Hope Centers were created, they operated out of a small center, giving compassion and help to hundreds of desperate women. Many more have followed, faithfully serving the cause when it seemed we would never win the war. The war does go on, to be sure, but only our Lord knows how many lives were saved through the efforts of the people who gave and continue to give of their talents, energy and resources.

I would like to briefly introduce the members of my family who are able to be here tonight. My Mother, Barbara Johnston and her husband, Robert; my wife, Karen, and son Tristan; my sister Cindy Johnson; my brother Barry and his wife Monika; my brother Tony and his wife, Rebecca. My younger sister, Angela and her husband, the Rev. John Hill and their five children live in Casper, Wyoming and were unable to attend.

Again, thank you for honoring our Father in this very special way. May each of us be renewed in our zeal and determination to fight and defeat the proponents of abortion and euthanasia. During this intense period just before our national elections, let's remember how important it is to elect those men and women who will stand up for the unborn. Thank you!

It Takes A Lifetime

No matter how many years we've been married, there are times when things get rough. Sometimes it's a small matter. Sometimes it's bad enough that we wish we could just crawl into a quiet hole somewhere and never have to come out again. Sometimes the problem is directly related to our spouse. Sometimes it's just a combination of circumstances over which we seemingly have no control. All you have to do is go on to some of the blogs and Facebook sites to read the cries of sadness and discontent that many women are having in their lives, some with their husbands, some with their children, some with their jobs.

In our culture, it's not hard to attract and obtain a mate, in most cases. But building a life with another person over forty to sixty years requires more than a fairytale approach. Ah, if parents would but try to impress upon their children that it's critical to choose someone to marry with whom one is in agreement about such things as the Faith, family finances, priorities. There are more than enough surprises that crop up later. It is certain that all marriages, made in heaven or otherwise, have their ups and downs. But if these basic values are held in common, even in hard times, a couple is much more likely to stand up through the storms of life if they already have common ground on things that matter.

Pastors and their wives are vulnerable to pressures and temptations that all couples face. Since we are not superpowers, we are not above any of the human dynamics that exist all around us. There are no shields around us to protect us from all the human emotions that everyone else experiences. And just about the time we think we are above all that, we take a tumble.

If ever there is a situation where a young woman should know how to cook and manage a household, keep the laundry caught up, the house tolerably clean, and all at the same time, it is in the parsonage. It is sad for me to see that with so many women in the workforce today, there are few role models teaching girls these basic wifely tasks. Strangely, men expect to be fed when they commit to marrying a woman. They are happily planning for someone else to keep their clothes ready to wear and their living quarters clean. There is the occasional man who prefers to do all his own cooking and cleaning, but I haven't seen too many.

Now, I'm not implying that clergy wives are expected to do a better job of these things than all other women. I only know, after raising five children, and having a perpetual house full of company over the years, that there are some things that can make life less stressful and your home more inviting and happy. For instance, if your husband finds an atmosphere of love and support when he does come home, he will be more inclined to come home, than if he comes through the door, tripping over chaos and mess, only to be met by an exhausted, quarrelsome wife.

I'm not ignorant of how hard it is to keep all the fires burning at the same time. When I first married my late husband, in fact, our parsonage had a wood burning stove on which I was expected to cook and keep the hot water coming! I didn't even know how to build a fire, much less how to produce edible food on the stove top. Fortunately, there was a second stove, a little gas range with no oven thermostat, in which to burn things. Since I didn't know much about cooking anyway, it probably could have been worse. Amazingly, the Australian women made the most amazing sponge cakes in those appliances!

The laundry and toilet (WC) were outside. Yes, we shared them with the fuzzy spiders and toads and whatever else came in the night. There was not one square inch of carpet, and there were no screens on the windows. It wasn't a bad house otherwise. There was a study, with its own outer door, but none ever came to that door. Rather, everyone came to the back door, through the kitchen. A generous spinster lady, who was closing up her house to move into a nursing home, donated all her furniture to the parsonage. The only new items we had were the wringer washing machine and new linoleum for the living room.

Lest you think this was poor housing for the pastor of such a big parish, allow me to explain that it was probably typical of most clergy housing in those days in that place. This was in 1961, and for years I had been using an automatic washing machine in my Mother's home, and was used to a big beautiful gas range on which to cook.

Our house was about a block from the mother church, so it was very handy for the kids and me to walk for services, etc. The office in the church was not large enough for a library, so most appointments were at the house, in the study...or around the kitchen table.

Three days after I came home with our third child, the Lebanese shop keeper on the corner offered to purchase the parsonage IF we would be out in three days. (Is that what it means to sell a house "as is"?) I wasn't even aware that the house was on the market. I just have memories of sitting on the bed, telling a couple of dear ladies into which boxes to toss things, so that it could all be moved in a hurry. I had a relapse from the delivery and was not in very good shape. But I survived.

Since the sale was so sudden, the congregation had no idea where to move us in such a hurry. One of our members owned a duplex, and one half of it was vacant. At that time, by the way, we had two foster sons, 12 and 13. So there were seven of us, plus a dear friend who came to help take care of my baby for a while, all moved into a two bedroom apartment with a tiny kitchen and bathroom.

It was a blessing that there was a beautiful public park across the street, and we were able to spend many hours there with the children during the months that ensued. Our other form of entertainment, when we had guests (yes, we entertained in the tiny kitchen) were listening to the hilarious noise the water made as it gurgled down the drain of the sink in the tiny bathroom just off the tiny kitchen. When that became old, we would watch for the tiny mouse who scampered around behind the TV in the corner.

We were in that apartment six months while the congregation bought property and built a new parsonage. It was very cold, and we endured lots of sniffles and colds. But it was worth the wait, as the new parsonage was near the school, and it was all fresh and clean.

We splurged and purchased a "damaged" sleeper sofa for the living room of the new house, and I was given some cash with which to buy material for curtains. Growing up, I had watched my Mother make draperies and I knew how to use pleating tape, etc. It was, therefore, a great time to actually be able to express my own taste in decorating, and it was fun working with the ladies who volunteered to help. It was probably the first time they realized I was more than an air head, a real grown up who knew how to measure and cut and sew something that turned out really professional.

I'm getting off track, though. What I want to say is that it is not just the terrible storms that are possible in any marriage that are the challenge. I think possibly the thing most clergy wives dread above all is "the other woman". There is such a conflict between striving to be a Godly wife and competing with other women who may have more money, better looks, are sophisticated or possess a better education. There are women in every place who make it their goal to attract every male they can, one way or another.

We are all aware of the women who hang on every word our husbands utter, who volunteer for every job under the church roof, bring in yummy baked goods, all to please and win his admiration. I recall one very beautiful woman who came to the parsonage one time to drop off something for my husband. She planted herself on the sofa across from him, and when she crossed her legs, she displayed the most beautiful pink lace petticoat, among other things. My husband kept company with us for a few moments and then dismissed himself to take care of a phone call. I was so proud of him for having the presence of mind to make a point without causing a scene. He told me afterword that we would all be horrified if we knew the view pastors get from the podium. Sometimes, he said, one wishes to avert one's eyes, and there is nowhere to look. I fear in our present culture there is little modesty nor respect for the Office, and I really do pray for men in the public ministry. Their burdens of responsibility are already so heavy that one is saddened to think about members who purposely or otherwise make it harder by their sultry attire or brazen behavior.

This whole conversation reminds me of the fact that these things tend to occur more frequently when the pastor and his wife invite a familiarity with members. It's one thing to love the people and interact with them in the work of the congregation. Even socially, it is good for the family to have contacts with members of other families. I can assure you, however, that it's almost inevitable that something unpleasant or awkward will happen when members are encouraged to address their pastor by his first name, or when he tries to be "just one of the boys". That is why so many seasoned pastors and their wives will advise you to speak about your husband as "Pastor" or "my husband" and avoid his first name. That practice helps them remember that he is indeed their spiritual father, maintains the respect for the Office, and also makes it possible if and when the need for discipline should arrive. It is hard to admonish people with whom you are buddy-buddy.

Now, since we know that the ground is often fertile for someone to cross the line with inappropriate behavior with the pastor/member relationship, it helps if we try to understand how easily it can happen and how some of us wives might inadvertently set our husbands up to fail by not only our own shortcomings as loving wives and Godly partners, but in failing to recognize the signs when something might be amiss.

When you think about it, pastors, more than nearly any profession, are in the sometimes awkward position where they cannot be rude nor offensive to people, especially women. What a dear price he pays if the pastor tells a woman to back off, for instance. I know a pastor who was placed in a very unpleasant position when a female member made advances towards him in his study. He was polite but firm in his attempt to discourage her, but when he tried to open the door and invite her to leave, she blocked the door and actually struggled with him. Later in the week, he was met at his front door by the police, who hauled him off in cuffs, in front of his little children and wife, under arrest for assault. The situation was indefensible. He had no witnesses. It was his word against hers. In the end, for the sake of peace in the parish, he was compelled to resign his Call and leave.

Pastors are admired by a great many people, partly because they are well groomed, intelligent, polite, and they listen to problems of heartache and family woes. Women who are ignored by their spouses at home find this attention very attractive and alluring, and it is easy for someone to imagine that the pastor cares more for them than is realistic. In rare cases, the pastor feeds these fantasies, much to his discredit, and inappropriate relationships result. If the pastor is not happy in his own marriage, if his wife is disengaged from his life and work, if the female member is especially solicitous and even lovely, it is a very flammable situation.

While I understand the flesh is weak and that our pastors are only human, there are ways to avoid these situations, and there is no earthly excuse for any pastor getting past the point of no return. I assume our men are taught such defenses at seminary. One pastor I worked for felt he should counsel women in the sanctuary. He felt there would be less danger of anything getting out of control in that atmosphere. (It doesn't say much for confidentiality, though.)

I knew another pastor in Australia whose study was not at the church, but out behind his home. It was decorated very nicely, with comfortable furniture, etc. While visiting with him, he admitted that he personally felt it necessary to have a relationship with any woman he counseled! He insisted it was the only way to really help someone in deep distress. I was horrified to think that someone would go to him with every hope of getting real pastoral help and find herself being seduced by this man. I cannot imagine that had his wife known, she would have approved. But who knows? Some women can be convinced that a lot of strange things are ok!

Another pastor I knew made it a practice of making appointments with troubled women after office hours so that there were no staff people about. While I can respect a person's desire to have confidentiality in such matters, I felt the pastor really invited the possibility of scandal for them both by doing it that way.

There were a few unbalanced females in the parish we served in Australia. One was a young woman who was a recent convert. But her family, who were not Lutherans, had badgered her with the threat that if she didn't have a "religious experience", she was not a true Christian. So, many mornings, as early as six a.m., she would appear at our front door, and Kurt would have to sit with her and try to reassure her that she was saved through her Baptism, and that an experience was not necessary.

The other lady was an older woman. I don't recall what her problem was, but I suspect it was something like anxiety attacks. She would call the house during dinner nearly every evening and beg him to come to see her. We tried to visit her as a couple, and eventually, I think she must have moved away.

Probably the most annoying intrusion into our marriage was a female church worker who was hired by the congregation. Since Kurt was so busy, he insisted he could not do justice to a vicar, and perhaps they were convinced this "trained" person would be able to take some of his load off his shoulders. But, there she was. And before long, her attentions became more than just that of a colleague. She made endless lists of people she thought he should visit, and presented all manner of possible contacts for him to follow up on. In other words, rather than relieve him of some of the mundane work she might have done, she created more things, and especially things that would allow her to follow up with HIM. She began bringing him little gifts, and began stopping by the house to take him to chapel when he had not asked her to.

No good would have been served had I made a disgruntled scene every time our lives were interrupted by this kind of thing. None of the cases described was a life-threatening situation, but I have a feeling they must have made some waves or I would not be able to recall them so vividly. I suggest you have a little corner in your world in which you can pray alone every day. I managed to come to grips with many things through prayer, which in my case was done at my clothesline. With five babies, you can imagine all the cloth diapers I hung in my day. (Disposable diapers did not yet exist.) I would consciously pray for situations and people in our parish while pegging those diapers up, and my most fervent prayer was that I would be given the grace to love them, even the ones who might be openly unkind to me.

That reminds me of my favorite "clothesline story". One day my husband came home from a sick call and found me at the clothesline. He reported, "I went to see so and so, but her mother said she was in bed with silas." (She meant sinus.) Half listening to his story brought my reply, "Who's Silas?"

Having been on both sides of things, having been on the clergy side, as well as the lay side by virtue of my work as church/school secretary in two congregations, I would like to emphasize more training be given men and women who are planning to go into full-time church work with regard to ethics, and the principles of Christian behavior between staff members.

I listened to a District President many years ago, who lamented that in his visits to church offices all over his area, he was appalled how many problems there were with this. I have seen myself too many cozy friendships develop into irreversible heartache, and most especially in the home for the wife, of both pastors and teachers. One spouse is left out of so many things when that husband or wife goes off to work in the church building with co-workers. One wants to assume that the spouse is safe with Christian colleagues. One is only as safe as the ideals and policies that are in place and practiced by everyone.

I believe that the pastor needs to set the tone with this in his own church. If there are no boundaries in place, he and the Elders and/or Board of Education need to create them. There's no point instilling an atmosphere of legalism in the place, but everyone representing Christ to members and school children are to be held to the highest standards of behavior, and when something goes amiss in a church setting, the danger is that it tends to destroy the confidence of the people and disillusions many people about the church and Faith altogether.

While there is no guarantee that our being the perfect wife will prevent anything disastrous happening with our husbands, it must be admitted that there are some pastor's wives whose necks should be wrung for making life literally unbearable for those living in her household. Constant complaining, criticizing, lack of interest in her husband's work (which happens to be theology and the care of souls), unreasonable demands on his time are just a few habits I would discourage. No pastor is perfect, and dealing with problems all day and then dreading to return to his own home because of a hostile wife is a sad state of affairs.

Some have said to me, "Yes, he can be nice to the members, but when he comes home, it's a different story." This is a grievous situation, and I really pity the family that must live in this hypocritical scenario. Whether the husband has delusions of grandeur, whether he is perpetually worn out, or whether he has a foul temperament, if the climate at home cannot be improved with joint effort, I would be inclined to risk his wrath and call in a circuit counselor, or other colleague whom you trust. To suggest counseling for a pastor is a complicated thing, because due to his own training, he knows the questions and answers already. Some men simply think they can live outside those guidelines they prescribe for others.

Herein arises another question: Should a pastor's wife have her own pastor, apart from her husband? I've had many women ask this question, which leads me to believe that perhaps there are too many of our pastors who do not make themselves approachable so that their wives can come to them with things about which they are worried. A wife should be able to talk to her husband about nearly anything that is troublesome.

I have seen it happen when a small problem is not taken care of right away, it can mushroom into something more serious. I know that in the later years of my own marriage, my husband was gone out of the country so often that we often found it difficult to settle some issues that required finalizing. There was not time to really get to the root of some things, and he would leave me for days, to stew and fume about issues over which I had no control.

This was never done out of any kind of malice. But I mention it because I don't think men always understand how pushing some things under the carpet is not a healthy approach to happiness. If pastors can spend hours discussing problems with their members and boards and committees, they can most certainly afford their wives and children the same courtesy. The man who is away from home a lot simply must make the time to be sure all is well with the wife, and the children as well, no matter what else has to wait.

It is a wise couple who recognize that sometimes a situation, whether in the marriage or with a child, may need professional counselling. Where possible, try to find a Christian professional. I have seen sad consequences arise from dealing with secular counselors who tend to make things worse than they were, adding yet another layer of mental or emotional anxiety to the problem.

It is hoped that most problems of our clergy couples will be minor and that many differences will be settled as one or both of you mature and grow up. Many conflicts are born of childish selfishness, stupid ambition, self-centeredness, and the need to always be right. As you learn to identify your priorities and put your family affairs into perspective, the bumps will gradually smooth out. While the ride won't always be smooth as glass, the trauma that goes with these upsets as a young bride and groom tend to become less and less as the children come along and as things change in the home.

Probably because of my age, and due to the mindset of women in my generation, I am not inclined to advocate the husband assuming a huge share of the household tasks. Our younger generation may have a different outlook on this matter, but personally, unless the wife is working full time at a job that takes her out of the house every day, I am troubled to see women who demand that their husbands do half the housework.

When I was teaching in Australia, and my children were too young to be very helpful in the home, I found I would rather economize on something else and pay someone to come in a couple times a month to do the floors and bathrooms than to ask my husband to do them. If your husband really loves yard work or gardening, if he gets relaxation and pleasure from woodwork or home repairs, that's one thing. When we were setting up our household, my husband wisely devised this plan: "You will be the minister for the interior, and all household affairs are your job description. I will be the minister for the exterior, and all the bills, dealing with salesmen, anything that must be done on the outside are part of my job description." At first glance, this may seem out of balance. But the fact that my area of responsibility was defined turned me loose to do it all any way I wanted to, without having to consult with him, etc. It was liberating.

Australian women were very good housewives. They had shiny floors and tins full of home baked goodies. They ironed all their clothes and made many of them. One friend of mine said, and it really struck home, "Anyone who can't keep a house clean is just plain lazy." She had six kids.

It is a challenge to keep a nice home. I won't deny that, especially with a young family. But it is the kind of work that women should take pride in doing well, for her own sense of well-being, and for the pleasure of her husband and family.

I am the first one to condemn a pastor who can't make it home to dinner at least six out of seven nights a week. There is no excuse, unless there is a medical or spiritual emergency, for him to fail to arrange his time in such a way as to be with his family as its leader, as father and husband. If he isn't at home for that evening meal for other than emergencies, I believe he is doing a cop out. Some pastors must be lovingly shown that they are using the parish as an excuse not to fulfill their role at home. Sometimes, people don't realize it until a bad pattern has been established. If your husband has already slipped into that unfortunate trend, try to gradually pull him out of it. It's not easy for a man to recognize that he has begun to enjoy the feeling of being needed by people in his care, that he has developed a kind of power trip for himself. Some have called it a "messianic complex". While things appear to be going smoothly at home, he forgets that he has an infinitely important responsibility towards his wife and children, and perhaps his grandchildren.

When our children were young, we were invited to the home of a local pastor and his family. We had a lovely evening and the dinner was delicious. When the wife and I were cleaning up in the kitchen, she confided that it was the first time her husband had been home for dinner in many weeks. Only a few years after that, I saw a divorce notice in the local paper. How sad.

A woman told me recently that she still had resentment in her heart against her father/pastor, who was the kindest and most generous of men, but who was so detached from his family he never realized how much they were hurting and from what desperate financial straits they suffered. Charity of all kinds begins at home.

Some people are better time managers than others, and perhaps a few helpful schemes should be discussed and agreed upon before a couple even arrives at a new congregation. For one thing, the pastor needs to post "office hours" and clearly indicate that he has one day a week off. He must stick to that, too, unless someone literally dies. There needs to be a way that members know they can find their pastor in his study or at the church at certain times. This eliminates a lot of interruptions from folks who call at meal time. It allows the family to have a decent schedule for time to do things together.

Neither of these means the pastor cannot work on sermons at home, or study, or write. But his physical presence in the home means more than he realizes. Especially when the children are very young, the pastor should spend as much time with them as possible. These times together are bonding and permanent, not to mention, they are good for the wife to have a little time to get things done that are difficult with little ones to watch.

It doesn't work in every church, but my late husband was successful in consolidating board meetings into one evening a month. If they had extra work to do, they could do it on their own, but he would go from meeting to meeting to see if there was anything they needed from him, take care of it, and move on. The only meeting he had on a separate night was his Board of Elders, and they met for two hours.

When elders were elected in that congregation, they were given a Book of Concord. The first hour of the meeting was for study of that book, and the second hour was dedicated to business. Because the elders were instructed in the Church's position on various matters, if and when conflict arose, they were united behind the pastor with their support, especially when it became necessary for action, such as discipline.

With regard to endless counselling that goes on in the church, I have heard it said that after the first hour, people tend to start repeating themselves. Rather than go on all night, it is sometimes better and more productive to set another appointment and resume another time. Not every pastor is gifted at counseling. I always thought the pastor's responsibility was to hear confessions and absolve his members. Naturally, in cases of serious illness and death, and in preparation for marriage and baptism, pastors are required to comfort and instruct. In my opinion, we could do with more Christian psychologists to whom pastors may send their members, especially in cases where the problem is complicated, prescribed medications are needed, or long-term or family counseling is needed.

Many wives do not realize that they are the only one in their husband's life who can save the pastor/husband from totally losing himself in his work or jumping at the demands of all the members. Sometimes the answer is as simple as arranging pleasant evenings or special outings that he would not normally have time to think of himself. I believe it's critical for the pastor's wife to understand that she is the key, not only to his effective work, but to his temporal happiness. She, and only she, can love him in the way that he needs and longs to be loved. The members can show him all kinds of favors, but they cannot love him as a man, as only his wife can.

So, when the attention seems to all be going his way, instead of getting miffed and feeling left out, remember that you are really the only one whose opinions matter, whose love is forever, whether he flubs it or not. He depends on you a great deal to nurture his children, to prepare them for life, to support him and them in the special way that only a wife and mother can.

In a conversation with a young woman recently, we were discussing the whole matter of how much men require respect, whereas women require love, in a relationship. She surprised me by making a remark that implied that her husband had made it impossible for her to respect him. How sad. I said, "Surely he must do something for which you can respect him? Doesn't he provide for you and the children? That in itself is praiseworthy." She was unwilling to go into it further, but I wanted to tell her that a man cannot really be a good husband unless he knows that at least his wife respects him and his work. Just a little bit goes a long way towards building a reciprocal relationship that every marriage should have.

It is so difficult in today's culture for a man and a woman to work on anything long term, especially their marriage. The marital relationship is so complex that a successful, happy marriage takes a lifetime to build. Like a glorious cathedral, it takes years to complete, and then when it is finished, there is constant maintenance. Therefore, it is really important to understand that minor losses are to be expected, and as long as there are also some victories along the way, in the end, there will be something of great worth. In a matter of years, the union takes on a life it was intended to have, and you can look back and see how it all happened, without your knowing it at the time. Like a beautiful tapestry, from the bottom side, all you see is the tied off, messy threads. But when it is finished, and one is allowed to see the top side, it is glorious and has a logical pattern.

Some time ago, I engaged a young man, a friend of our family, on the subject of his inability to make a long-term commitment to any one woman, resulting in his remaining single during the best years of his life. He had enjoyed many serious relationships, but at some point, with each of them, he had given up and gone his own way again.

I told him that the kind of relationship he wants requires a lifetime. I used the analogy of a builder who dreams of a beautiful building in the heart of the city. In the beginning, the builder has all kinds of ideas for his masterpiece. It all looks great on paper, and he is secure in his belief that it will all work out, and that many people will benefit. He has a partner, and in the beginning they share the dream with equal enthusiasm. The loan is secured, the laborers are hired. All is well.

After a few weeks of work, one can see the foundation taking shape. The layout looks just like the man's dream. One day, the partner announces that he doesn't like the look of the entrance to the building. He argues with the builder, but they cannot agree. After much bitterness, the partner pulls out, and takes his men with him. There stands a partially finished building.

The builder is still hopeful, despite all the problems. Then one day, the partner returns and says, "Let's give it another shot. But we have to do something about that entrance", he insists.

The builder doesn't agree, but says he is willing to try to make the change if it doesn't affect the final cost. Once again, the building crew goes to work on the building and the frame for the walls go up. The electricians have finished their work. It starts to look the way the builder hoped.

One day, without any warning, a terrible storm blows into town. No one is ready for the force of the winds, and a lot of damage is sustained. Both builder and partner are devastated.

"We'll have to begin again", says the builder.

"I'm sorry, friend, but I cannot do this anymore", replies the partner.

Without the help and commitment of the partner, the builder loses all hope and motivation. The site is closed down. The building stands there, stark against the sky, just a skeleton of what it was intended to be.

Just as any project requires dedication, commitment, and determination to stay with the job until it's finished, two people who decide to build a life together must stay at it, even if the first plan fails. Life happens. Living with another human being necessitates that lightning will strike, floods may come, hurricanes will blow, and illness and death are not unusual.

If we all give up before the marriage is built, there will be mere shambles all over our land, mere hopes and dreams extinguished, and nothing remaining but rubble. This not only bodes badly for us as individuals in such marriages, but think how the nation-wide impact this "here today, gone tomorrow" lifestyle is affecting our next generation, and those to follow.

GOOD NEWS! There IS No Typical Pastor's Wife!

Someone may ask from where the idea came that all pastors' wives are to fit a certain mold, fulfill certain responsibilities, etc. No one knows for sure, but maybe it is because in earlier years, the role of the clergy wife tended to be cut and dried because pastors tended to marry the young women who happened to be available. Due to the proximity of seminaries to other institutes of education, it was easier to meet available prospects at teachers colleges or nursing schools.

Absurdly as it seems now, it was advisable that a man leaving seminary was married before he reached his first parish. This, despite the fact that he had to remain single while a student and was not allowed to court a young woman, or even associate with young single women before his certification. If they were lucky, they found a girl while they were on vicarage, but it was unlawful to become engaged until graduation.

When, then, the pastor's wife was perceived to have had more education than the farmer's wife, etc., the other ladies of the congregation, many of whom did not have those advantages, would acquiesce the role of leadership to the pastor's wife. As well, in most cases, the pastor and his wife in those days were held in high esteem, both in the church and socially, so appointing her as chairman of the ladies organization was no doubt considered an honor and privilege which they felt no one else quite deserved.

Thus, whether a pastor's wife was suited for public life or not, whether she had the makeup to lead or not, it was expected that she would automatically fill those shoes. One can only imagine how nerve-wracking it must have been for some young women, just married, perhaps with a new baby, starting out as the chairman of an organization of older, seasoned women. But somehow, they managed.

In my days as a new wife, at the ripe old age of twenty, I was the youngest pastor's wife in the district. My husband decided to tell the women that he didn't think it wise for me to be their chairman until I had been there for a while. He explained that I had enough to do to set up housekeeping, to make visits with him, take care of the new baby that was on the way, etc. *(I avoided holding office for several years by being pregnant.)* Perhaps your husband can do the same thing for you, if the issue arises where tradition deems it your duty.

On the other hand, if you are inclined to enjoy administrative activities, if you are handy at delegating work and motivating others to do useful things, then, by all means, feel free to accept the task. It would still be a good idea to weigh the pleasure you receive or the good you might do against what the cost to your family and home will be. Someday, when you look back, you won't want to regret letting your house and family go to the dogs because you had so much to do with running the ladies guild. Anyone can chair meetings, but you alone can be the mother to your children and wife to your husband. Only you can create the kind of home that results in harmonious family life. Many times you will be on your own with this duty, with unreliable assistance from your husband. Another bit of advice is that the more involved you become, the more public exposure you have and the more opportunities there might be for evoking criticism.

In recent years, with the advent of more women acquiring formal education and many entering professional fields all across the board, it should not be assumed that the leadership duties among the women in the congregation should fall to the pastor's wife. Neither should anyone take for granted she will conduct the choir and teach Sunday School.

It should be understood then, that unless a woman really desires to take the role of leadership, there is nothing to say she must. It may prove difficult, in a small congregation, where resources are few, for a woman to say "no" when asked to serve. For this reason, it is a good idea for the pastor and his wife to agree on priorities for the family, so that if the moment arrives, you won't be pushed into something you will later regret. Young women with young families have plenty to do to keep a functional home, and maintain stability in the family where the husband is often absent, without adding responsibilities that result in unnecessary stress. And yet, an older woman, whose children have grown up, and who love sociability and fellowship, connected to church gatherings might find the role fulfilling and she might be a great asset.

It may help you, when asked on the spot whether you can serve in any capacity, to say, "Let me think about it." Or "I need to check the family calendar." That gives you a chance to talk to your husband about it, and to decide whether your time and energy really allow for you to accept, as well as then cheerfully follow through with whatever the job requires.

An older and wiser woman told me, when I was still in the parish: Ask yourself these questions:

> Is my husband happy about my doing this?
> Is this a job that someone else could easily do?
> Do I need to commit myself to it long term, or just once?
> How many times a month does it meet?
> Does it require preparation, or do I just show up?
> Is it something I can do just occasionally, like choir for special services?
> Will I have to neglect my family a lot if I undertake this job?

If I don't do it, can I expect others to do anything?

You'll notice that the first question regards seeking the advice and consent of your husband. Your husband is busy. You don't want to always have permission to do something. You're a big girl now, and I suggest this only because his memory is better than yours about what happens when you overbook yourself. He knows if you get totally involved in something, he won't get fed, and that tends to be important to men. He also understands what stress will do to your health in the long term. He can remind you, too, where your first devotion lies, to insure the children will never feel as if church work is more important to Mom than they are.

Whether or not you become heavily involved in the activities of your congregation, you can show an interest in the things others are doing. If the pastor's family is not interested enough to think something is valuable to do, why should the members? So, even if you are not at the head of things, it is important to know what is going on, and let the ladies know you think they are great.

Since we know that where people gather for any reason, there is potential for conflict, due to our sinful nature, one enters activities with realism and is not taking offense at everything that comes her way. Remember, others may be equally offended by us, even when we don't realize it. It is a good opportunity to foster a cheerful, forgiving spirit, refusing to let the undercurrents get to you. Since you and your husband are servants of Christ in that place, humility and kindness are the best weapons you can carry.

Sadly, there is a lack of understanding of our doctrine of church and ministry in many places. If a congregation has never been taught what "church" is, what "pastoral ministry" is, and how they should interact with one another, according to our *Book of Concord*, there are likely to be issues. I suggest that you find your husband's copy and refresh yourself on this doctrine. It is not your place to teach it, but it will help you and your family to understand it yourself. Knowing will help you support your husband and know that he is doing his job well, and when things get bumpy, you will have a clear conscience about your own response. Encourage your husband to choose this topic for one of his Bible studies, or his studies with the elders, helping to create and maintain a God-pleasing working relationship.

When we hear from members of the Council of Presidents that many problems in congregations come from unhappy pastors' wives, our first reaction is "What a sad commentary!" Because these statistics are most likely the same in districts across our Synod, not isolated cases, we immediately question what is wrong in our church. First of all, what has happened to the traditional role of the male being the head of his household, being able to love and protect his wife and manage his family in a way that should result in harmony and joy? At what point in our history have young women lost the nurturing instinct and talent for keeping a peaceful, happy home for her husband and their children? Where did the concept of service fall through the cracks to leave an attitude in many cases of entitlement?

At the same time, when did congregations cease to honor and love their pastor and his family and concern themselves with taking care of their temporal needs? When did congregations begin to think of their pastors as employees that could be dismissed on a whim?

At a glance, it would seem as if pastors' families might well expect nothing but problems everywhere they go; and equally distressing, as if congregations may well anticipate clergy families who just don't measure up.

But we're getting ahead of ourselves. Let's first find comfort that there are no rules set in stone by which every pastor's wife must live. Let's assume that every woman whose husband will be called to a congregation or mission field is a God-fearing woman who is gladly anticipating a wonderful relationship with God's family. Let's assume that each and every congregation is excited to have been blessed with a new pastor, especially a pastor with a family, and that they are eagerly awaiting a mutually joyful experience.

What about the God-fearing part? And, are you happy about your husband's choice to study for full time parish ministry? These days, we cannot assume that everyone who is preparing for the ministry was born "Lutheran" or even "Christian". There are many men who have had long successful careers in the secular world to whom the Holy Spirit has spoken. One does not automatically assume that his wife is also a Christian. Perhaps he is a convert, and she is still outside the church. Or, even if she is an adult Christian, it does not follow that she will be thrilled to give up her life of relative ease and freedom and follow her husband to the seminary for four years, with a family in tow.

Thus, the statistics that our District Presidents have given us may reasonably reflect unhappy possibilities and reflect situations that may very possibly interfere with, or even undo the work of a faithful pastor, and at the very worst, destroy a congregation. Initially, these numbers tell me that there are a lot of unhappy couples in our parsonages, unhappy families creating not only serious problems for their congregations, but miserable couples raising children who will very likely grow up bitter against the organized church and sickened by the hypocrisy they have seen.

These are serious problems. One immediately wonders how we can help couples living in the parsonage to avoid situations that can, in fact, undermine the ministry that the pastor is attempting in the congregation. Can it be that the pastor/husband/father develops a shift in his attitude towards his vocation once he has a Call? Is there something in the pastor's wife that causes resentment before she even gets to the first congregation? Are families who leave comfortable living styles behind finding it too difficult to face the lower salaries and more modest home? Are children in the parsonage resentful for being uprooted from their homes and schools? What happened to the "servant mentality" among some of our clergy?

Every couple has problems to work through. The clergy family is no exception. So let us work through some of the things that might be hard for some folks, and see if we can find some answers, so that the pastor's work may be more effective, so that wives don't get lost in the shuffle, and so that children of clergy families don't grow up bitter and angry at the church.

The few books that were published in years gone by for the wives of ministerial students seemed to have been primarily promoting things like keeping the living room clean in case of visitors, refraining from making dear and personal friends in the congregation, being musical and offering your services in the choir or playing the organ every Sunday, and heading up the ladies organization, teaching Sunday School, and always smiling, etc., etc.

There were so many dos and don'ts that it doesn't surprise me that many women have grown up vowing never to marry a pastor. What realistic woman believes that all those attributes are possible for a single person? For that matter, which of those qualities are necessary for the vocation of being a loving wife, faithful mother, and friend to the lonely? Some of the warmest women I know are the least likely to have perfectly tidy homes all the time. Even fewer of them play the organ. And only a few married with the idea that they wanted to be a church secretary.

I think it's pretty safe to assume that most of your husbands asked for your hand in marriage because they were madly in love with you and wanted to spend the rest of their lives with you, wanted you to be the mother of their children, wanted you to help him create a little piece of heaven on earth, regardless of where you lived. No doubt they were thankful if you shared a common faith and had other things in common.

I would be very surprised if any of them spotted you and thought, "Ah, yes. She would make me look good. She would be a great Ladies Aid Chairman, and I'm so glad she can play the organ and sing. No doubt she'd be a good Sunday School teacher as well."

Dear friends, there are as many different kinds of pastor's wives as there are pastors. Then multiply that by the different personalities congregations have! You might be one kind of pastor's wife in one congregation and a totally different kind in another congregation. So then, let's try not to set too many boundaries for ourselves before we even get that first Call.

When my late husband asked me to marry him, I really had no idea what a pastor's life was like. In fact, my Mother was horrified; she knew I couldn't cook! Had she known that I would be cooking on a wood burning stove in a 40-year old pre-war house; had she known that I would be having five children and two foster children; had she known I would be hosting members of parliament and church officials around my table; had she known. . . well, you get the picture. She would never have allowed me to leave the country to marry a pastor.

Kurt & Bob in our first car in Toowoomba

Kurt – Niagara Falls 1960

Kurt – the vicar

**Brothers -
Kurt & George**

Paul McCain, John Stephenson presenting festschrift

Friends to the end - Herman Otten, Kurt, and Walter Otten

Forgiveness Is Costly

I remember the exact moment. As I unloaded my groceries into the trunk of the car, I was struggling with the age-old question, "What, then, must I do to be saved?", juggling the truth that we can do nothing by ourselves to keep God's commandments. For some reason, the Lord's Prayer rushed into my mind, as if by direct inspiration, to tell me how simple it is to be forgiven. God's wonderful, unfailing and forgiving love for us enables us to overlook and forgive the faults and sins of others.

We don't make a bargain with God that "I'll forgive so-and-so, and now You forgive me". But his mercy overflows in us and enables us from the heart to be forgiving towards others.

Right! That knowledge gave me such wonderful satisfaction and a real sense of peace. And that conviction held fast until the first time it became particularly relevant. There had been, long ago, an incident in which I had been terribly crushed by the actions of a fellow Christian toward me. Not a careless, drunken stranger, but someone that I trusted and admired. Opportunity for reconciliation never seemed to present itself, and it was as if the person involved was incapable of asking for my forgiveness or did not desire it, whether or not I was ready to give it.

While I thought that I had forgiven the offense, it nonetheless kept rearing its ugly head into my life, causing me to remain very uncomfortable about it. How I longed to be free of it!

The relationship remained strained for all those years. While I felt I should be able to approach the other person and speak about it openly, it was just "too risky". Why should I be the first one anyway, when the problem wasn't mine alone? Maybe she had been so little affected by it that she had long forgotten, while it continued to torment me. Why create a new problem? Besides, when we forgive someone, we are removing the accusation and should be prepared to behave differently towards them. We aren't allowed to lick our wounds any longer. I wasn't sure that I was ready for that sacrifice. We might be required to make some investment in renewing the friendship, or, heaven forbid, we might discover we actually shared the blame in the first place. The longer I waited, the more I realized I couldn't do it. I could develop a tough indifference about it and shove it into the corner of my mind. But that brought no peace. Why couldn't God just wipe it out?

This thing had to be resolved. I asked myself: Do I hate this person because of what she did? If so, I should not be communing. What if one of us were to die suddenly before peace could be achieved? What would it cost me to make the first move? What if she didn't react the way I hoped? What if she made light of it? Nothing would be solved. What if the situation gets worse instead of better? I may even jeopardize other friendships by making peace with this person. Could I be trying to drag out a kind of "punishment" for this person by withholding friendship?

Finally, none of it mattered. I was forced to see clearly that forgiveness is not "something nice we do for therapeutic results". God does not say, "You will feel ever so much better if you make peace with this person." He says, "Seventy times seven. Do it." But because we cannot muster the genuine thing by ourselves, we beg Him to help us through His Holy Spirit. The result is the gift of peace, relief, and the opportunity for renewed relationships.

Where do we go from here? "Let this mind be in you. . ." If we really want to be forgiving people, we don't save this attitude for the rare occasions when there is a sad case of betrayal, slander, denial, etc. When Christ forgave the crowd at the foot of the cross, I doubt that they heard Him or realized that he had forgiven them. They were so busy with their evil they did not notice. Every day, deliberate and unconscious giving and taking of offense goes on around us. With a God-given forgiving spirit, our precious "self" esteem yields to God's esteem for us, and along with that comes His power, not ours, to forgive.

One of our stumbling blocks in our progress towards forgiving is our own pride. How the devil loves to use that, and how pious and "right" he lets us feel under its auspices, when in fact, pride is one of the most singularly unattractive characteristics any of us can have.

Shall we risk losing God's forgiveness by refusing to ask it of others or to give ours? Shall we invite and embrace a hardened heart and claim it as a self-defense against our enemies? Oh, yes, forgiveness is costly. But the price is not so bad as the weight of the baggage of ill will and mistrust that we will carry around otherwise. When we forgive, we are not concluding that the person has suddenly become perfect. We are not saying we will never disagree with her again. We are not saying what she did was alright. But we are following God's way for us. Freely we have received the balm of reconciliation, and freely we give it.

The Greatest of These

Interesting, isn't it, that we tend to think of one another as souls at the time of a death more than otherwise? Why is it so unusual or difficult to think of fellow Christians as souls while they are still living? We speak of "his soul being with God" when someone leaves this life, yet we don't act toward one another as souls who, together or separately, will spend eternity in heaven or hell.

Two areas of thought provoke these questions. First of all, I believe that when we think in supernatural terms, we are closer to serving the people in the parish in the proper way. Numerical goals and clever strategies crumble into dust in time of real spiritual and human crisis. Each and every soul, whether there are twelve or three thousand, is so precious that I fail to comprehend how anyone awaiting ordination can take the responsibility with anything less than humility.

Every single soul belongs to God and looks to the Church for the only Medicine there is to fight the cancer of sin. Only the sincere desire and the Holy Spirit can provide the grace necessary to make a pastor's wife the loving and caring person she needs to be, someone who recognizes people as God's children and the stranger at the door as an "angel unaware". Then she can practice "the greatest of these".

Secondly, we who are preparing to serve in His holy Vineyard are given advice to develop the "hide of an alligator" to protect ourselves from the offenses of others. (I don't know what kind of hide others need to defend themselves against our offenses!) I would like to think that means we shouldn't let every little thing people do or say "get under our skin". Perhaps Luther's explanation of the Eighth Commandment would be better advice. ". . . but defend him, speak well of him, and put the best construction on everything."

It helps me to think like this: Jane Doe is going out of her way to insult me and hurt my reputation. I find this very painful to live with, and it doesn't look as if she will ever change. But while Jane can annoy my intelligence and deeply hurt my feelings, she cannot hurt my soul unless I let her. If I give way to the devil and allow myself to conjure up evil retaliation, then I do my own soul damage. And so it is sometimes in the parish. Others can take away everything we have, but they can't touch the eternal part of us unless we allow them. We are responsible for our own actions and not those of others.

The wise and strong pastor/husband will avoid revealing things about the members of the parish to his wife that will distress her or tempt her to behave in an unloving way. She should never have the burden of keeping a confidence. That's not her job. Emotional beings that we women are, it is almost impossible to leave things alone once we've been stirred up. We tend to feel we need to "fix things". Some things must be borne and left to God to mend.

Someone near and dear to me has said that in conflict, it is a good practice to assume the misunderstanding is on your part, be prepared for reconciliation where possible, and put it behind you. That's almost as difficult as Luther's advice, but there it is!

Cindy, Barbara, Danny, Kurt, Kevin & Colin
- Back yard of first parsonage

Bringing Up Children In The Parsonage

PEOPLE HAVE BEEN having babies and rearing children for a very long time. From the creation of the world until today, mothers have experienced the joy, the responsibility, the pain and often hardship, of rearing children... in times of war, in times of plagues, in times of economic depression, in times of moral decay. Yet, for most children, HOME and MOM have always been a happy mainstay in life. Motherly love has motivated self-sacrifice and hard work that has fed, clothed and provided the needs of children since the beginning of time.

Mothers are really special. I mean REALLY special. Mothers have God-given qualities that just fit the bill for the job for which they were created. The trick is to recognize those qualities and fine-tune them for the special needs of your family. Especially in our day and age, when public morals and values are so bankrupt, when we are told over and over, "Things are different now", *Christian mothers will want to draw on every ounce of Biblical wisdom and maternal commitment they can in order that their own children will grow up into useful, God-fearing adults.*

Our Christian families face enormous challenges today to share the Gospel with their busy, active children, and to pass on the values and beliefs they cherish most. Rearing children is not a nice hobby we can put down when we grow bored or frustrated. At the time of each child's Baptism, parents and sponsors promise God they will raise up the child in the

Apostolic Faith. That's a big promise.

Our first baby, like most I suspect, was more or less an experiment for me. Having been the youngest of two children at home, and not being around families with babies, I hadn't the foggiest idea what to expect. *There I was, ten thousand miles away from all my family and people with whom I had grown up, and I have to take a brand new infant home from the hospital!*

Two things saved me. The first was my Mother. Although she never visited us in Australia, and I frequently felt completely on my own, I recalled something she had said so often, "Children are just like little wads of clay. You can mold them any way you want to. You can have a patch of weeds running around, full of thorns and ugliness, or you can plant beautiful flowers, weed those beds that bear wonderful fruit and trim the edges for a garden." *Obviously, one takes more energy and commitment than the other.*

While we love our babies and thank God for them, in most cases, it is we who are given the real work of not only seeing that they are fed and clothed, but it is we, our husbands and we, who are to, from infancy, lead a child in the way he should go. . . for his own happiness.

In our present culture, where society calls a spanking physical abuse, and where we are not allowed to raise our voices in public when our children need it, it is very confusing to know what we are to do. So, let's wade through some of this and see if we can find some hints that work and are really good for our kids. Let's see if we can make things easier to understand and actually put into practice.

For instance, the way little ones behave in public is generally the way they behave at home. There is no magic wand we can take along in the car to bring about special behavior when we leave home. Good manners and obedient behavior, therefore, are desirable, for the sake of the child, but also for all who must occupy the same space with them. Good manners and obedient behavior are not found in little chips that are inserted in the neck of the baby at birth. It falls to us to teach our own children, not leave it to the company they will be keeping who will certainly share their manners and values. *If, in fact, you and your husband share values that are important to you, then those are the things that only you can teach your child.* A wise pastor/father once told me that he counsels young parents to teach obedience at home, not at the grocery store, or church.

A young father told me recently that because of his work schedule and that of his wife, whenever they were taking care of their three-year-old, either alone or together, they worked hard to keep a "positive" atmosphere. In other words, each would try to keep her equally fond of the parent she was with, so that when one of them left, she would be content to stay behind with the other.

He said they thought it was working fairly well until the first time one of them had to say "no" to her in church. She reacted in a shocked, angry manner, causing them all embarrassment. She had always been so pliable at home. Only at that point did they realize stronger medicine was going to be necessary. *It's a lot harder to break a bad pattern than it is to create a good one.*

This is a perfect case example of parents who went to great lengths to work around the child, instead of teaching the child to work around the daily activities they were to share in the home. We sometimes gasp at the behavior of the little people of this present age, and wonder what has happened to the "seen and not heard" attitude of generations gone by (whether or not we approve of that attitude!) Some of the difficulty comes when young parents, right from the beginning, make little idols out of their babies, become consumed by them, enchanted and amused by every move and sound they make.

If we think about it, any of us would imagine we were pretty special, like a celebrity with a fan club, if people paid that much attention to us. It wouldn't take long for us to figure out that by screaming, we would make them worry, if we smile, they will go to the ends of the earth to make us happy, and so on. Through the eyes of a baby, if mom smiles, "I've done something to make that happen." If mom looks worried, or angry, "there must be something wrong." Either extreme can be overdone, obviously. We have a lot of grown up problems throughout the day, and our attitude towards them is not something that is ignored by the child. Each child, however, will ordinarily learn that not everything that happens in the home is due to them in some way.

It is written somewhere that children most likely develop their sense that they are loved by the way the people around them look at them and respond to them. A person can grow up believing he is ugly and worthless by the early responses given them as they are growing up. If this is true, then neither do we want to convince the child that he is perfect, smarter than everyone around him, and in need of all our attention.

Without a word spoken, children pick up on people's real feelings. The balance, therefore, becomes critical: we don't want to create self-centered little divas and little boys who really believe they are destined to rule the world. At the same time, we don't want to create the impression that the child is somehow a disappointment and an object of rejection.

It seems to me that it might become a great burden for a little person to have parents with such high expectations all the time. Do they worry, do you suppose, that they might at some point fail to please? Do they think they have to keep up this "adorable" behavior or the parents won't notice them any longer? Just a thought. It would be wise to give the baby/child the necessary attention to confirm our affection, to assure good health and development, but at the same time, get on with our own routine so the baby observes there are other things in our lives that we must take care of?

The question is, then, are you a parent, do you and your husband plan to co-create a person who ultimately will be independent of you, a person who is secure in his own space, without everyone oooing and ahhhing all the time, without the need to perform on demand for company? You say, "We just want to make him happy." Do you desire happiness for the moment, or happiness as a way of life? Happiness tends to come, in the well child, with knowing what is expected and being taught how to achieve it.

My second source of help came from, of all places, my husband! Who would ever guess that a recent bachelor would know so much about raising children? It seemed to me he must have just been born with all the answers, just a fluke of nature. But after a lifetime of living with him, I've realized that apart from the little bit of boy that he still had in him that allowed him to enjoy the company of children, he was being a father as prescribed by Scripture without pontificating about it all the time.

He was secure in his understanding of God's directives for him as the head of our family, as well as a loving and devoted father and husband. He took as fact that children require several things in order to grow into God-loving children of the Lord. Here are just a few of them:

Children belong to God. We are in His place to teach them how they are to live. We, as parents, will someday stand before the Throne of God and answer to Him for the way we teach our children.

Everything we do for our children is to be motivated by our love for them, just as God's Law and Gospel are given us because He loves us.

Just as we don't wait until children have a working knowledge of nutrition to begin feeding them, we begin immediately to prepare them for a God-pleasing life through teaching them responsibility, respect, reverence and love for fellow men, appreciation for the beauty of the world and most of all, teaching them to know their God by word and deed.

Children cannot be loved too much. They can only be loved the wrong way.

Children need the active participation of both parents for balance.

Children growing up without firm boundaries and rules are unhappy and make everyone around them unhappy. Children need consistency, and they work and live at their best with routine and regularity in schedules.

Children need to learn to understand that not everyone gets treated the same in this life; that there is no such thing as "fair". Just as God sends different blessings to different people and allows different crosses, sometimes parents must provide different needs for each child. Children who know they are loved can learn to accept this and rejoice with others when they receive, and sympathize with others when they suffer. *(Not a bad lesson for us either!)*

Children soak up attitudes like little sponges. Right away, they can sense whether dad is just doing a "job", or whether he has a real shepherd's heart. They can tell when dad is working on a sermon, not because he is disagreeable, not because he pushes them aside, but because he has his "important books" out, and he prays a lot, and he talks about God's Word and how it relates to the family and the people of the congregation. Children who regularly see mom studying her Bible sense it is a special and necessary practice for her. And regular family devotions put a seal on the families who walk with God together. An atmosphere of bitterness and antagonism can creep into their personalities, potentially remaining with them into adulthood. Those feelings will most likely always be associated with their early years in the life of the church.

Our relationship to our children is very like our Father/Child relationship to God. If the plan was inspired by God for our welfare, it stands to reason that it should work well for us parents as well. Let's look:

We love Him because He first loved us.

Babies learn to love because parental love provides everything he needs.

We love God's Law because we know it is for our welfare. It is written on our hearts and in His Word.

Parents begin laying out some boundaries within which the baby must learn to live. This plants security.

We have free will and can depart from the Law by choice. Consequences follow.

Children begin to challenge the boundaries. Parents must see that the consequences are interesting enough so that the temptation will grow smaller and smaller.

When we sin, we confess our sorrow to our Father and ask forgiveness. We live in thankfulness and peace that He does forgive, that He doesn't keep tormenting us with our past sins. Only Satan does that.

We teach our children from the beginning that if they do something wrong, they tell us right away. They show contrition. We remove the fear of punishment by forgiving them, and then the incident is forgotten. We prevent further humiliation by not rubbing it in over and over. The child, of course, cannot be protected from the consequences of his action. If, however, he conceals the wrong that he has done, or through stubbornness he is prevented from feeling sorry, then a suitable punishment is necessary in order that we may bring the child to the point of seeing he has done wrong and must not do it again.

Children are really such a joy, such a miracle that takes place right before our eyes. Anyone my age will tell you it happens and is over before you know it. My husband used to say something, that at the time really annoyed me. In our case, it turned out to be right. But young wives usually balk at these things. He always wanted to take our children with us everywhere we went. We rarely went anywhere alone. He would say, "You, I will always have with me. The children we will have for a very short time." Because of his persistence, we have wonderful memories racked up in our family, and the children enjoy a very close relationship with each other and with us.

It seems like such a short time ago that I was spending literally hours doing laundry, hanging those hundreds of diapers on the line, day after day, year after year, going through endless mountains of ironing, cooking for hundreds of people, chasing after that inevitable one lost shoe every Sunday morning, wearing out the carpet in the back of the church, pacing with one baby after another for what then seemed forever.

I often questioned how mothers would ever get to heaven if they died young, because just getting to church with little ones and hearing only snatches of the service, especially during the Christmas and Easter seasons, sometimes didn't seem worth the effort. Each child possessed one church outfit, and it was wash, wash, wash. However, I've noticed the survival rate of both mothers and children is quite high!

God does give the strength. He replenishes the energy and the motivation. He loves mothers with a special love. He knows it's a 24-hour a day job. He knows we weep with fatigue and worry. But He also foresees that we will weep tears of joy when these little ones grow up and approach the altar for marriage, and when they bring their own little ones to the Font. He knows that sooner or later, we as parents will identify with Him, His parental love, His joy and sorrow in taking care of us. We share in His creation, we share in His caring, we learn his patience, His wisdom, His LOVE.

Acceptance

It's something we all need, even if we think we don't want it. But it is safe to say, I think, that every clergy wife hopes that she and her family will find it in their parish.

The parish is a group of individuals, not a clump of mankind. Each person is different, just as the members of your family, only more so. Each member comes from different ethnic, economic, political backgrounds.

At your entrance into their, yes, their, congregation, the members are already quite established. Some are very close, some are on the fringes. But the fact that they all gather regularly at the church indicates that there is one common bond, and that's their Christian Faith. Because they are baptized children in the family of God, each is very special, even the ones that act a bit like black sheep sometimes. Most times parishioners will behave like God's children towards you. But on the occasions when they don't, it helps to remember that not every Christian is at the same level of sanctification at any given time.

Some Christians are quite mature in their faith. For whatever reason, they don't regard it too difficult to think and act as the holy people of God. But many of us are on the long train of life, together, but at different places along that journey.

Some of us are just behind the engine, invigorated by the new-found Gospel and feeling lots of steam. Some are cruising along the track, just happy to be pulled along. Others are in a dark tunnel, waiting to emerge again, while yet others are around the bend, but will rejoin the rest eventually. Some are still in the caboose, wondering where the rest of the train is.

So someone you love dearly, while heading to the same destination as you, may be in a different car of the train. But that doesn't change your basic relationship with him. You anticipate the final arrival, when we all hop off and are united before God, where He alone will receive us all as His dear, special, unique children.

If the train jerks around a little on the journey, and we lose our footing, we pick ourselves up, laugh a little, and go on. We can't jump off the train while it's moving. We don't want to leave the train before it reaches the place we really wish to go.

It may not be a beautiful train. The seats may be sticky, the windows may be smeared and dirty, the tiny restroom may smell, the dining car may be crowded and expensive. The people sitting behind us or across the aisle may be unpleasant. We may feel weary from travel, or we may be feeling very lonely. We may get sick and tired of the whole adventure – but we stay on the train.

So, what will we do to occupy **our time** on this journey? That will depend a lot on those around us. Are we traveling with little ones? Are our companions our own grown children and their babies? Do we have an aged parent along? Maybe we have in our carriage the tiny tots Sunday School class. Perhaps the ladies aid or the choir. Worse luck, it may be the entire voters assembly. But maybe it's the shut-ins or the people in hospital, or that hermit neighbor from next door. What if you are lucky enough to share a compartment with just your husband? Wouldn't THAT be nice? I think we both know for a fact that if that happened, you wouldn't be on your own very long!

In other words, while it is good and desirable that each of us enjoys this life we've been given, and little time to ourselves occasionally, we should look around us on this train of life and think what it is we might be doing to ensure the trip is as pleasant as possible for others and that we might all arrive safely. This applies to all Christian men and women, not just clergy families. When we start looking at our journey as a self-serving, on-going holiday, we have lost the concept of our Christian calling.

What, then, about the stranger that hops onto our train when it makes its brief stops along the way? What is our response to the man who climbs on, worn out from life? Maybe he jumped off the train earlier and got a bit bruised up and sorrowfully climbs back on. Will he find rejection?

Or, what about the raggy family with grubby little kids that climb on in search of some refuge from the world that hasn't been very kind, looking for rest, some warmth?

What of the old lady, who's so weak she needs help up the steps. Her family dropped her off at the station because she's a burden to their lifestyle. Will she find a seat in your carriage?

Or the young man who has had many failures at school and can't hold a job, the lass who trusted a man for love and security and now comes with a baby to care for alone. Will they catch you averting your eyes to look out the window?

Miles down the track you get used to your carriage, and its collection of humanity. You manage to be a little helpful and companionable. Then out of the blue, someone else on the train, coming from another carriage, bursts through the door. She strolls down the aisle and begins criticizing everything you've been doing. You recognize this woman. You've had trouble with her before. Your husband probably has, too. How, then, will you deal with this insult?

They say clergy families live the "fishbowl life". Not really. They actually live in the ocean of humanity, swimming with and against the flow, in full view of everyone all the time. Remember, all the passengers in your carriage have been watching you all along. They know whether or not you are patient and kind, tolerant, helpful. They've heard and seen your attitude toward the others and their problems. They will know whether that woman's criticism is valid or not, and they will make their own judgment. You will have to deal with the nuisance value of it like you would that from a naughty child. In other words, you will have to ignore it.

Where do we get the strength to ignore, or better yet, to forgive? In my life as a pastor's wife, there were two places that I can distinctly remember being quite alone. One was sitting long hours on the beach watching the children at the waterside. The other, less exciting, was at my beloved clothesline, where I hung literally hundreds of diapers over the years.

In those two places I used to pray a lot, and one very regular prayer was for the grace to love God's people. I know that prayer was answered. And I firmly believe that when we pray for something we know is God's will, He will bring it about.

We don't always have to figure out how things will be solved. For instance, a case in point: Perhaps there is a person who has been a thorn in your flesh for a long time. She has made friendship impossible. The sad part is that she is the wife of a friend of your husband, and her hatred makes any normal relationship impossible for them as well. She has sent rumors throughout the church, resulting in considerable personal agony.

Now I firmly believe that if you pray for God to heal this relationship, He will. Knowing this, you are reluctant to pray that prayer. Why? Because if it indeed "works", you will have to develop a new attitude yourself toward her! You've built up such a good defense for so long, you can't imagine feeling good about her, or being able to relax around her. In other words, it's easier to leave it as it is.

The crux of it is, then, that we don't have to stew about this kind of problem if we can simply pray that God will plant the desire for genuine reconciliation. God arranges the dynamics. Quite frankly, sometimes I think we enjoy being victimized. We need just one little headache to complain about. And if God takes it away, we have to be happy. Complaining is a real pleasure for some of us. But, can you imagine, when we do arrive in heaven, and in the blink of the eye, all this nonsense will be gone forever, we may feel as if we have wasted a terrible amount of energy and time cultivating these hurts in this life. Think about it. Pray about it. Unload the pain, give up that cherished hatred. Owning it can only make you sick and disgusted with yourself. Blessed are the peacemakers.

"The Proppa Banner"

Having just come out of the four year seminary tribulation, where it seemed as if he was continually defending the Faith, rather than being taught it, I believe the young Kurt Marquart was probably in a perpetual "defensive mode". While he was tender-hearted and pastoral in his approach to his congregation, there was little trust given those in power on the Synodical level, nor at our educational institutions.

He had witnessed up close and personal the way men who challenged the system could be disenfranchised. Men who had spent four years training to be the under shepherds of Christ were discounted as "having psychological problems", "defiant", or were "not team players". All these thoughts can be verified by other materials written by others who were there at the time.

Had Kurt remained after his fourth year, at which time he would have worked on his STM, the administrators very likely imagined they had another year during which to fabricate something that would disqualify him from being certified. Having been caught off balance, they had no choice but to let him through. Since his grades were exemplary, they could hardly fail him. The worst they could do was give him a Call to a tiny mission field down in the Baptist Belt of Texas, where his accent and liturgical dress would be such a turnoff, he would not succeed as a Lutheran pastor.

Eighteen months or so were dedicated to Trinity Lutheran Church in

Weatherford, Texas, during which a building project was finished, and two confirmation classes were completed. Then the telegram came from Pastor Noack which read: "What is your age? Are you attached? Return prepaid." This telegram still sits on my desk, as a reminder of how God works.

It was around this time that I met Kurt Marquart. That story is elsewhere in this book. I had no previous information about him. I knew only about the seminary at St Louis, as Texans were rarely told about the Springfield seminary. I knew nothing of the Herman Otten Case. I knew nothing of his European background.

It was to this unknown individual that I attached myself through marriage, ten thousand miles from all with which I was familiar. Much of his past was not revealed for years, because we were living in a different world and time, in a new life for both of us.

One would be stupid to think that such recent events, however, did nothing to color his attitude toward many things. My personal experience was with the local scene, with the men, women and children of our three congregations. The way I witnessed him relating to those people gave me the opinion that I had of him. He was gracious, patient, but also firm enough so that they took him seriously. He was only twenty-seven after all. He spoke with such authority that before long, no one thought of his youth, and many were surprised, when meeting him for the first time, having read his articles, that he was not an old man!

While his pastoral personality was congenial and kind, he took no guff from quarters in the district or national body. Almost immediately, he was placed on the national CTICR, the body that studied and reported on theological and interchurch matters. The Queensland District was chaired by Pastor F.W. Noack, and at his request, Kurt was always formulating language for resolutions, and official statements used by the District, often countering the same from the Synod. While the ELCA was said to be "the conservative" Synod of the Lutheran Church, there were still those who, either in error, or on purpose, attempted to water down, or do away with, articles that were needed to keep the church body soundly in adherence with The Word of God. Kurt's combined knowledge of theology and language provided invaluable skills for such work.

As in all bodies of people with varying degrees of enthusiasm for their own point of view, there arose controversies in the Church. It was one of Kurt's gifts to read things and immediately see the issue, to judge whether it was correct or tainted, or just plain wrong. To the typewriter he would fly, and hours of careful research would ensue, resulting in documentation which would be disseminated to various committee members to be debated by various entities in conferences, and brought up at district conventions. To this end, the little typewriter went with the family everywhere, and some work was always in progress, whether we were at home, at the beach, or elsewhere.

Perhaps because of his determination for accuracy in everything he wrote, or the fact that he was so serious about these matters, in some quarters, I'm sure Kurt came across as someone with ice water in his veins. While never attacking individuals, he would dissect issues in such a manner as to confound those with whom he disagreed. In some parts of the country, as a result, he developed the reputation of being a "warhorse", "a firebrand", and he struck frustration and hatred in the hearts of the liberals.

Very early in the piece, he had dealings with the leadership in Adelaide, because he had to travel down there every three months or so to meetings of the CTICR. During one of those visits, he had dinner with Dr. H. P. Koehne, who was at that time the Vice President of the ELCA. He was a kindly man, and apparently a wise and brave man, because he approached the subject of "presentation".

"Kurt," he said, "God has given you a brilliant mind. The Church needs your gifts. You must continue to provide light on issues that are perhaps beyond some of us. Your information is absolutely correct. You are careful to see to it. It's all in one's 'manner of presentation'. You need to work on 'the proper manner' of telling folks the truth. Then, they will sit and listen, instead of bristling."

Kurt was one of the best mimics out there, and when he came home and told this story, he used the Australian accent and expressions so that one always knew which man was talking. Dr. Koehne, it seemed, had a bit of a sinus problem, and so his words came out more like "the proppa banner". From that day, the power of persuasion became something for which he continued to strive until his death. He learned from this kind man that one's reputation can get in the way of what he has to say, and that to open the ears of your hearers, you must smile a bit, joke a bit, and then when their defenses are finally weakened, they are happy to listen to what you have to say. Combining those techniques with the Truth, which was all he really wanted to share, his ability to teach and lecture became known everywhere. If his name was on the program, people who would not have otherwise bothered, came to hear. God used him mightily.

The wonderful thing about all this was that Kurt really never knew how excellent his work was. It was important to him, but I never heard him say, "God has given me great abilities." He was always effacing and deflected attention to others. In all the years I was with him, he never really spoke ill of anyone, with the exception of one man, of whom he quietly remarked, "He has no character." Otherwise, it was always "the issue, the issue, the issue." He had no interest in money, most likely because he never experienced having any, and he never talked about salary, but rather "God will provide".

Unexpected Houseguest

Part of my pastor/husband's responsibility in Toowoomba was to make regular visits to members of our parish who are confined in the local hospitals. It was a rare week when he didn't have someone very ill who needed daily visits until the crisis had passed.

Making these rounds sometimes found him coming into contact with people who were not from our parish, but who were seeking spiritual comfort. It was his pleasure to stop and spend some time with these individuals, and usually, he never saw them again.

One day he came home from his rounds and announced that we were going to have a houseguest for a while and that a spare bed needed to be prepared. This must have been before our first child was born, because after that, we didn't have a spare bed! Anyway, he said that there was a young fellow who had been working with a travelling circus, who, while setting up the tent, had bashed his foot with a sledge hammer. He had not healed well enough to continue with the troupe, and the hospital would not release him unless he had somewhere to go until he was better.

You guessed it. He was coming to the parsonage!

I can't tell you where this man came from, nor do I recall his name. But he was in our home for several days, sharing our meals, and lying around, getting better. I do remember that he didn't have a change of clothing, and so it was necessary for him to stay in bed while his things were laundered!

One of my friends and I had made plans to go shopping in Brisbane on a certain day, and it was not possible to cancel this arrangement, since other ladies were also involved. Brisbane had wonderful, air conditioned indoor malls in those days with all kinds of specialty shops that were not available in Toowoomba. The buyers had more international resources, and it was possible to find really pretty things. These were coveted occasions, and I had been looking forward to it to break up my endless pregnancy! So I went merrily on my way, knowing that we would not return til the late evening hours.

Brisbane was two hours away by car. The first leg of the trip was the drive down the winding range, with brilliant bougainvillea covering the sides of the steep mountain walls. In those days, there were only two lanes, and many cars and trucks coming up the range would only get half way before they overheated and had to stop to cool off. If the driver didn't get a good running start at the bottom of the range, he rarely made it to the top, even in low gear, without having to stop. If he landed behind a big truck, he had to crawl up the range without passing. The drive down, on the other hand, was almost as harrowing, since it was easy for your car to race out of control, going too fast, and running into others. There were safety ramps where men could pull off if their big trucks got away from them.

At the bottom of the range was Helidan, famous for its spring water pool. Temperatures being ten degrees warmer down the range meant that the pool was warmer. The Spa was always crowded, as there were two big pools as well as several snack bars. It was a happy place to take a family.

Further along, we drove through Ipswich and Indooroopilly towards the outskirts of the big city itself. The countryside was cluttered with unexpected flocks of wild, exotic birds swooping across the road, bottle trees next to jacaranda trees, heavy with their purple blooms, gum trees, with their peeling bark revealing stark white trunks, and the unique Queensland houses, all high on stilts, with children playing in the coveted shade beneath, where their mothers hung the wash.

Brisbane is a beautiful city, with a river that winds its way through to the ocean. The homes vary, but the old architecture, with the wide verandahs and corrugated iron roofs, on stilts, was the most common. The flora was amazing, with huge poinsettia bushes growing happily in front of the homes of just about everyone. It was like having perpetual Christmas. The buildings in the city were massive and primarily stone, and the sidewalks were wide and inviting, so that foot traffic was natural and heavy with shoppers and business men as well. From banker to delivery boy, all the men wore shorts with long socks during the heat of the summer. It was the era of mini skirts, and all the women, whether young or old, fat or thin were showing off their long, tanned legs. Such fun! So many sights!

Numerous tea shops competed for the foot traffic, and were nestled in crannies everywhere. They showcased irresistible delicacies, such as lemon squares, Lamington bars, scones and sponge cakes, fruit tarts, all topped with mounds of real whipped cream. Stopping for a cuppa was tantamount to the American coffee break. The shop girls came in swarms, and office girls carried trays of goodies back to their bosses. Morning and afternoon tea were ceremonies not to be ignored. When women went "down the street", or shopping, they tried to punctuate their trips with a visit to a cake shop.

At least three casket shops could be found on every block. What is a casket shop?, you ask. Are there so many deaths in Australia? The Golden Casket was the name of the state lottery in Queensland. The lottery money was paid into the hospital systems throughout the state. When it was almost time for a drawing, a sign would be propped up under the window of the shop reading, "Casket Closing Soon!"

The four of us roamed in and out of the shops for hours, totally unaware of life home on the Range. Cell phones, thankfully, did not exist in those days. When you left home, you could be free of all that bother.

Kurt, on the other hand, was not enjoying his day all that much. When I went away, which was not often, his ability to stay on task seemed to collapse. There he was at home, with this stranger all day. My husband was very tall, and possibly a little formidable to someone who was crippled. But he was not at all adept at fending off any kind of attack. He obviously didn't consider this when he invited the gentleman to stay at our home. In actual fact, he used to enjoy imagining all manner of dangerous developments. It was as if he was continuously writing a mystery novel in his head, with all kinds of probabilities of suspense in every shadow. But being left on his own for hours on end was apparently a bit unnerving, and he started imagining all kinds of scenarios that would necessitate his using some tactics of self-defense.

When we finally returned home, much to my amusement, I found Kurt wearing his dressing gown, roaming the house, awaiting my return. The mere fact that he was even wearing his dressing gown was strange, since it was summer. But the most amusing part of it was that he was wearing it inside out! Hidden inside the gown, with its head in the pocket, was our wood chopping axe!

It seems he felt much safer, having his pregnant wife return home. The house guest was probably never aware of how much horror he struck into the heart of his host. After only a couple more days, he moved on, and we never heard from him again. But we never forgot him, obviously. Needless to say, I never let Kurt live down that axe in his pocket!

My First Trip to New York

It was, if my memory serves me, in 1963 when Kurt was invited by *Christian News* to attend, on its behalf, the Lutheran World Federation Conference in Helsinki, Finland. At that time, some of the Scandinavian churches who were still true to the Lutheran Confessions had not joined the LWF for reasons of conscience. As well, many in the United States were being enticed with membership, but few understood the ramifications that would come with that choice.

Some always believe there is strength in numbers, and belonging to the LWF afforded special advantages that were denied those who stayed outside. Especially the poor congregations in Europe and Scandinavia were punished financially by their refusal to join, making their ministry and mission doubly hard with insufficient funds to do what was really needed. Salaries for pastors and teachers were inadequate, to say the least, and money for building schools and churches was reserved for those who gave in to the pressures of the LWF. The incentive to join was great.

The trip to the conference would be followed up by a lecture tour across the U.S. to many Lutheran congregations, where Kurt would explain the pros and cons of membership in the LWF. It is believed by some that his efforts were largely responsible for the Lutheran Church – Missouri Synod staying out of fellowship with the LWF.

Danny, our first born, was almost one, and I was expecting Cindy, who was giving me reasons to be acutely aware of her already in those early days with morning sickness, the likes of which I had not known in my previous pregnancy. I was so sick the doctor had to give me medicine against nausea, which made me very drowsy. Nevertheless, it was decided that since Kurt was to be gone for so long, it would be good for me to go to the States and stay with my parents for a few weeks. We had no money, so we had to borrow enough from Peter Boesch for me to make the trip. Uncle Peter was very careful with his money, and drew up a repayment plan which was to be followed to the penny!

So it was, that while Kurt flew West, through the continents of Australia and Asia and over to Finland, Danny and I flew out of Brisbane, East to Fiji, Hawaii, California to Texas.

It was the only time Danny was ever with his grandparents without the competition of his siblings, and he was doted over and enjoyed the royal treatment that goes with such rare occasions.

When it was nearly time for Kurt to have finished the conference in Finland, the plan was for Danny and me to fly to New York, where his parents lived. I would meet them for the first time. We would hook up with Kurt briefly, and then he would begin his lecture tour, while I returned to Texas.

My parents took Danny and me to the main airport, which was at that time Amon Carter Field. That was the major Fort Worth airport before the big Dallas/Fort Worth international terminals were built. It was a lovely airport, and I recall the huge gilded State of Texas on one wall.

Our flight was very rough, which was not helpful in my condition. We were literally lifted out of our seats at one point due to turbulence! It was a direct flight at any rate, so at least I didn't have to change planes with Danny.

La Guardia Airport was my first meeting place with Kurt's parents. There stood that diminutive couple, with a beautiful young girl, who was Kurt's sister, Mourka, waiting at the gate when we were finally allowed off the plane. With effusive hugs and greetings, we were immediately wrapped in affection and led to the baggage claim area. We were surrounded by incessant questions and pronouncements of how happy they were to finally meet their daughter-in-law, and everyone competed for holding rights to Danny.

Having secured our bag, and more than ready to head back to Nyack, where a nap was a promising idea, we were not allowed to go until we sat down inside the waiting room, where Kurt's mother insisted we first have a cup of homemade soup to sustain us for the drive. It was as if we had arrived from a month at sea and could go no further without nourishment. But she was insistent, and so we sat, and so we drank.

Kurt's stepfather, Uncle Lulick, was a frail little man. But his physique had little to do with his gusto on the freeway! With the typical Napoleon complex of a short male, he embarked on our journey with frightening speed and determination.

Before we got to the bridge that crosses the Hudson River, somehow Uncle Lulick missed the turnoff. The traffic was flying past us, when he suddenly stopped, threw the big car into reverse, and backed up so he could make his turn off. It was a pretty hairy moment, the sort of experience you never forget. Uncle Lulick also had trouble on inclines at intersections. He was driving a standard transmission, and if he had to stop on an incline, he would invariably roll backwards. Half of us were looking forward, while the others were checking out the rear window!

We succeeded in making it to their home without further incident, unloaded ourselves, carried our things upstairs, were introduced to the bathroom (it was explained that the bathroom had quirky habits of only working part of the time), and then shown where we would sleep. . .in Mourka's bedroom.

Kurt's parents lived in Nyack, New York, just across the Hudson River from NYC. It is a lovely place, with hills, rivers, and established homes, and happened to be the place where Russian refugees and immigrants settled after the war. Lulick, Margarite and Mourka lived in an upstairs apartment in a large house in an old neighborhood.

Mourka was in high school and still lived at home. Kurt's brother, George and his wife and son lived somewhere not too far away.

The apartment was small, with a living room, eat in kitchen, two bedrooms and a bathroom. It was cozy, if close. There was no television. Once a week, friends came to play bridge, so Russian chatter filled the air, as did lots of cigarette smoke, and vodka kept everyone cheerful. Mourka and Danny and I spent quite a bit of time outside, exploring and getting to know each other.

I knew that Uncle Lulick was an artist, as was his twin sister. His occupation was to design and supply color codes for beautiful handmade rugs. He would go into the city, bring the backings home, fill them in with patterns and colors, and take them back to be made at the shop.

Kurt's mother had been on the staff of the Tolstoy Foundation Home for many years. That was a place established by the daughter of the famous writer, Tolstoy, where many Russians lived who needed help getting started in their new country. Kurt's mother was very intelligent, and had indeed enjoyed being a baroness in Russia. But because she could not write English it was impossible for her to get decent work. At one time, she scrubbed floors in a local hospital. Before she died, she was written up in a local press for her collection of international dolls for which she had made native costumes. They were on display at a local library branch. She was a beautiful woman, had endured many hardships in her life, and I was happy to finally know her.

Uncle Lulick was an opinionated man, quite certain that he was right about most things. One day, he insisted I sing so that he could tell if I had a decent voice! He declared that it was clear and on pitch. O, thank goodness! He required a lot of attention, as his health was not good, but more as a result of his disposition. He was not used to sharing attention with anyone, especially a baby. It was evident at that time that he was still in charge of the household.

When, at last, Kurt arrived in New York, we all went to the airport to meet him. He landed with a thin dime in his pocket and needed to borrow money to buy stamps for all the postcards he had written on the plane!

It was such a joy for his mother to see her son again. Uncle Lulick was less thrilled, but that was not unexpected. Mourka loved her big brother, and so the visit was happy with lots of catching up to do.

Kurt wanted to take me into the city to some special places. We went by bus to the city. Keep in mind that I was drugged for morning sickness. Even though we were able to leave Danny behind with his grandparents, it was an effort for me to put one foot in front of the other. Kurt was notorious for walking everywhere, if possible. Fortunately, to get to the Statue of Liberty, it was necessary to get off the bus and find the subway. Each time I would take a seat on a bus or train, I would fall asleep. Poor man. He would have to wake me up and shepherd me out and onto another conveyance. Fellow travelers must have thought he was escorting a drunk!

After all that effort, by the time we got where we needed to go, the last ferry to the island had left and the tours were finished for the day. Kurt had never been out to see the Statue himself, and he, too, was disappointed.

The Empire State Building would have been a good alternative, had I not been so sick. The idea of going that high in an elevator was out of the question.

My few memories of the city include a lot of traffic, mostly honking taxis, stacks of garbage along the curbs, and very, very tall buildings which I personally found claustrophobic when we were in sidewalk traffic. The desire to return there has never been very strong. The international flavor was great, with representatives from every imaginable country. Standing in any line, one could overhear several languages all going on at the same time.

After the long bus ride back to Nyack, we returned to find Danny's grandmother had been having an all-day birthday party with him. She had streamers and balloons all over the apartment, and I think they must have had a grand day, just the four of them.

One day, while Kurt was still in Nyack, we were driven to Big Bear Mountain, a very scenic place, by one of his relatives. It's a beautiful part of the country, and I'm sure there were many things we might have seen had we had more time and I had not been feeling so pregnant.

Even today, when I hear news stories coming out of New York, I recall those days with the Russians in Nyack. It was not simply a geographical experience, but one full of cultural distinction for this young Texan. As my first year in Australia had taught me that Americans were not the only ones who knew how to get things done, the Russian family in New York opened another window to a part of the world of which I knew nothing. The fatigue and grief that lay just under the surface all the time was something I had not witnessed anywhere before. Knowing now what I know about the history of the family and what all they had to endure to find a safe life, it all makes perfect sense. One simply wishes to have been able to experience meeting these dear ones after gaining a few years of maturity, to be able to understand better, to be able to love better.

Great With Kids

A new testing came along with the arrival of our first child, Danny. I had no little ones in my history, apart from the Sunday School class I helped with as a teenager. We had no neighbors with babies. So, in my mind, little kids were there to be subdued, and the most pleasure I received from their company was the fun of teasing them. In fact, the grownups in my acquaintance claimed that I had the "teacher look". At the time, I didn't understand what that meant. Later, I realized it meant I could outstare any little kid, and reduce them to tears if necessary. Not a good beginning for a new mother.

Kurt, on the other hand, while a bachelor until so recently, was amazing with children. He was not afraid to hold babies, and toddlers followed him around as if he was the Pied Piper. Of course, it doesn't hurt when they all think you're Jesus, I guess. Whenever and wherever he sat down, the kids flocked around him, sitting on his knee and at his feet. If you want to develop a complex as a new mom, that's the kind of company you want to keep, right?

It is probably typical of all parishes that the folks are curious to see if their pastor can relate to children. Some have the amusing idea that pastors are too holy to enjoy the joys of marriage and fatherhood. Even my old boss in Fort Worth said that he could not envision Kurt any other way than to have a thick volume of Walther under one arm. I was pleased to send him photos of Kurt with his kiddos.

The congregation had not seen children in the parsonage for many years. Our little ones were immediately adopted and enjoyed the luxury of aunties and grannies all throughout their early years of life. It was never difficult to find someone to watch them, because they were well behaved and polite. I was able to accompany Kurt to New Zealand when our second child was only three weeks old, and Danny was scarcely more than eighteen months.

The Australian government was very clever about encouraging women to remain at home with their children. I suppose in an effort to grow the population, first of all, there was a $2000 grant given to anyone who immigrated who would stay two years. Naturally, there was vetting, and it was necessary for you to have secured employment and sponsorship. Then when your child was born, you received a check, followed by monthly checks per child, called "child endowment". It was sent directly into the mom's bank account, so that dads could not drink up the money.

In this country, we tend to call this process "taking advantage of the system". However, since our salary was far below the national average, we had no difficulty in accepting it. The drinking problem was pretty serious in those days, and many families didn't have employed fathers as heads of the household. This support enabled women to take decent care of their children, without having to go out to work.

This is not to say there were not stable families in Australia. I dare say divorce was not nearly as commonplace as it has been in the States. There were far fewer unmarried couples living together. In fact, many of our pastors would not marry a couple who had been living together until they separated and lived alone for a time. I'm sure it's much more lax now. As we lived there for fifteen years, it was sad to see the worst of America and Great Britain infiltrate the culture there, adulterating what had been a pretty decent culture.

It is probably safe to say that our little family was "different". We were not European. We were not American. We were not Australian. We were The Marquarts. A unique family culture developed over the years that was right for us. Kurt was a very good disciplinarian, and I don't recall any of our kids being rebellious. If they were unhappy, they were very clever to keep it from showing.

Despite the constant duties taking their Dad away, the children had profound respect for him and his work. There was never any talk of "church work more important than family". But each certainly had its place, and they trusted their Dad and Mom to make sure their needs were met. Kurt, for the most part, enjoyed the respect of his members and colleagues, making the possibility of a "persecution complex" unnecessary and unlikely. Even if someone was at odds with him, the kids were never aware. In fact, I don't think it really worried Kurt all that much if someone disagreed with him. He knew his job, he knew what God had to say about shepherds and flocks, he knew how fathers deal with children, since God left the perfect example. As the spiritual father of so many, it was the most ordinary thing in the world for him to think of his members as his children, too. And they seemed to sense that.

As our children grew old enough to go "camping" with their dad, it was his favorite thing to do. Mind you, there was no camping equipment, no tent, no bed rolls. Just a hunk of cheese and a loaf of bread, maybe some drinks. Driving ten minutes from Toowoomba resulted in being "out in the bush". One just drove into someone's paddock, parked the car, made a little fire, and sat around telling ghost stories. Since there was always a baby, I never had the thrill of going along on these overnighters. Sometimes, other kids the same age as ours would be invited to tag along. That, at least, meant there was more interesting food!

Kurt loved to tell the kids what life was like when he was young. He and his brother, George, got into some interesting antics that made the children roll with laughter. Their favorite, I think, was when their parents would have adult parties. They would make little tickets, set up a little table, and stand at the bathroom door, charging admission to those who wanted to use the facilities. They loved going around after the parties, emptying the wine glasses, but were never keen on the caviar. He brought the kids to hysterics talking about the fancy dress parties they had at their home. One man dressed as a devil, and under his long pointed tail was tied a mustard pot!

When the family was on the run, after leaving Russia, they had adventures that would terrify most of us today. One place they stayed in was so dilapidated that they hung an ammunition box out the window, in which they kept their cheese and milk cold. As an adult, Kurt still bore the scar above one of his eyes from a shell that exploded, when he and George hit it with a rock! He told the kids how he and his brother, while living in Vienna, would put a penny on the tram track right at the last possible moment, so that it would run over it and flatten it out. While he was an academic, he had a fearless child inside!

Because he enjoyed childish things, Kurt took kids with him to the swimming pool, to the park, anywhere where it was impossible to "play" without the presence of a child. When the kids were young, the local County Fair was a great family outing. To walk around the booths, observing farm animals close up, and to ride the exciting carnival rides that were brought to town were about the most exciting thing in the world. That was their first exposure to fireworks displays as well, and their needs for thrills were easily filled.

Then one year, when we returned to the States, we made our first excursion to Six Flags Over Texas. The county Fair was no longer the source of much enthusiasm. Kurt loved the roller coaster and was so glad when his eldest finally measured tall enough to ride with him. Some of us were not thrill seekers, but enjoyed the swirling tea cups, and milder swings, you know, things that don't usually make you sick!

With all the family friendly things one can find to do anywhere in the world, nothing, nothing compares with the beach. That was the place we all loved more than anywhere else to go as a family.

Overheard

Since I am often left to my own resources when it comes to attending activities, it has long been my habit to leave early and arrive before most others. OK. I don't like to be late. I don't like to enter a space when everyone else is already seated.

Every time I walk into a room full of people who have already settled in with their friends, I am reminded of the day I visited a friend of mine who happened to own a huge hatchery. She had said to meet her out back "in the shed", so I went out to find her. While exploring the property, I ventured into the long shed that housed all their laying chickens, or chooks, as they are called there. In this shed, there were probably a thousand or more hens, four to a cage. It was clean and airy, and the girls were all busy, pecking away. It was quite noisy.

The instant I walked through the door, every last one of them stopped clucking and all heads flung around with thousands of beady eyes looking right at me. This experience reinforced my need to be early!

Recently, I was excited to be able to attend a lecture by one of our finer guest theologians at the seminary. As usual, I found my place in an empty auditorium and got comfortable while the others strayed in from their lunches and began settling in. Since initially, I didn't recognize anyone I knew, I began people watching, as I am prone to do, since I don't play with my phone in public. There were two men in the row in front of me, down about four seats. But they were speaking loudly enough for me to overhear their conversation. While I missed the first part, I picked up the thread. Let me share it.

"What every happened to so and so?"

"I haven't seen them for a while, but I know she left him a while back."

"You're kidding! They were so happy. They haven't been married very long!"

"I know. It was a total surprise to me. I think it was to him as well."

"Well, what happened?"

"O, you know. He was really excited to be starting with his seminary training. Moved her and the little one here and got started with his Greek. He was really a good student and every opportunity he got, he was in the library, studying. At first, she didn't seem to mind too much, but after a while, well, it was kinda like he just left her behind in his enthusiasm."

"How's that possible?"

"Well, I guess he didn't take the time to talk to her about what he was learning. More and more, he just shut her out. I think she was interested in the whole thing, but he was never home, and when he was, he was studying for a test or writing an assignment."

"So, what you're saying is that he kinda outgrew her, left her behind, so that they had little in common anymore?"

"I guess. Seems as if it would have gotten even worse when he got into the parish. You know how it goes when you start sermon prep every week, and have meetings and bible studies to prepare for. Some women have little patience when they think they are taking care of the family all alone."

At this point, the speaker was being introduced, and they had to discontinue their visit. I was distracted by their conversation all afternoon, as I recalled the number of times Kurt spent time sharing ideas for papers, letters to the Editor, or lectures he was working on. He literally followed me around the house in our early years of marriage, reading to me something he felt was especially interesting. At first, I thought it peculiar, but as I began learning more and more, I was so pleased to be learning things that I knew meant a lot to him. He never read trivial things, never fiction.

When we attended one of the first faculty potlucks after Kurt joined the faculty at the seminary, as usual, the men were in their circle, and the women in theirs. I tried to be interested in recipes and problems with children, or home decorating, or the latest movie, or the fact that Mrs. So and so was looking for just the right matching towels and shower curtain to hang for spring. That, it seems, is what "normal" women talk about. But I really wanted to be listening to the guys. I was shocked and disappointed the first time I heard one of the wives say, "I just hate it when they talk theology! I'd rather listen to them talk about golf than theology." When I hear that kind of comment, immediately I think how sad that such an important and interesting part of that man's life is boring to his wife, and that they are missing so much because he is not encouraged to discuss it with her.

This is a two-way street. Some men don't think their wives are smart enough to understand what they are doing. Some may not be at first. Some women are so busy, they don't want to be bothered listening to "that stuff again." The truth of the matter is, the couples who don't attempt to share these "things of God" are walking parallel lives, but they are not living the kind of life that is possible if each takes just a little time to share.

Most people know how smart Kurt was. He certainly didn't need my input on anything he was writing. But he did say more than once, "I figure if you can understand this, then the reader will, too." He didn't mean this as "You're so dumb." But he always wanted to state things in a way that the average listener would get the benefit from it. No point using language that only the elite could follow.

Often when we travelled by car, he would give me a lecture to read aloud so that he could hear what it sounded like out loud. Or perhaps he would pick up on something he could say in a different way to make it more clear, or more interesting. If he wrote letters to the Editor in Australia, he normally asked me to proof read them ahead of time to be sure he didn't forget something I thought would be useful.

The point of all this is that we shared something that was the core of his work, and in the end, the core of our life together. No matter what other issues arose, or disappointments, we had that in common, and he knew that not only was I interested in his work, but I was proud of him. When he was invited to lecture somewhere, if I could, I went along. Having me in the audience was important to him. My opinion was important to him.

The best part of it all is that I learned soooooo much. I felt so blessed to have access to information that very few enjoy. After the first year, I realized that he knew what he was talking about, he researched everything, he left no loopholes, and I could trust everything he wrote to be the truth.

Yes, in the end, he, too, left me behind. But not because he wanted to. The joy of it is that he prepared me to live without him, because I learned so much with and from him. The pastors I have been blessed to have since Kurt's death have continued to teach and nurture what Kurt began. I understand that not every woman is going to envy this. Not every woman needs to be a perpetual student of the Word. That's ok. But I suggest any wife will be happier if she knows what her husband has on his mind, and especially if it is useful to her and the family. Think about it. And husbands, take this to heart, and don't leave your wives behind. Someday, when the kids are all gone, will you have anything to talk about? Start preparing now.

The Lord Is On Your Side

Over the years, when visiting with groups of ladies at the seminary whose husbands were at different stages of their training, there have been expressed various levels of concern, and even fear of what lies ahead in their futures as pastors' wives. For those waiting for the time to come, I suspect it would be foolhardy of them to not have some desire to prepare as best they can. That's not easy, given the fact that no one knows where they will be sent, and therefore nothing about the congregation they will be serving.

Some of the fears I hear expressed, however, are of a nature that can be confronted before certification. Those fears of poverty, shabby housing, difficult people in the congregation, church-in-flux, etc.

Some of our Lutheran hymns suggest that life can get tough. They can also provide power and reassurance. Think about it: "And take they our life, goods, fame, child and wife." Few parishes will exact that much from us! "But even if these be gone, they have yet nothing won."

I think it is a mistake to set out even thinking in those terms, that every parish has those who are "out to get you". The only enemy we have that can do any real eternal harm is the devil himself. He is the one, he and his angels, against whom we must arm ourselves and our children. For it is he who works overtime in the parsonage, casting doubt and suspicion into our lives, tempting us with material goods, creating discontent and fear within our hearts, and attempting to destroy the work our husbands are sent to do. And make no mistake, there are pastors whose work is hindered by a wife whose faith lies where it should not.

From my experience, poverty never killed anyone. In our household, we were discouraged from thinking in these terms, that "we are broke", but rather that we were experiencing "a temporary financial inconvenience". How can we say, "It's not fair!" when we are surrounded daily by God's abundant mercy and love? No one dies from wearing recycled clothes when they are worn with thanksgiving. When cash is low, the cook scratches her brain for clever ideas for making the money stretch. When sickness visits, we endeavor to learn yet more patience. But hardship itself does not kill. It should rather drive us even more to feed on His Word and His Sacrament, to nourish an undying trust in Him.

I have also heard some of our women express the fear that their future congregations may expect more of them than they can offer. Try to remember your marriage vows. When your husband makes his ordination vows, that doesn't change anything for you. There is nothing in Scripture describing what and how a pastor's wife is to be. We do read in Titus, however, that the older women are to teach the younger women about holy living, to keep a happy home, to obey their husbands, to love the children, to be holy.

Our behavior often says more about our faith than what we speak. A well-behaved family of children in the pew says a lot about your family life. Your unpretentious love and concerns for the members of your parish says a lot about you. Your husband is the called teacher. Attempt to avoid <u>doing</u> as much as <u>being</u>.

At a recent gathering of student wives, someone drew a human graph, a clever way to demonstrate the various feelings the ladies had about their husband's decision to come to the seminary. Some of the words were: *excitement, anxiety, joy, challenge, desire.* It was interesting to me that one of the feelings that was left out was *"humility"*. I would very much hope that when you arrive at your parishes and see day by day the very unique privilege and responsibility you have, that you will feel very humble. Why has God chosen you to be at the side of a servant of the Master of the Universe? What does He hope from you and for you? Only trust and faithfulness. That will keep you busy enough!

Be still my soul; the Lord is at your side.
Bear patiently the cross of grief or pain.
Leave to thy God to order and provide;
in every change He faithful will remain.
Be still my soul; thy best, thy heavenly Friend
Thro' thorny ways leads to a joyful end.

Funerals ~ Why We Go

I notice, in the newspaper obits, more and more announcements of "As per .....'s request, no services will be held." It saddens me, to think that some people, despite the clearness of Romans, think we live and we die to ourselves. Of course, it's everyone's right, I suppose, to have an opinion about this whole business. I've certainly been in a position to listen to all the reasons people have, like "I don't want to go to church every week and think about that coffin sitting down front." So they opt for a dismal funeral parlor somewhere, a place that has no cross or symbol of that person's lifelong belief in the afterlife. Sometimes they don't want a funeral because they know the members of their clan are at each others' throats and figure any attempt at civility would be purely hypocritical. Then, there are those of us who think, "I don't have anything nice to be buried in!" Just kidding!

So I'm just running these thoughts through my mind to get a handle on why I go to funerals and why I know, that despite the fact that they certainly are trying for those left behind, they are, as Paul says, a good thing.

Funerals, to my way of thinking, are almost as much a cultural, tribal thing as a religious thing in many ways. From what we read in Scripture, when someone died, they mourned, wailed, tore their clothes, etc. Like their weddings, sometimes these things went on for some time. Today in Africa, people come from miles away, on foot, and there are two or three days filled with feasting (which the family must pay for and provide), and whatever festivities are deemed right for the occasion. If it is an old person, they celebrate. If it is a young person, they mourn and comfort one another. I believe, traditionally, the funeral has been intended to actually mark the fact that a person spent time in our midst, that he/she mattered to someone, that he/she was a member of the Body of Christ. At the departure of that part of the body, the other parts feel the pain of separation, one way or another, some more than others. But because the body has changed forever, it is an occasion to contemplate the Creator of the Body, and rejoice over the life of the part that was with us and lived our common struggle. Somehow, it is a public acknowledgement that we realize the contribution that person made to our own lives and that we were grateful for that, grateful to God for giving us all to each other.

Doing funerals in the church invites prayers of thanksgiving to God for having given us this person, and through that person, the gifts that were shared with the whole. The service allows for comforting prayers for those who are torn apart by the loss. It reminds us of the promises of God, that He never leaves us nor forsakes us, especially in times of great sadness. It also shows us, by the attendance of others, that we are not alone. The Body will continue to support us, with love and in some cases, tangible help. Nothing is more depressing, I should think, to a family than to have no one attend the funeral of a loved one. Having attended hundreds over the years, I know that the families observe very carefully who is NOT there, and they are insulted by that absence, unless there is a good reason. It's not keeping score, it's a reaffirmation of the fact that that person's life was recognized as being worth an hour of prayer together with the family.

As far as one's own privacy is concerned, no one knows more than I how stressful it is to have to be paraded out in public all the time. Especially when you have lost someone very significant, like a parent or spouse. I learned a long time ago that as long as we are members of the human race, we don't really have a right to exclude our fellow Christians from our lives. Yes, there are some things you can keep personal. But the wedding or death or baptism or confirmation of anyone is a public matter in the Church. We all have to go through these things, and in the end, they are a wonderful occasion to receive the love of the brothers and sisters with whom we live on this earth. It is often the one time people break down their inhibitions just long enough to tell you that they really loved your ..... and what a difference he/she made in their lives, how they will miss them, how they hope you will be ok, etc. It is a simple exchange of human concern and love, and as I told Mrs. Bunkowske years ago, when she announced that when Gene died, she would have a private funeral for the family only, we are in no position to prevent others the opportunity to mourn, and more importantly, to receive the comfort of Christ in His Word through the Pastor at the service. Death is not a private matter. Every death ultimately effects each of us, directly or indirectly, but in no place more so than in the congregation.

The funeral service also makes a statement. It testifies to the fact that the person who has gone to the nearer presence of God lived, understanding that he/she was a creature of God's own making, that his/her life was blessed and directed by God, that he/she lived by Faith in the promise of Salvation through Christ, that he/she recognized the sinful condition of his/her own life, and lived under grace. And, yes, we know that it is a time when the Gospel is proclaimed, the words that pour oil over the stressful days of getting ready to bury this loved one, and infuse everyone once again with the strength, under God to carry on.

You will say, we all know all this. God knows we know, so why just go through the motions. It's not just going through the motions. It is the upholding of the members of Christ's Family by others. When we go to a funeral, we don't go for our own sake. We go to uphold the family who has just been shattered. We don't have to utter a word. Our being there is all that is required. From the beginning, God has worked through tangible means. Not just spirits, but real flesh and blood, real grape wine, real water, real humans. That is the state in which the world operates. Some say, I am spiritual, not religious. Finally, that means worshipping the god within. Christians make a public statement of worshipping a God in common, united, in a structured expression, through the liturgical funeral service.

IV
LIFE IN THE ACADEMIC WORLD
1975-2006

Acapulco

The Italian liner, *"The Marconi"*, pulled into the harbor at Acapulco in the evening hours in mid-December of 1975.

 Standing at the railing, all one could see were the myriads of twinkling lights, stretching from the shore to the tops of the hills that surround the port. Their reflections danced on the ripples of the quiet water that was pleasantly splashing against the side of the ship. The motors were cut off, and at last the long trek across the Pacific was finished. The next morning, we would all hop off this floating hotel that had been our home and embark on a new life.

Our introduction to Acapulco was, however, not to go all that smoothly. While most of the nightmare that was awaiting us was not of our own making, it took quite some doing to get out of it and be on our way. This is what I recall:

During the three months of farewells in Australia, being feted by every local, circuit, district and national entity of our Lutheran Church of Australia, though mightily distracted, we had to pack up our family. Three stages of this were necessary.

The first was to pack up our household things, cooking utensils, bedding, keepsakes that should be waiting for us when we arrived in America. This then necessitated our borrowing duplicates of all these things from our friends to use until, some ninety days later.

The second, and the hardest, was to pack up the study, which consisted of hundreds of books and documents. We had been specifically instructed to pack these into small boxes, and they would then be sent to Sydney and put on our ship and would sail with us. Every book, it was advised, needed to be wrapped first in newspaper to absorb any humidity that might be incurred along the way.

The third step, which could only be taken during the final days, was to pack the clothes in which we would travel, and things we would need on the trip. Keep in mind that these tasks were to be undertaken with the man of the house out of the house 99% of the time!

Leaving our home of fifteen years was a deeply emotional experience. Our congregation had become our family, and it was painful to imagine we might never see any of them again in this life. At the same time, our heart strings were being pulled from the American side, since we would finally be able to see our families again.

After many farewell gatherings, it was a welcome relief to finally be on our way. Much like being pregnant nine months, it was good to finally give birth to our new life. But not before a last minute wedding, and the funeral of a dear soul, who swore we could not leave until she died. I was mopping floors and throwing things in bags right up until the last minute before we left town.

Interestingly, our departure from Sydney Harbor was on the Last Sunday of the Church Year, November 22, 1975. It's nice to have that connection every time that Feast is celebrated in the church year. While it was exciting for the children to be going on this great adventure, it was agonizing for the pastor/husband/father to leave his parish.

At the time of our leaving Australia, Danny was thirteen years old. Cindy was eleven. Barry was nine. Angela was five. And Tony was a mere eighteen months old. One of the main reasons we returned by sea was that each member of the family received 35 cubic feet of free baggage space. This enabled us to bring Kurt's library back with us. The cost to us was $350 per person, and because of his age, we paid $35 to bring Tony back!

We discovered that the reason the rates were so low was that this was the final voyage of the *"Marconi"*. In fact, there were some factions on the crew that were so politically involved in something that was going on in Italy at that time, we were told, that at a whim, they just didn't stop in some of the places along the way that they were supposed to, and some passengers were virtual prisoners on this voyage.

We, on the other hand, had been anticipating a single cabin on D Deck, sharing bathroom facilities with many others. When we boarded, we were led to two cabins, connected by a bathroom of our own on A Deck! Just God's way of making it nicer for us all!

After a day in New Zealand with a school teacher friend, another day in Fiji, with an all day tour of the island, another day in beautiful Tahiti, we finally landed in Acapulco. The idea was that we would fly from there to Fort Worth, Texas, where my Mother lived, and then buy a car and drive to Springfield, Illinois. Our cargo would be shipped. But we had made no arrangements for that last detail. For the boxes, that is.

As it turned out, getting the boxes off the ship almost made Mexican captives out of us, as it seemed the people who packed for us, put all our small boxes into large boxes after all. The crane on the ship was not able to lift them out of the hold! One crane was actually broken trying.

We stood on the shore, anxiously watching and waiting, wondering if we would ever see our things again. It was beastly hot. No one spoke English. A few of our things had made it to shore and were sitting in piles, some of the boxes damaged, so that beautiful sheep skin rugs were poking out and causing great temptation to the multitudes of beggars who continually circled us like sharks.

Of all days, we landed on the feast day of some saint in Guadalupe. No businesses were open. Everyone was on holiday! How in the world would we make arrangements for our things to be shipped?

God is good! Of all the people in the world to appear was a lovely lady from Great Britain who turned out to be a customs officer! She cut a rather formidable figure, and her red hair got the attention of the natives right away. Her Spanish, though seasoned with a British accent, was very effective in shooing away those who had been almost physically attacking us. As well, she knew what calls to make to find out how best to help us.

Already in those days, bandits controlled the roadways between Acapulco and the American border. We were told we could truck our things, but not only would we have to pay the driver, we would need to hire two armed guards to accompany the truck, and that each truck would go only a third of the way. Literally Highway Robbery!

Finally, it was decided that we would have the crates taken to the airport and have them flown as cargo all the way to Illinois. That seemed to be the safest way to deal with things.

In the meanwhile, this dear Brit took all seven of us to her home, let us shower while she prepared us a meal, and we had a chance to pull our wits together and regroup. Angels certainly come in all shapes and nationalities. Hers was an extraordinary act of kindness. Her husband and children were so gracious. One had to wonder how often they had received total strangers in their home! Or maybe they just enjoyed being with English speaking people!

After a while, we were taken to a place down near the docks that had the dubious name of hotel. It was certainly not the kind of place one imagines one would like to stay in Acapulco. With all the beautiful tourist hotels within view, there we were in a dump of a place, with doors made of corrugated iron, concrete floors bereft of any covering, and run by very suspicious looking personnel. While Kurt was with us, they promised a cot for Tony, and gave other assurances. The minute he left, they pretended they didn't understand English. We locked ourselves in our room and sat on our beds, waiting.

The plan was for Kurt to be picked up by the driver of the truck that was taking our things to the airport. He would take care of paying for it all and they would bring him back to the hotel. Sounds simple, doesn't it? Nothing is simple in Mexico.

As it was the big Feast, with the setting of the sun came parades and bands and fireworks. For hours, the trumpets and drums and singing & yelling wound through the streets of the city. Sleep was impossible for the noise, and the children became afraid, especially as the hours passed and there was no sign of their father! Kurt had all our cash, all our passports, everything with him.

While we were cowering in the shabby room, he was bouncing along with the driver who was trying to bargain with him about how much he was going to have to pay for all this service. At the outset, one price was quoted. As they drew closer to the airport, the price escalated sharply! Kurt stood his ground, but apparently it was very unnerving.

When they reached the airport, the truck was unloaded, and there was another customs person with whom to deal. The British agent had called, so they knew what they were supposed to do. In some cultures, however, apparently it is ok to break your word. So once again, Kurt had to haggle with those in charge and was most likely over charged. It was always a joke in our family that all our boxes were labeled as "household gods", instead of "household goods". The crates were to be flown to Chicago, which was the closest the airlines could take such a big cargo shipment to Springfield.

It must have been after two in the morning before Kurt finally arrived back at the hotel. The parade had finally died down a little, and so traffic was easier to navigate. He was safe and had all his papers intact. So his personal angel was on duty that night. Although we had an early flight out the next morning, we did manage a couple of hours of sleep, and then made a trip to a local restaurant, where Kurt devoured a Spanish omelet, and the children and I all had waffles and pancakes. Somehow, few things tame childhood tensions better than good food. In the light of a new day, one would never have known what a harrowing twenty-four hours we passed in Acapulco. The sun was glistening off the beautiful water in the harbor, our ship was no more, the horrors of the previous night evaporated.

Just to seal the deal and make sure her wards were safely on our way, the lovely British agent actually came and drove us to the airport. She assured us she would keep an eye on our shipment and make sure it got off as soon as it could be managed. There was no immediate hurry, since we were making a stop in Texas on our way. Her efficiency allowed us to leave our household goods behind with reduced apprehension. It was a unanimous decision that we would never have survived that stopover without that customs representative.

We loved Acapulco and always thought it would be fun to return there for a vacation. That was not to be. It most certainly provided us with some colorful memories. Somehow, after that experience, we were emboldened to think nothing worse could befall us than what we endured in Mexico. Little did we know!

(It is interesting that in all this chaos, only one smaller box was lost. It went with a research scientist somewhere in South America. We had one of his. In a month or so, we finally made the exchange, and in total, only one slipper was lost.)

Seminary Calls/Rescinds Call To Teach

While it was not uncommon to hear that one of our colleagues had received a Call to a new parish, it was not until 1969 that one came into our lives. Kurt was very content with his position in Toowoomba, and I suppose his reputation protected him from "run of the mill" congregations wanting him.

Shortly after my Dad was killed in his plane crash, a letter arrived from Bethany Lutheran Theological Seminary in Mankato, Minnesota. It was a Call Document for a position as lecturer at their institution. Bethany was well-known as a bastion for confessionalism, and it was an honor to be considered by them. It was the single time in my fifteen years in Australia that I was homesick, and I really wanted Kurt to accept that Call so that we could return home.

It had been an emotional burden to me that I could not be home, as the only daughter, to help my Mother in her new status as widow. While the three of us had agreed, when I left the country, that if any of us were to die, we would not attempt the funeral, because of the distance, and expense, her remaining years were to be considered. I really wanted to be home. I can't recall his rationale for declining it, but I was very depressed when he said he could not go.

A few years later, he received word that he was to receive a Call to teach from the Lutheran Seminary in Adelaide, South Australia. While he loved the parish ministry, this was something he would seriously consider. The future of the Lutheran Church in Australia would depend largely on what kind of pastors came out of that seminary. After the uniting of the two church bodies, the seminaries also combined into one. As throughout the rest of the new church, there were more liberals than conservatives also at the seminary.

Within a few days, while Kurt was giving favorable consideration to this news, before the official documents arrived, it was learned that Dr. Henry Hamann, Jr., who was on the faculty of that seminary, warned the Board of Regents in no uncertain terms, that if they issued that Call to Kurt Marquart, he would resign. The Board rescinded the Call.

I thought it ironic, that some years later, when Dr. Hamann was a guest lecturer on our Concordia Theological Seminary campus, that he was in the Systematics Department, of which Kurt was Chairman at that time.

Dr. Hamann served our seminary on a number of occasions, and we were quite good friends with him and his wife, Ricky (Erika). During his last tour of duty, he was diagnosed with prostate cancer, and it became necessary for him to be flown home to Australia as quickly as possible, as death was eminent.

Henry and I met almost the first week I was in Australia. He was a guest in the home of our friends, Harold and Sylvia Stehn at the time. There were several other pastors there, who were also attending a conference in town. When I entered the room, he was instantly on his feet. I was introduced to the gathering and made the round of handshakes. Finally, after a few minutes of chatting, Henry said, "Will you please sit down so that the rest of us can!"

Our conversation went something like, "Do you play squash?" "No. Sorry" "Oh." Over the years, we managed to enjoy being in one another's company. He told me once that when he first met me, he said to himself, "Kurt's got the most beautiful pastor's wife in the country!" He was very frank and pretty much always spoke what was on his mind. While one could say that he was rather a flirt, it was obvious that he adored his wife, and no one ever felt threatened by him.

When I went to the hospital that last time to say good bye to Henry, he knew he was very sick, that he was flying home just as soon as his bookings were complete, and he had had many visits from colleagues from the seminary before I arrived. When he saw who it was, he said, "I hope you're not going to recite the 23rd Psalm! Everyone who comes in here recites the same thing!" He was such a character! I kissed him on the forehead and said, "God keep you Henry Hamann. I love you." I gave his hand one last squeeze and left him to the mercies of God, and prayed that Ricky would be able to deal with that long flight alone, with Henry. He died shortly following the arduous trip back to his home. Ricky died soon afterward. They say she died in her sleep, peacefully, joining her man.

Henry's father, Henry, Sr., was on the faculty at the seminary for a long time, too. The story was told about him that he went through the open door of an elevator shaft and fell some distance, without a scratch being suffered.

Ah, the Australians gave us such a colorful life! Henry loved telling the story about what happened when he had to find documentation of his birth. He was applying for travel documents or something, and it was necessary that he have a birth certificate. I think he was born in India. In any case, he had to do a search to prove who his parents were. He somehow reached the place of his birth and discovered that the hospital where he was born had suffered a terrible fire, in which all the records were destroyed. Thus, his official documents read: Father: Henry Hamann, Sr., Mother: Unknown.

Henry was good friends with Norman Nagel, both having shared their British experience. Norman is a brilliant theologian, beloved by students and colleagues everywhere. His British accent is lovely, and his use of the English language is stellar. The only frustrating thing is that he tends to taper off at the end of his sentences, so that you catch the first half, but not the finish of what he is saying. Some might have said "he mumbles" rather much, and frankly, he didn't seem to care. At any rate, one time when he was lecturing in Fort Wayne, following his presentation, Henry accosted him with, "Norman, you simply can't impose on people that way!"

Throughout all the years these men wove themselves in and out of our lives, I noticed that all brilliant individuals are just a little strange. Just a bit unique. No matter how much they give, in terms of speeches, sermons, lectures, papers, they continue to maintain that amazing quality that makes us want to come back.

Since the Lord was after all in charge, before long, the last Call arrived, the one that would take us to Concordia Theological Seminary, which was at that time located in Springfield, Illinois. Kurt had gone to the States over the summer to teach a class there, after which the Board of Regents interviewed him for a full time position. Dr. Robert Preus was putting together his new faculty after having recently been elected as President, and he wanted Kurt very much to be a part of that.

There was not much discussion when the documents arrived. We all loved Australia, the children were good little Aussies in every way. The parish was growing, the school was grown to its max, and a second one was being built. Kurt was serving on a number of boards and committees that were helpful in steering the "new church" in the right direction, and we knew that his leaving would create a big void. Nevertheless, when he received the documents, his only question was, "Why is it a temporary Call? Can I rightly leave a full time Call for a temporary Call?"

So he called Dr. Preus on the phone, which was a rare thing for any of us to do in those days, and discussed this aberration with him. Robert was quick to answer, "Think of the things that would disqualify you from a temporary Call, Kurt. If it's not likely that any of these things would happen, then you don't need to worry about anything remaining temporary."

On the basis of Robert's assurances, in his announcement to his congregations, he included the remark, "The battle for confessional Lutheranism is going to be fought at that seminary, and that's where I have to be."

We began, then, the closing of the Australian chapter, which had consumed fifteen years of our lives. The members of our congregations had become family. It was painful on many levels, walking away. The Australian Lutherans loved their pastor very much. Things were never to be the same for them again.

And the Marquart Family, which had been indulged by these generous and loving people, left the security of God's provisions through His people, and entered the academic world, an environment where you are on your own. You work, you get paid, you take care of yourself.

When we left Australia, Kurt was being paid $115 a week. We had a house provided, and a car allowance. The rest was taken care of by gifts in kind from our members, and from extra work that Kurt did, lecturing overseas, etc. We didn't have money to save, or manage. We lived day by day, and the Lord provided the life we needed. When we arrived in this country, while the salary was obviously higher and benefits were included, the expenses were worlds apart from what they were in Toowoomba, and there was a matter of managing what little we did have to go the farthest.

At one point, with our children ranging from 15 to 3 years old, we were so stretched that Kurt went to his boss, Dr. Preus to ask for an extension, or else, as he put it, "I'll have to go pump gas somewhere." It was at that time that his salary was increased, which was only right, since he was doing more and more outside of his job description for Dr. Preus.

However, during the interim time with the temporary administration, after the illegal firing of Dr Preus, Kurt was refused raises for more than three years, because they claimed he was already above the district scale. We were thankful he was awarded tenure before this crowd took over, as there is little doubt they wished to dispose of this nuisance, and obstruction to their plans to close the seminary.

Kurt was on the faculty of Concordia Theological Seminary for 30 years. That's a lot of students over those years, many of which asked him to preach at their Ordinations, and invited him to lecture in their circuits over the years. He would have gone on for a long time yet had he not become ill with ALS, which finally killed him in 2006.

Gleen How

During the war-torn years of the Vietnam crisis, Kurt and I spoke many times about attempting to adopt an Amerasian child. Being in such close proximity while living in Australia, we thought it would be a relatively simple matter. But after several attempts in all the appropriate places, we were informed that the Vietnamese were no longer allowing Americans to adopt their children, because it was still very uncertain, with the chaos of war, which parents were really dead, and not just missing. Until they were sure a child was really an orphan, they would not give them up to international adoptive parents.

When we returned to the States, therefore, having gotten settled here with our brood of children, with everyone in school, and the house large enough to bulge just a little more, we went to Catholic Charities to make enquiries about Amerasian children. The woman we needed to see was not in her office, so I left a note on her desk with our phone number. I could never have dreamt how my life would change from that day.

There was a rapid influx of Vietnamese, Laotian and Cambodian refugees flooding into Fort Wayne at that time. Catholic Charities was working like gangbusters to bring them in, but then had very few arrangements in place for their housing, schooling and employment. Thus, congregations were adopting families, and clothing and household goods were being scrounged up everywhere for hundreds of new people. Schools were making adjustments for all the children who knew little or no English. Simple jobs were searched out, sewing for the women, janitorial and factory jobs for the men, etc. The demand was always greater than the available jobs. Therefore, skilled men and women were being hired to wash dishes and scrub toilets just in order to survive.

When the Director of Refugee Resettlement Office got back to us, it was to ask if we had

Kurt with Vietnamese God children

room in our family for a young Laotian boy. He had been living with a bunch of young men who were older than he was, and the agency wanted to get him into a home and attend high school. The prospects of his doing well on his own in the U.S. were not very good in the situation in which he had found himself.

It was a big consideration for us. It's one thing to take a young child into one's home. It's quite another to

Kurt and Barbara with Wynn and Ann Nguyn and God children

take someone into the family's private life who had had the kind of exposure to trauma, deprivation, and desperation that these refugees had seen. Phayboun had been fending for himself for a long time. He and his brother had left their family, made a run for it, dodging the military, and had wanted to come to the States together. But Phayboun had been selected by the people who make these decisions, and the older brother was left behind to wait his turn in the filthy camps where food and comforts were rare.

We were vetted by the Social Services people for foster care. There were probably reasons why we should not have taken Phayboun, but there was such urgency to place these people that I'm sure a lot of rules were stretched. The fact that Kurt traveled a lot and was not always around was a concern. But we decided to give it a shot and if it didn't work out, at least we would have tried.

Kurt moved his study into the dining room so that Phayboun would have his own room on the opposite end of the house from the younger children. He was kindly cautious, and it was rather a big sacrifice for him to relocate his work so that Phayboun would have this advantage of his own room. It was the only way Kurt had any hope of monitoring the safety of his own children, while allowing for some privacy for our new boarder.

Phayboun was delivered to the house by one of the agents, carrying his whole world in a brown paper bag. He was a handsome boy, beautiful smile, shiny black hair. His English was not very good, but he could communicate most of what he needed to. We managed to enroll him at South Side High School, where there was a program in place for remedial work for the children of Asians coming in. He rode the bus across town in all kinds of weather, and for the most part, made good grades.

He had a sunny smile and I believe he made a big effort to fit into our crazy family. He got on well with our three boys, and was polite to the girls. We helped him with his homework, and he joined in all our family adventures. It was not always idyllic, and as I look back, I'm sure our children were not particularly thrilled with the arrangement. But they went along with the plan that we hoped would result in at least a temporary respite for Phayboun.

The beauty of it was that Phayboun opened many doors for us into the Laotian community that would not have been available to us otherwise. He knew everyone, and everyone knew him. He helped us cross-reference families, jobs, housing needs for families and worked part time while attending school. He went to church with us every week, but he was never confirmed. He said he had been baptized, but we never really knew for sure. In the very least, one could say that he was sent to us at a unique time to help us do unique work among the poor.

The Asians culturally do not like confrontation, and they will answer "yes" to just about anything you ask. If we asked, "Do you want to go now?", he would answer "yes". "But maybe you would like to go later." He would answer "yes". No matter what the question, the answer was always "yes". But we always knew what he wanted when he said he needed to go the **gleen how.** That was the green house where some of his friends lived. He liked to visit them on the weekends, because the women always made egg rolls and other delicacies that he missed. Saturdays were cooking days, when the women would make all the noodles and egg rolls, even the rice, that would be used all through the week. It was like one big party, and he learned to cook some pretty tasty dishes.

I used to call Phayboun "my sunshine". He and his affection for us came at a time when our own children were less and less interested in their parents and family life. The two were not connected. It was just the natural development of boys to start finding their fun with kids from school, etc. Phayboun was happy to come home from school and rest, do his homework, and help in the kitchen. His happy disposition always lifted my spirits. I believe he missed his own mother, and very likely his desire to help in the house and yard were his way of bridging that painful gap.

As it turned out, after about two years, Phayboun moved on. It became known that he was a few years older than he had reported to the government, and he was hanging out with some pretty rough people. When we discovered pots of marijuana out in the woods behind our place, we decided it was time for him to find a place of his own. It would not have been smiled upon by Kurt's bosses to learn that we were growing pot on campus. He bundled up his things and found lodging with some of his friends. We bumped into him once in a while. On Mothers Day, he would be in the parking lot of the church with a potted plant or some other gift for me.

After meeting Phayboun, we became quite involved with the resettlement of literally dozens of Laotians and Vietnamese. Zion Lutheran

Church had adopted a number of families as had Redeemer. At Redeemer, where we were members, the entire family of Phommachans was instructed, by Kurt, baptized and confirmed. One of the seminary students who rode with us to church just happened to have been a translator during his military service in the Vietnamese war, and spoke and read Laotian. He was such a blessing during this time.

During these years, it fell to me on many occasions to drive individuals to job interviews or to the bank, or to the hospital. I had three couples to whom I taught English in their homes. One of the couples I met with twice weekly told me how they found Christ. The husband told the story of how he found a Bible under the floorboards of a fishing hut in Laos. By reading it, he had become a Christian and was secretly baptized, along with his wife and children. He was so thankful that his children could worship freely in this country.

For Christmas, I gave them a manger scene. Tears came to their eyes, and they told me they would have to set it up in their bedroom, since the relative with whom they had to live at that time was Buddhist and would never allow it in the house. They would set it up during the day and take it down before the others returned from work.

Khamby, a scrawny little man, was one of the first Laotians I met in the larger community. He was in English classes and was always looking for work, so that he could support the family that was still vegetating in the camps in Thailand. Finally, he received word that his family had been accepted, and they were, in fact, on their way.

The Phommachan family travelled a very long way before their arrival at the Fort Wayne International Airport. The children were pretty young when they struggled off the plane, carrying their meager belongings. Ketmany was about five, and she was so tired, she could not walk. Our bonding began as I carried her to the car. The kids were all enrolled in schools, and they picked up English quickly, since as their family became acclimated, it was necessary for them to act as translators for their parents.

The house that was initially provided by Catholic Charities was adequate, but was bug and rat infested. While not perturbing the family that much, since they were used to such things in the camp, it was a bit disconcerting to me to sit on the couch with baby roaches crawling all over me. Sitting next to me, in a trash basket, was a huge dead rat that had been trapped. The children were disappointed, since apparently he had provided amusing games before his demise.

Hours were spent, wiping out kitchen cupboards and spraying for vermin. I think they all found it quite amusing, when I think of it, since they would not have bothered. As they began to accumulate a few household goods to add to the comfort of the family, generally, they took very good care of things. I was amused to discover one day that the whole basement was full of used clothing they had gleaned from numerous sources. Deprivation makes us greedy to finally attain things for our children. It was amusing to me that one of the first things the mother wanted to find for herself was a girdle!

Not surprisingly, shortly after the mother arrived in Fort Wayne, she became pregnant. Everyone was excited, and plans were underway for a new baby when Ali had a miscarriage. She called me at home to say she was sick and needed to go to the hospital. I was due to take her older children to school for special language classes, but I told her I would take her first, drop them off and then come back to her at the hospital. I was gone over an hour, returning to find her in the same spot I left her. I asked what they were doing for her, and I was told that they had to give her a pregnancy test before they could continue treatment. When I asked them why that had taken so long, they told me they couldn't find a pregnancy test in the hospital! I was furious and replied, "If this woman had lots of insurance, you would have run every test in the book on her !" By the way, the doctor's name was Dr. Amature!

After hours of futile waiting, we were sent home. The nurse told Ali that her baby was dead and that she would miscarry. I took Ali home, and told her to rest and call me if anything happened.

Later in the day, the father, Khambay called to say she had lost the baby and that I was needed to come. When I arrived, the house was full of all the male Laotians from the community, all sitting in the living room. I went into her bedroom to find Ali sitting on the floor on a grass mat, all wet with perspiration, shivering, holding a little package wrapped in a paper towel. She said, "This is my baby. We will bury it."

I immediately found dry clothes for her, put her into a clean bed and kept her warm and quiet. Then one of the daughters and I made some chicken soup and made sure she had something hot to eat. She was very sad to lose her American baby.

Before too long, another baby was on the way. This time, she carried to term, and Anna was born, healthy and beautiful. New hope for a new life.

It was a happy day when amassed funds from all the working members of the family enabled them to purchase a house. In that culture, it was not only a status symbol to own property, but it was critical to be in a position to be hospitable to other members of the Laotian community, and many parties ensued.

Ali was a good mother to her children. Sadly, when Anna was about five, Ali developed cancer and soon died. I was at their home shortly after she died. The family had her laid out to receive visitors, who came with fruit and cheese on plates that were scattered around her room, and each person left cash on the bed at her side. The explanation was so that she would have money to spend in the next life, and the food was in case her spirit roamed at night.

I sat in her room, thankful that her weeks of pain were behind her. She was so beautiful and peacefully accepting. The event was soured by the wretched funeral director, who sat at the kitchen table with the children, ascertaining whether or not they had a life insurance policy on their mother. He refused to remove the body unless they could prove they could pay. As someone mentioned to me, "Didn't he realize those people dealt in cash?" I vowed at that hour to be sure to make clear to my children that under no circumstances should they turn me over to that man when my life ended!

Ali had a Christian burial, since she had been baptized and confirmed in the Lutheran church. At the funeral home, the Buddhist monks sat in their circle, doing their thing, while we Lutherans and Catholics who knew the family visited in a large room together. As each friend of the family passed the casket, they left cash as well as some fireworks in the coffin. I never new whether the undertakers removed those things before they closed the casket for the last time.

We were invited to go along with the family to the "crematorium", which turned out to be a brick factory. We disembarked from our cars on a wet gravel driveway of the business and filed into a warehouse where there were two huge ovens where bricks were baked. The concrete floor was wet from rain, and crunchy, and all the Americans stood in shock, sharing looks of despair, and grief, and shame, while witnessing the eldest son pull the switch that ignited the oven that was to annihilate his mother's coffin, which he and an uncle had lifted up into it. There was no Hollywood niceness about this cremation. My heart bled for the children and I was never told why it was necessary for the whole family to endure that cold experience.

Ali's ashes were to be taken back to Laos with the eldest son to be placed in a wall there with other members of her family. For weeks, we were told by excited children that they had seen the spirit of their mother in a squirrel that they saw jumping from one branch to another in the tree outside their home. A relative in Laos wrote that she had seen her sister's spirit flying in and out of her house through the windows in the form of a beautiful bird. It is not too hard for me to imagine how these "signs" might be used to comfort the grieving. But it troubled me that they were not secure enough in their Christian faith to realize that Ali, who confessed the Faith before her death, enjoyed a far better condition than that of a squirrel or a bird.

I don't know where all the family is now. Three of the girls appeared at my husband's funeral, after many years. They were all married or in college and attending a local congregation. Each was more beautiful than the next. They gave me a framed photograph of themselves at their confirmation, in which Kurt and I were also, and a plaque with the Lord's Prayer engraved on it. Someday, I will track them down and we will have a reunion and talk about the old days. Each of them is so much a part of my heart that I will never be free of them. They gave so freely of their cheer and hope and gratitude. The tensions that we overcame with language and cultural barriers were broken down after years of friendship and trust. What a gift they have been to me. How I love them!

What If Something Should Happen?

You've heard it a thousand times. Your friends and family members say it. "You should be prepared, in case something should happen." Or the TV commercials, pushing life insurance, "in case something should happen." Or mother's advice, "You should train for a career, in case something should happen."

The implication is that if something should happen, it must surely be something bad, right? Like illness, a sudden death, a job loss, a government overthrow. Or maybe fear of a storm blowing away all one's possessions. Or some drunk driver might total your car, or worse, kill the breadwinner in the family. Lots of things "could happen". That's what the insurance market tells us.

I knew a pastor in Australia who refused to purchase insurance against the loss of anything. He had given his wife a lovely sapphire ring. She wanted to insure it against loss. He argued that it was a lack of faith that resulted in folks spending tons of money on insurance, and he refused to be part of it.

Anyway, I digress. Every time I hear that expression on TV now, I have to smile. It reminds me of the many times, when I would encourage Kurt to take some kind of precaution, saying "But what if something should happen?" His immediate response was always, "I surely hope something will happen. It would be depressing to think I could go through life and nothing happen."

It was his joy in life to play with words. He manipulated the English language more than anyone I ever met and delighted in the sometimes humorous results.

Vienna

The year was 1986. Another Luther Academy conference was being held in Ratzeburg, Germany, and Kurt was assigned a paper. The job coincided with our twenty-fifth wedding anniversary, so we decided to go together, and then visit Vienna while we were in the area.

Kurt and his brother, George, had a history in Vienna, having lived there during the war. Some of the most interesting times of their young lives were spent roaming the city, dodging street cars, etc. It seemed to Kurt like a good time to include Tony on this adventure, and taking a tour of the places where he and his brother had gotten up to their most memorable antics. All the other children had left home, the benefit being Tony's, that he could travel with his parents.

Our first stop was in Norderstedt, a suburb of Hamburg, for a visit with Kurt's father, Kurt Arvid Marquart. To reach his home was quite cumbersome, first taking a train out of the big city, out to the suburbs. The scenery was captivating, rushing by retaining walls, covered with very artistic graffiti, and big posters advertising products in a much more provocative way than I had seen in the West. Along the tracks were dozens of tiny cottages with fenced-in gardens, measuring no more than twenty feet, by twenty feet in total. Kurt explained that because of the density of the population and the often crowded living conditions, some people purchased these small retreats along the tracks as escapes for the weekend.

The first train would take us only so far. At a secondary station, we found two choices: one was another little shuttle kind of train that would take us within a mile to Norderstedt. The other was a bus that ran within a block of Grandpa's flat, but it ran on a schedule which rarely suited us. And so, the train was it. Out in the middle of nowhere, the train would leave us, and with all our baggage, and inappropriate shoes, we had to traipse along gravel roads to the neighborhood where Grandpa lived. Even if it was only a mile, it was still difficult for someone with short legs to keep up with the lanky guy who loved walking everywhere he went. Every time we had to do that, I thought I was going to die. But I obviously never did. The ordeal certainly did nothing to endear me to those visits. Kurt Marquart, Jr., did not believe in spending money on cabs when one could walk.

The little community of Norderstedt had a couple of nice little hotels. They were equal distances from Grandpa's. One offered breakfast. The other did not. So many of our meals were taken at Grandpa's. It was always a risky business, because despite the fact that he was a good cook, one could never be quite sure of the freshness of his ingredients. One time we went there to find he had had a duck in the oven, turned off, for a couple of days. I cannot speak for the times when various of our children visited there with their father, but while his hospitality was great, there was always some doubt in my mind about the food.

Grandpa's tiny apartment was in government housing, where retired people living off their pensions often lived. His friend, Suzie, lived next door, and together they shared the tasks to keeping going in their final years. (Suzie died before Grandpa.)

(Grandpa Marquart had been off the radar for over thirty years, and no one knew where he was during that time. Eventually, as he aged, he grew

curious to know what happened to his sons, and he reached out to their mother, who was in New York. Having gone through several wives over the years, he was at last living on his own in very modest circumstances, surrounded by his books and keepsakes. Typically, older men become very sentimental about family, and it seemed important to him to connect with his boys, and maybe in hopes of being on the receiving end of some charity. I don't know.)

Grandpa Marquart always wore a suit outside the house. We were greeted, therefore, in that spirit of feeling special, important guests in his home. He had been out shopping for things he believed we would enjoy, like chocolate liquor beans, and there was plenty of vodka on hand. He was not a fan of food from the West, like pizza or hamburgers, and we discovered that he had roasted duck in our honor, and did as much as possible to arrange for enough seating in his cozy two-room apartment.

The visit provided a good opportunity for Tony to observe his father and grandfather together, even though neither he nor I could understand what they were talking about half the time. From one of these visits comes a story of how Russian soldiers cope with the philosophy of never drinking without a proper toast. It seems they could capture a cockroach, which was not a problem, tie a string around its middle, and let it crawl around the table. When the roach would fall off the edge of the table, they would toast, "Farewell, Comrade Cockroach." Then they would pull it back up with the string, and toast, "Greetings, Comrade Cockroach!" This, of course, could go on all night, allowing much toasting!

I knew Kurt never fully recovered from his father leaving his life as a child. Especially since he fell into the cruel hands of a step-father who hated him. While ambivalent towards his father, he never failed to stop in Germany to visit him when he had lectures in any part of Europe. His father was a professed evolutionist, having been a scientist by trade, and the concern for Kurt was always wanting to help his father reach an understanding of, and grasp the Gospel for his own before his death. Many phone conversations between the two revolved around this effort.

With Grandfather Marquart, a little time went a long way, since I spoke no German and he spoke little English. He was a determined fellow, pushing his vodka and chocolate as a means of showing meager hospitality. I'm sure he imagined that if he spoke his German very loudly, I would be more inclined to understand it, making it a tad stressful to be enclosed in such small quarters for very long. He tried, however, to make our visits as rewarding as he could, always roasting a duck or goose, and setting an elaborate table. Suzie was always part of the gathering, and I seem to recall she had some connection with the U. S., and her English was better than his. It was obvious that they depended upon one another quite a bit for company and entertainment.

During our time in Hamburg, we made day trips into the city and along the river. It is a beautiful city. On another occasion, when Kurt and I were there on our own, we took a bus tour of all the consulates in the city. It was then that I learned that Hamburg has more canals than Venice. We heard the incredible story of how Hamburg had once burned to the ground, and since then, only stone buildings were erected in the city.

The ancient cities of Europe are wonderful to visit. To walk on the same sidewalks as generations of others is to connect with the past in a special way. One finally has a sense of belonging to something that has gone before. The cemetery in Hamburg is enormous and holds the remains of thousands of victims of war and plague. Kurt's grandfather is buried there. The Elba River is a major waterway for ships coming in and out of Hamburg, supporting industry and economy. But more than that, it is just plain beautiful. The architecture of the government buildings is timeless, the likes of which are not possible today.

Finishing our visit with Grandfather, the three of us went back to the train station where we boarded a train to Ratzeburg, just northwest of Hamburg. The conference would begin the following day. Accommodations in Ratzeburg were very nice, but we spent little time there, as most of our meals were taken at the conference hall where the papers were read.

Negotiating our way around Ratzeburg was invigorating. Surrounded by four lakes, it consists of two small islands, connected by an isthmus, a small strip of land. We stayed in one part of the city and walked to the other side of the city for meetings, meals and vespers.

The outstanding attraction of the town was its cathedral, or dome, where those attending the conference observed Vespers every night. The famous pipe organ was being serviced during our visit, so all the chanting was done a cappella. The strong male voices of conviction ascended into the high, vaulted ceiling, joining centuries of songs of praise by the faithful of the past. The only illumination was given by candles around the chancel where we sat.

The cathedral, built in the 12th century was of solid stone, with columns measuring ten feet in diameter. It was dark and cool inside during this summer visit. In its shadows, one sensed the thousands of pilgrims who had passed through the ages, with their sacrifices of prayer and praise to the only Source of help during wartime and famine. The pews worn from men, women and children listening to hope in the Gospel. The floors worn from the kneeling! What a wonderful feeling of continuity, of being connected with the Communion of Saints from another time and place.

The village of Ratzeburg was beautiful, providing lots of unique places to visit on foot, including brightly colored houses, with ornate fronts and pretty gardens, paths along the water, frequented by many geese and ducks, unusual shops, etc. I don't believe there was public transport, and everyone walked everywhere.

Attending the conference were men and women from all parts of Europe, providing a unique opportunity to connect with pastors and families with struggles, as well as victories, different from our own.

After a few days, when the conference had ended, the three of us boarded a train and went through Germany to Austria. I recall little of that trip, except the disappointment of getting a rather boring cookie, after ordering a croissant! My male companions thought that was amusing. I did not. Much of German food, to me, was lacking. Even the sausages, that one would expect to be very good, were bland.

When we arrived at the massive train station in Vienna, the first thing we had to do was to find a place to stay. My husband never believed in spending money on places to "sleep". His idea of travel was to get there, to meet people, or see things. Hotels did not interest him in the slightest. Walls in the terminal were covered with advertisements for various lodgings, but none of them suited him.

We stared at the wall for what seemed a very long time, when out of the blue came a hunched-back old woman, like someone out of Hansel and Gretel. She spoke enough German to be able to converse with Kurt, and told him that she ran a boarding house. She had no car, but she would take us there by bus. OK?

So it was that the three of us chased along behind this sprightly lady, who said nothing along the way, but who first coaxed us on one bus, where we listened to the amusing singsong announcements by the driver, none of which we understood. We left that bus and boarded another, getting farther and farther away from the heart of town.

Finally, we were led off the bus and down a street where we entered a gray, stone building. There were no markings on the building. We had no idea where we were, but were more or less dependent on our tour guide at this point. She led us to a small elevator, into which the four of us squeezed with our belongings. On an upper floor, she led us out and down the hall and opened the door to a delightful one-room apartment with a communal bathroom just outside the door.

So, there we were, with twin beds and a pull-out sofa bed, in a little room with big windows, which opened in the curious European way onto a view of yet another gray stone building. Tony was spooked, first by the woman, and then by the silent building, in which there didn't seem to be any other living soul. At night, Kurt had to sleep with his bed across the door to allow Tony to feel secure enough to go to sleep!

The landlady made a point of explaining to us, using the water meter as a visual aid, that we were allowed to use only so much water. Therefore, when she discovered we were washing out a few things, she was annoyed. She didn't like underwear hanging around the room either, so she took me up into a spooky attic, where there were clothes lines stretched for the likes of our backward American family.

Every morning, early, our landlady would rise and go across the "Kennedy Bridge" where she procured fresh hard rolls for us, and would bring butter and knives on a tray, boiled eggs and tea for our breakfast.

In no time, Kurt got his bearings, and there were certain things he was he wanted to show us. The first day, we went to Shoenbrunn Palace. Built some three hundred years ago, Shoenbrunn was the residence of Empress Elizabeth during the early years of her marriage. Later it became the summer residence of the Habsburg Family, and its halls and secret passages were the playground of the sixteen children of Empress Maria Theresia. The famous Shoenbrunn maze, once the private garden for the royal children, has since become a public park where many children are allowed to wander. The grounds of the palace are meticulously groomed, and the many acres of garden, 50-foot hedges, ponds and statues make for a beautiful day's outing. During the good months of the year, concerts are conducted on the platforms of the palace gardens, and beautiful lighting and special effects may be seen on TV specials when these are broadcast.

Another exciting visit was to the giant Ferris Wheel located in Prator Park, where there is also a very good zoo. The Ferris wheel has carriages the size of railroad box cars and go up as high as 213 feet, overlooking the city of Vienna. It was very meaningful for Kurt to be able to ride the wheel with his own son, so many years after being a twelve-year old himself. The Ferris wheel was built in 1897 and was the inspiration of Ltd. Walter Basset, an English engineer, who at 33 years old, designed and supervised it's building. During the bombing of the war, it was damaged, but it was decided that it would be too expensive to dismantle. Rather, they replaced only fifteen of the carriages. The Ferris wheel had been erected to honor Emperor Franz Josef I's 50th Jubilee.

During our short visit, Kurt was able to take us to the location of the apartment building in which he stayed with his family. It was still very much the same on the outside. Much of the city had been damaged during wartime, but had been rebuilt to much the same designs as it had previously been. We were able to visit some of the special sites commemorating Mozart as well. All in all, it was a very good visit, and while brief, it was the one time I was able to peek into Kurt's past in a concrete way. We were unanimous in our wish to return another time and go deeper into Austria, which is a beautiful country.

Four Star Hotel It Was Not

On many occasions, when my late husband would travel abroad to lecture for the conferences that were held for confessional Lutherans, he would be asked to bring his wife along. Since, for ten years I was working full-time as church and school secretary at Ascension Lutheran Church and School, it was not easy to extricate myself for prolonged travel. So it was that Kurt became accustomed to striking out on his own and doing everything at minimal expense, since he was easily satisfied by modest accommodation and little food.

When the invitation came from the brothers in the Scandinavian Lutheran Synod in Oslo to give a paper at their Luther Academy Conference, the temptation was too great to pass up. I managed to work ahead on church bulletins and newsletters at the church to allow a full week off for myself without much inconvenience to anyone there.

It was the middle of summer when we landed in Amsterdam, the place where a lot of international flights go for passengers to proceed to other parts of Scandinavia and Europe. From there, we flew to Oslo, Norway, where we were picked up by a local pastor and taken to the youth hostile where the conference was housed. Located in the outskirts of the city, one could just see one of the many fjords through the tree tops on one of the hills where we walked in the evenings. It was a residential area, and I enjoyed the varied architecture of the homes, no two alike.

Since I understood no Norwegian, I found myself taking little strolls, some of which led to a little gas station across a busy freeway, where one could purchase all kinds of necessities, like bar soap! Walking required hiking up slopes and almost racing down little hills, with few flat surfaces anywhere.

I had never stayed in a hostile before. Accommodations were certainly adequate, but with the common showers and toilet down the hall. It seemed to me that the facilities were just bare enough to encourage everyone to congregate, rather than spend time alone in their rooms, reading or relaxing.

Everyone, mostly men, with a sprinkling of women, attending the conference stayed at the hostile, and meals were taken together three times daily, providing opportunity to meet new acquaintances, as well as reunite with old friends. The first afternoon we were there, while scouting out the neighborhood from the window in our room, I thought I smelled a familiar fragrance. Looking down into the patio, I saw my first boss upon arriving back from Australia, Pastor Charles Evanson. He was teaching in Lithuania on behalf of Concordia Theological Seminary and was attending the lectures. What a nice unexpected surprise. It had been many years since I had seen him.

One day, when Kurt was not scheduled to teach, we walked to a nearby bus stop and took public transport into the city of Oslo. After being in our dead inner cities, it was very stimulating to walk in busy foot traffic, poking into interesting shops and beautiful old cathedrals, smelling of centuries of the faithful. The Norwegians are a beautiful people, mostly blond with blue eyes, healthy from outdoor sports, smiling and all seeming to be on their way to something important. No one strolling, everyone striding, with purpose. I thought it peculiar that the young women all seemed to have such great figures. Someone enlightened me by telling me that more than half their women have breast augmentation. That took care of that delusion, and I realized no amount of exercise would ever give me those results.

One night, about one a.m., the fire alarm in the hostile started blaring, and people came through the halls, knocking on doors to make sure everyone got out of the building. Sure enough, there was the smell of smoke, and there was a huge fire engine in the front yard! For a minute, I wondered if Pastor Evanson had fallen asleep with his pipe lit! Eventually, the source was found, and it was determined that the sound system in the main hall had some faulty wiring which started a blaze there.

Since it took a day to restore things, everyone decided to take a day off and go for a tour together. Several people were in our car, as we went down to the main tourist attractions, which included a museum made exactly in the same shape as the Kramer Chapel in Fort Wayne, sure proof that the same architect designed them both.

We were taken through the huge, ancient homes and chapel that had been moved into Oslo from around the country in which previous generations of Norwegians had dwelled. Very stark, but quite practical, obviously constructed to protect the inhabitants from the savage winters, one could almost see the families eating around the rough tables, and tucking their children into the set-in sleigh beds. Heavily insulated from the elements, they were by necessity dark inside. One imagines that it got pretty depressing by the end of winter, without the benefit of sunshine for so long.

Our host was very gracious and spent a great deal of time telling us the history of everything we visited. Perhaps he was taking pity on the wives, who had endured so many of the lectures that might have been construed as dull, since they were mostly in a language we could not understand.

Parting company at the end of the conference was bitter sweet. Leaving those very fine pastors and church leaders behind, knowing how difficult their work was in that part of the world, was a feeling I won't soon forget. The government, as well as the Lutheran World Federation were obstacles at every turn for them, and finances were very difficult. Many of them had little or no salary with which to support their families. Their congregations were small, the economy difficult. Certainty and deep faith drove men like that to hang on, and one had to admire their cheerfulness.

The last night was spent in a hotel attached to the railway station, because our departure was early the following morning. The room was very small, but clean and adequate for one night. It was also very expensive. But we chose it so that no one would have to be inconvenienced by bringing us into town in the morning. It also afforded us the evening to ourselves and our own resources to scout around town and see the city by night.

The town centers are heavily populated by people of all ages, sitting around fountains, on the steps of the parks, wandering musicians, and lovers everywhere. It was a very pleasant scene, at least on the surface, to see the community enjoying just hanging out together, and everyone greeted us everywhere we went.

The train we boarded was to go through the rest of Norway, Denmark and Sweden on its way to Hamburg, Germany. It was very modern and comfortable in coach, and we enjoyed the companionship of two young students across from us, who, as it turned out, were studying Luther and the Reformation at university.

We had one last look at the beautiful landscape of a very unique country, and hurled our way south in this very efficient train. At one point, we had to drive the train on to a ferry and cross a body of water. I cannot recall where it was. But it amazed me to be able to go below deck and find actual train carriages on the ferry! One does not think of them as that big and strong. There was a large cafeteria on the top deck where we were encouraged to have lunch while crossing.

Eventually, we arrived at the monstrous train depot in Hamburg. It was more like a huge shopping mall than a depot, and nearly anything one would want to buy could be found there. Making our way out the front door, we found ourselves on the main street of downtown. Kurt had been there many times, and so I assumed he knew where we would be going for the night.

The busy street was lined with one hotel after the other, and as we dragged our bags along, I was hopeful that we would soon settle on one and be able to situate ourselves in time to go out to eat. It was very disconcerting to me that as we passed each one, Kurt would declare that it was too expensive! He insisted that as we walked down the way, out of the heart of the city, things would be less expensive.

Naturally, he was right. But just as the establishments became less expensive, so did the inhabitants and clerks looked less reputable. Knowing how cheap Kurt could be with such things, I had the foresight this trip to bring along some of my own money. So, when we climbed the darkened stairs into a smoke-filled reception area, which had required us to ring a bell to enter yet, manned by two very questionable looking women, I stood my ground, stayed on the street, and said I would not enter. Kurt laughed at me. He said, it's only for one night. I said, "It's a brothel!" He said, "It doesn't matter. You just keep inside your room with the door closed." I'm betting the rooms had no bathrooms either.

When he saw that I was determined, since I literally turned on my heel and started walking back towards the city, he finally followed me. I picked a hotel that I thought would be ok, and we checked in. The man at the desk said, "O no. You don't want to be in a place like that. They rent rooms by the hour there!"

I still wonder why European elevators are so small, but nevertheless, we made it to the second floor, and the man showed us our room, which was very pleasant. We took a while to freshen up, and then went out to find a place to eat. Hamburg is a beautiful city, too, but I liked it better in daylight.

When finally we got to bed that night, we found we had to keep the window open since there was no air conditioning. It was somehow providential, then, that there were call girls just under that window, turning tricks all night long.

We were in Hamburg three days. There were some friends Kurt wanted to visit just outside of town. They were from Africa, and Kurt had met the father at a bus stop one year when he was visiting his father. The next year, when he was again visiting his father, at the same bus stop, the same man appeared. They became friends, and Kurt had been to their home many times.

After doing my duty with the family, I talked Kurt into a bus tour in Hamburg, a trip that went around the city by every embassy in town. No two were alike, and it was very interesting, as the driver told us many historical things about the city that neither of us knew before. For instance, Hamburg has more canals than Venice! And after the great fire, nothing was built of anything but stone. Sitting on the banks of the Elba River, Kurt reminisced about his childhood, and how precarious life had been for his family in those times and places. Just when one thinks they really know a person, an entirely new layer is peeled away, and a new perspective is gained which helps to understand so much. No doubt many Europeans have similar stories to tell. Perhaps that is one reason they seem to have so much more depth, and maybe even a bit more tolerance when it comes to hotel rooms.

The Russian Project

Google notes that the Iron Curtain fell in 1991. It was a momentous development and one which Kurt Marquart never dreamed he would see happen in his life time. Communism was so entrenched and so powerful in the Soviet Union that it was deemed inconceivable.

It took a few years after the "fall" for church bodies to react to the amazing mission field that had opened up. Like Kurt, they never planned for it because it was not expected. Slowly, as churchmen from the U. S. started penetrating the bodies of Lutherans in the European countries that had been held hostage for so long, lines of communication were opened and created between our LCMS and the Lutheran Church in Russia, Latvia, Estonia, Ukraine and others.

Because Kurt's mother tongue and family culture were Russian, he was a natural resource while plans were being made to help the pastors and people. Pastor Wallace Schulz was an active participant in these plans. As soon as they could arrange it, he and his wife, Kathy, were living in Russia, getting information first-hand about what the situation was, and those things which might be attempted to rebuild the church. This initial information was critical.

Professors from Concordia Theological Seminary were sent to Novosibirsk to train pastors for the church in Russia. There was a small seminary there, and the goal was to rebuild and strengthen what was there. At some point in the 90's, the "Russian Project" began, involving bringing men and some of their families to the Fort Wayne campus, where they were taught the basic theological courses that would qualify them to become ordained.

At this time, there were men from Kazakhstan, Novosibirsk, Ukraine, Latvia, Lithuania, Estonia, and perhaps also Belarus who sat in classes together, putting aside their century-old hostilities and cultural differences to learn how to proclaim the Word of God to the world.

Several of their families came along. One of the dorms was converted to serve as family accommodation, with central cooking areas, common areas, etc. The clothing bank was made available to them, and they were invited to use the gym, library and grounds for their children.

When we first learned these people were coming, I thought I might teach myself the Russian language. What a joke. I got the tapes and books, and after the first five minutes decided that the Russians would have to speak English. While Kurt grew up speaking Russian and French in his childhood home, we as parents didn't pass it along to our own kids. He always said that it couldn't be done well unless both parents spoke the language.

I had thought the Russian project would be an exciting time for Kurt, after so many years of having been removed from it. There had been no one in Australia who spoke Russian, so there were years when he had no practice. His obvious advantage was that he could teach his classes in the language, so that an interpreter was not required. The students loved it, and good communication was exchanged during that time, both on our campus and when he went to Russia to teach.

At some point, it became necessary to appoint one man who could coordinate the travels, the courses, the professors so that the work could go forward unhindered without chaos and duplications. Sometimes our men went to Russia, and sometimes their men, especially the leadership, came here. Finally, one of the professors was chosen to be the head of the project. Strangely, this appointment seems to have been made without any consultation with Kurt for his input.

While he hated the bitter weather in that part of the world, especially Siberia, Kurt continued to teach and provide support to his brothers in Europe. The fact that they had such monumental struggles endeared them to him and for years, they enjoyed close ties. Records indicate that he had the following schedule:

Summer of 1996 – Russia; Summer of 1997 – Russia and Kazakhstan; Summer of 1998 – Russia and Ukraine; Summer of 1999 – Russia, Belarus, and Kazakhstan; Nov, 1999 – Russia; March 2000 – Lithuania; Summer 2000 – Russia, Lithuania; November 2000 – Russia; December 2000 – Belarus; Summer 2001 – Uzbekistan, Moldova, Ukraine, Kazakhstan, Russia; May 2002 – Russia; Summer 2002 – Russia, Lithuania.

When you realize that nearly every January, Kurt was in Haiti at their seminary, as well as teaching a summer extension course to our men in the U.S. you can see that he was not home a lot. But he loved his international contacts and looked forward to every one of them. I think his favorite was the seminary in Kenya, where he spent his last tour before he got sick. He was there for at least four weeks, following throat surgery in 2004.

As I have written elsewhere, when it seemed as if he might have to face an early retirement from the seminary, he was not bothered. He said he wanted to teach as long as possible, but should he be retired, he would spend his time going around the world, encouraging the brethren.

O, Canada!

In the world of academia, faculty members are allowed to take off every seven years for a sabbatical. They may spend a year away from duty at half salary, or six months on full salary. At least, that is what it was in those days.

So it was that after almost eight years, we had an opportunity to return to Australia, at which time Redeemer Lutheran Church in Toowoomba sponsored a seminar. I can't recall how many lectures this involved, but it was also an opportunity for Kurt to go down to Adelaide for a presentation as well, while Angela, Tony and I remained among friends in Toowoomba.

Pastor Peter Ubergang, who replaced Kurt at Redeemer, had died from cancer but his wife was still in town, living with her sons. I had not met her before. When she greeted us at the church parking lot, she said, "OK, now I get to meet this woman who can walk on water." What a gracious thing for one pastor's wife to say to another. Instantly, it enabled me to assume that mainly good things had been said after I left the country.

It was a wonderful experience seeing all our members again. As we stood at the back door of the church, greeting folks as they filed out after the service, I was so relieved that I was, without exception, able to call each one by name. The folks our age had remained just the same. Only the children had changed, ever so drastically, in eight years.

The hospitality was amazing, and I don't think a day went by when our host had not arranged a lunch and dinner in the homes of two families. Our kids were a bit overwhelmed, but we loved every minute. After all, the soul of any place is the people!

In 1981, Kurt had another sabbatical. He had been trying to find a university where he could obtain an MA in the Philosophy of Science. His wish was to go to Cambridge. But the first year he applied, they didn't have a faculty member who could teach that. The next time he applied, the class was cut off at eight students and was already filled. Finally, he was accepted at the University of Western Ontario, and it was decided we would go there for the year for him to accomplish his goal. There had been pressure from time to time on his earning further degrees, so that should they wish to place him as the head of one of our international seminaries, he would be academically qualified. Academic degrees were not important to Kurt. He simply did not have time, nor the inclination to give up teaching to add letters after his name. However, he did concede that furthering his knowledge in the field of science would enhance his courses in evolution and would give credence to publications that he might write on the subject.

When the time came, the family started planning for a year in Canada. Our eldest child had just graduated from high school, but he was not eligible to hold a job in Canada. The policy was that no foreigner could take a job that could be done by a Canadian. We had to leave him behind, therefore, in the care of a seminary student family who agreed to house sit for us that year. His initial semester at our local university was a disappointment, and so he had to satisfy himself with a boring job for the year.

Before the school year began, we made a pilgrimage to London, Ontario to check out registration, housing, and familiarize ourselves with the huge institution which was, by the way, very lovely. We had one day only to explore our options for a family of six. The campus housing was all taken. Towards the end of the long day, at virtually the last minute, when we were about to despair of finding a vacancy anywhere, someone suggested some townhouses that might work. As God would have it, there was one large enough for us, quite near a very fine elementary school, as well as a high school, which turned out to be very good for our children, who were between grade 12 and grade one at the time.

Kurt's first experience driving a 27 foot truck was when I closed up my Mother's house. He and Tony came to Texas and drove back to Indiana with a load of furniture that had to be disbursed among various family members. I was rather impressed, since he had never done it in his whole life. When we had to go to Canada, we rented another big truck, and it was filled with as much of our furniture and as many household goods as would be needed for just the year. The things we didn't take, we put into the storage cupboards in the bedrooms of the campus house.

The station wagon was stuffed with kids, fish tanks, plants, mops, buckets, cooking utensils, and items required along the road. I drove the car. Kurt and one of the boys were in the cabin of the truck. A story about our misadventure when we hit the city was written by our first grader at the time. His teacher was impressed. Especially when the child noted that "mother had a nervous breakdown!" His teacher's comment in the corner, in red was "O dear!"

Our townhouse was one of four in a complex that was part of a larger cluster of similar ones. Of course, we had to park out back, so during the winter, we learned to plug in the car at night. The apartment had three tiny bedrooms, so the boys shared, and the girls shared rooms. One bathroom. Downstairs was a kitchen, living room and dining room. All very adequate. The basement was not finished, but warm enough and provided a space for Kurt to set up a small makeshift study, and where I began my first piece of fiction. It still languishes in a file somewhere, but it was a good way for me to pass the time.

There was a clubhouse a block away with a nice little heated pool, and daily trips for a swim helped fill the hours when I was alone. The children all walked to school, with the elementary school being just across a large field behind the townhouses. I worked as a volunteer there a couple days a week, helping slow readers and working with crafts. It was a pleasant place to be, and I made some nice friends in the process.

We had three pastors with whom we were friends while we were in London. The one we still read about was Pastor Robert Bugbee, who is now an administrator in the Canadian Lutheran Church.

I was impressed that despite the huge amounts of snow that came every day, the Canadians were very good about snow removal, and travel was never restricted due to weather. They must have plowed all through the night. Kurt rode the bus to school every day, and there was never a delay.

The house was set up, the kids were enrolled in school, the grocery super stores were located, and Kurt boarded the bus the first day for school. We were all pretty pumped. That evening, when he returned, he was very dejected. This was so unlike him that it was immediately a bad sign. He said, "I think I've made a terrible mistake bringing you all up here." "Why?" "Because I don't think I can do this course work." "Don't be silly! You're a genius. You can do anything." "The vocabulary is like a foreign language to me. Everything means something totally different than what it does in the theological world."

So it was that our year began. Every day, Kurt rose early, which was uncharacteristic in itself, never ate breakfast, boarded the city bus and was gone for the day. Every evening, he returned, ate quickly, and headed down to the basement where he focused on all the reading he had to do, and planned the outline for his paper. He gradually began mentioning his professors and seemed to be growing into interesting relationships with friend and foe alike. I'm pretty sure he was the only practicing Christian in the class, and the discussions he had with his advisor were quite lively. I know his goal, in the end, was not only to pass the course, but also to convert his professor, whom he was beginning to admire from an academic perspective.

We all liked London very much. Most likely, this was due to the similarities it had with Australia. We could even obtain some of the food items we had been missing since our arrival in the States, and the atmosphere was very comforting to us all. The children had fine teachers and good schools, which apparently cannot be taken for granted in Canada. They all found friends and had an interesting social life.

We had an interesting family next door to us. There was a single mom with two kids, and a live-in daddy, named Bryan. We got along just fine, except that the walls were not terribly soundproof, and their taste in music was most annoying to Kurt. He would retaliate by playing bagpipes on our record player as loudly as possible. Needless to say, this solved little, and changed nothing. In the end, we enjoyed quite a good relationship with these folks, and after we left Canada, we received a letter announcing the marriage of Bryan and the lady of the house.

The only really negative experience we had in Canada was the theft of Tony's bike from the small back yard. It was chained to the fence, but someone rather liked that neat American bike and made off with it. The children were amused that their father immediately went out into the yard and made photographs of the footprints that were in the mud! Despite his every effort, the bike was never recovered.

Finally the year was up, and it was time to turn in the final work for the grade, pack up the family, and head back to Indiana. Naturally, the day before we were to load up, one of the children spilled grape juice on the dining room carpet! Otherwise, it went relatively smoothly. Sad goodbyes were said to our neighbors and school teachers, pastors and members of the congregations we attended. The station wagon was loaded with the same fish and plants that we brought along, and it was a concern whether the American customs people would let it all through. The truck was loaded. The children were loaded. And Kurt sat at his little makeshift desk in the basement, finishing his paper!

Mission accomplished, paper dropped off at the University and off home we drove. It was a national holiday, which was to our advantage, since the customs inspectors would not want to mess with a lot of domestic rubbish and tended to rush folks through.

When we drew near Harlan, on highway 37, we experienced horrific weather, and the truck stalled on us as well. What to do? I think Kurt must have gone ahead to seek help, and we waited in the truck. As things turned out, had we proceeded as expected, we would have driven right into a serious tornado. So once again, God was taking care of us.

911

Through the generations, there have been major occurrences that left in their wake a world changed forever. In our age, the Japanese attack on Pearl Harbor in Hawaii was one. The domino effect of that raid went on to disrupt, and in some cases, destroy the civilization of numerous peoples, tore families apart as millions of brave men were killed in battle, and devastated cities all over Europe and Japan before it was over. The generation that was living in the 1940's and onward were the victims of that time, and for the most part, they came out stronger, wiser, and more aware of what was important to them.

On September 11, 2001, another attack was made on the United States, this time on the continental soil of our land. This time, it was not an army, but a hand full of evil men, supported by an evil regime who flew air craft into the World Trade Center towers and our Pentagon. A fourth attempt was made to fly a passenger jet into one of our government buildings, but was thwarted by a number of courageous passengers, resulting in a forced crash in Pennsylvania.

Despite the brief investigation of these attacks, thousands of pages of data are filed away somewhere, with numerous findings, the substance of which we will never know in our lifetime. And perhaps that is just as well.

While the truth may be different from what was visibly obvious to the rest of the world, the result of those attacks was that the nation was once again galvanized, brought together in spirit, against something. While it's disturbing to me to think that the nation cannot be galvanized to support something good, at least it was something to see that there were few Americans who watched that atrocity on TV over and over again, who were supportive of those who were behind the attacks. And typically, all the dignitaries repeated the mantra, "We will overcome this horrible attack!"

In the wake of the attacks on 911, the smug superiority that allows people in this country to have a false sense of security, resulted in higher attendances in our churches than had been the case for years. Families were drawn together, sensing the frailty of their bonds if something as big as the WTC towers could be blasted off the face of the earth. Communities once again adopted a somewhat humane attitude towards their neighbors and realized that only if we stood together could we survive, and maybe not even then.

I was welcoming students into the front door of the school that morning, when a mother ran in and said, "We're being attacked! A plane just flew into the World Trade Center. Turn on the TV!"

At that time, I confess I didn't really know what the World Trade Center was, but she was so agitated, I went to the fellowship hall and turned on the TV. About the time the picture came on, the second plane was about to hit the South Tower. Those of us circled around the TV witnessed in real time this horrific crash, not believing our own eyes.

It became immediately clear that this was an event of huge portent, and that we needed to decide quickly which classrooms should be allowed to see this play out. The very young students would be traumatized perhaps, and even the older students would be very troubled and frightened to watch as people leapt from burning buildings and hundreds of pedestrians on the street scattered and fled for their lives as huge billows of smoke and debris took over the city.

Not long after the first attack in NY, the Pentagon was hit by yet a third aircraft! Who would be next? How many targets were there? To see the huge gash in the wall of the Pentagon was very salutary. After all, that is the nerve center of our national security. If it wasn't safe, nothing was. Why were there no fighter jets in the skies, taking out the enemy?

It was some time before we got the report of the fourth crash, a jet that was hijacked and intended for either hitting our House of Congress or the White House. Were it not for courageous passengers, who were picking up news on their phones as their flight was being diverted, that plane would have destroyed yet another level of our political structure.

As I watched the first tower collapse, the only thing I could think about was that in those ashes were the bodies of thousands of real people, all drifting on the wind currents, scattering on lower buildings, down to the street, covering vehicles parked in the street, coating everything in sight. It was like a huge crematorium, and that feeling is still with me. As the first responders hit the area, I kept thinking about what they were inhaling as they fought to retrieve survivors, and then the days and days of digging through the rubble to find pieces of victims. It is difficult to imagine any war scene that would have been more traumatic to anyone.

When a nation is struck by a natural disaster, it is serious enough. There are victims whose lives are never the same. Yet, somehow, the country moves on. I don't think any of us have moved on from that day in September of 2001. The memory of the act, the realization of the murderous motivation, the reminder that we are not really safe from someone who is determined to kill us, keeps a part of us paralyzed, and we know we will never be able to live and breathe and travel and feel about others in the world quite the same as we did the day before.

The memory of 911 also keeps us aware of other countries in the world who have known nothing but fear and dread all their lives, mothers and fathers who don't know the luxury of waking up, going to work, sending children off to school, planning ahead. There are those who live under the cloud of hatred and discrimination due to the happenstance of their birth. Before they even take a first breath at birth, they are destined to be hated by someone.

Christianity has a history of creating, not destroying, loving not hating. Charity, not capturing. "They will know us by our love." And so, we know the enemy by their fierce hatred. There is no gray area here. It is clear. It was made even more tangible on 911. Come, quickly, Lord Jesus!

Dealing With Adversaries

Whatever Kurt ever believed or felt about anyone who disagreed with him, whether it took great effort on his part, or maybe he was just a very generous man at heart, he never bad-mouthed people to me. It almost seems supernatural to me now, when I try to recall a single incident when he said anything negative about a colleague, or at least about him personally. If someone did something publicly that was just plain wrong, he would discuss the thing that was done, and why it was inappropriate, or just not true. But there was always a little tag on the end, such as "but everyone has a blind spot".

There were some men in his life who were in outright opposition to anything and everything he said and wrote. Endless hours were devoted to responding to criticisms in publications that never ceased to arrive in the mail, just when something else was in the works. Distractions, much like our poor present President endures, to prevent the real work from getting done.

This constant writing warfare accounts for the fact that one could never find the top of his desk, and it would have been an act of futility to attempt any dusting in the immediate area of his computer.

When we moved into our private home on Tanbark Lane, a seminary student came to the house to install the computer that I assume the seminary purchased for his use. We could not have afforded it, that's for sure. While he composed hundreds of articles, resolutions and letters on that machine, he did not engage in regular emailing, nor did he do much research on the computer. He would never have condescended to spending time on blogs nor face book. It was a waste of his time, and his library had everything he needed. If not, he could get our seminary library to send away to another library for things he needed.

A colleague of his once said, after being on the stage with Kurt in another city, where presentations were being made at a pastoral conference, "My goal in life is to be able to remain as cool and collected as Kurt when he's being challenged." There again, the matter revolved around an issue, a piece of fact that could be verified, not some subjective prattle. I'm sure this drove some of his opponents nuts.

Students who studied under Kurt would verify the fact that he would be seen heading towards his next class with a stack of books weighing him down. Even when he travelled, he often went by car, rather than plane, since he always took a number of books along to back up what he was presenting. He knew the book, the page number, and the person who said whatever he was talking about.

Once, after we were back in the States a while, I noticed that his Book of Concord was falling apart, and imagined that it would be a lovely thing to get him a new one for Christmas. When he opened it, the first thing out of his mouth was, "Where is the other one?! Surely you didn't toss it." He had all his markings in the old copy and could not teach without it. So it fell to me to find someone through the library who could give it new life with new binding. So much for the electronic age and Kurt Marquart.

While he could be quite firm in defending his position in public, he remained a gentleman in his dealings with colleagues. He might say, "I'm sorry, but you're completely wrong" with such grace that they almost felt as if it was a compliment.

Marquart for President

In the months running up to the Summer of 2004, nominations were solicited by Synod for names for various offices, including President. Congregations all around the country were entitled to nominate for President and Vice President. I can't remember whether they got one or two nominations per congregation. It was always interesting to see the initial long list of suggestions from the membership of men considered good material for these offices. For the most part, they were the same every election period.

In 2004, however, a new name garnered seventy-seven nominations, enough to allow his name to stand on the final ballot. Kurt Marquart.

Kurt was not excited about administrative positions, locally or otherwise, and was content to be in the classroom teaching. Encouragement came from many quarters, however, and in the end, while he knew his chances were slim to none, he was determined to honor those congregations who had submitted his name.

Almost daily, we received calls at the house, when various entities unashamedly advised Kurt to withdraw his name. Why? Well, two other conservatives were also on the ballot, and as every good church politician knows, if you have to split the conservative vote three ways, there was little or no chance of defeating the incumbent. Why, then, did they not urge one of those gentlemen to withdraw? It has often occurred to me that had the churchmen in this country witnessed the outstanding leadership Kurt had shown his colleagues in Australia, they would not have thought twice about whether he was qualified to steer the great LCMS ship.

It was an interesting time. Some of Kurt's colleagues looked at us as if we were nuts. After all, who would vote for Kurt Marquart? Didn't he know there were others who deserved this position more than he? Who did he think he was? Factions were quickly drawn up, and we found ourselves on the outside of them all. Folks who showed support for Kurt were shunned. In fact, the atmosphere became so toxic that some of our friends were actually criticized and shunned for "supporting the wrong horse". People whom we had always counted as close friends were suddenly distancing themselves from us, and especially from Kurt. As we said a dozen times or more, "Well, at last we know who are real friends are," and they were becoming fewer and fewer.

With Mary, who pondered "all these things in her heart", I had my own ideas about it all. I am still convinced that had this election included our international brothers, there would have been no question as to the outcome. From the earliest days in Australia, until the bitter end, Kurt felt like an outsider. Yes, he graduated from Concordia Seminary, St Louis, but he was a foreigner, and never felt accepted as "one of the boys". He was a very lonely man, and there were few with whom he associated that he considered "close friends".

The men in confessional circles with an agenda would not support Kurt for President. Only those men who were concerned with theological solutions to the problems of our Church stood strongly behind him. They understood that he was not a politician, and that he depended on nobody's approval. If elected, he would perform the task according to the official teachings of the Lutheran Church-Missouri Synod, and few men alive knew and understood them more thoroughly than he did.

While understanding Kurt's talents, and knowing how clearly he understood why our Synod was in the position it was, neither of us had ambitions for national office. The idea of uprooting ourselves from our home and family to live in St Louis held no attraction for us, and we both knew that such a position would take him away from home and teaching far more than anything he was already doing. But we had already witnessed how God works in unexpected ways, and sometimes we had the responsibility to accept our role in service as much as the next guy.

So, off we went to St Louis for the convention. Anyone who has been in St. Louis knows how muggy and hot it is in summer. Going outside is avoided at all cost. It is said that in earlier years, people who came from Great Britain to work in St Louis for their companies were given hardship pay due to the climate.

Attending a national convention can be pretty exciting, for the guests, that is. For those who are stuck in their seats all day, maybe not so much. Few things are as impressive as seeing so many Lutherans in one place. Convention halls are usually quite large, with thousands of long tables set up with pitchers of water (I suppose it is bottled water now). In the back are rows of chairs and many round tables for visitors who are not voting delegates.

The front platform from which business is conducted is normally decorated in some way to express the theme of the year, and sometimes huge sprays of flowers take away from the starkness of the thing. Only when it hits you that this is not a gathering of men and women all on the same team does it begin to feel more like the Super Bowl, where no holds are barred, and everything hinges on the final scores.

There were meetings for Kurt to attend, and as the wife of one of the candidates, I had obligations as well. I believe it was the Lutheran Foundation that sponsored a luncheon for a number of women one afternoon. It was there that I met some quite lovely women, some of whose husbands had "skin in the game". The elderly wife of one of our sitting Vice Presidents quite surprised me by saying, "They should have used your photo in the campaign ads. You're much better looking than your husband." Is nothing sacred?

One afternoon, during a break in the schedule, Kurt and I went to the little court house that sits in the center of town, not too far from the Arch. I had not realized that it was the very place where he was naturalized as an American citizen during the years of his seminary training. It was a special walk down his history for us both.

After several days at the convention, when the voting was over, and all the floor committees closed shop, and people were pretty much reconciled to the fact that the incumbent had been returned to office, I was quite cognizant of why Kurt was repelled by anything to do with the administrative aspects of anything in the church. Even I, as an enlightened layman (as Dr. Robert Preus described me once) saw clearly how few things were decided on the basis of Scripture. Many important resolutions that had been submitted by concerned congregations were killed in the floor committees and never made it to the convention vote. The system that regulated who spoke from the microphones throughout the hall was obviously controlled by people who didn't want to hear the opinion of the opposition on some points. At one previous convention, Kurt stood at a microphone forty-five minutes to speak, and the chairman refused to hear him. It took little of this nonsense for me to become disillusioned by "the system", and the realization that Kurt was not going to preside over Synod was not at all hard to take.

Naturally, those people who had been so anxious for him to withdraw his name blamed him that neither of the other confessional men was elected. The fact of the matter was that with the combined votes of all three men, the incumbant had still garnered the majority.

Nothing was ever the same after that. I actually believe that Kurt had already begun his decline with ALS, but we didn't realize it. His colleagues used to make fun of his clothes. He wore running pants and soccer shirts, in stark contrast to the black attire that he had always worn. In retrospect, it is my firm belief that he had begun wearing those slippery fabrics, with no buttons nor zippers, because he could no longer manage his dress clothes. He could not snap his clerical collar in the back, he could no longer tie his shoe strings. He had difficulty combing his hair, and that's when his crew cut dawned. Many things make sense now that were of nuisance value at the time. He had few casual clothes and tended to just grab what he had, rather than shop for anything new.

Naturally, his sense of his Office required him to continue in full dress for class and when he lectured anywhere. Towards the end, it was necessary for me to completely dress and undress him, bathe, groom, feed him, and while he gave up driving with a fight, I became his driver, even to his CTCR meetings in St Louis.

I believe it was when we registered for our rooms at the hotel in St Louis, the year of the convention, that some of his colleagues were sitting in the lobby, drinking and smoking cigars. One of them yelled out at me, right there in front of everyone, "Why don't you make Kurt dress decently?" Inspired, my response was, "Why don't your wives make you stop smoking those stinking cigars?"

As I reflect on those days now, I realize that the open acceptance he received from his friends in Haiti must have been a real comfort to him. They had no idea of his reputation in this country. He was kind and generous, and fun to be with. What little they had, they shared with him. The same might be said about his friends in Europe. Especially the students in Russia and Ukraine loved him and were so excited when they knew he was coming to teach.

As I reflect on those sad days, the days of church political nonsense, I realize it was then that I joined the ranks of every pastor's wife who has to sit by and watch her husband ridiculed, criticized, judged unfairly, misunderstood. As I watched the once adored "prince of the Church" slowly lose the support of his colleagues and "friends", I appreciated more and more his courage to always follow his conscience and do what he knew was right in the eyes of his Lord. I'm sure he wanted to be appreciated, admired, and held in a bit of esteem, not unlike all the rest of us. Gradually, these things meant less and less to him.

While he had always been the highlight of the annual Symposium, he really didn't want to undertake another paper in the end. "I've said all I have to say," he told me. Rather than sitting up nights, researching yet another paper, he wanted to give his all in the classroom. He wanted to use his time teaching the students doctrine, helping them understand "church and ministry", building them up to serve the Church well.

He was consumed with the fact of poverty and hardship that faced his brothers in countries less fortunate than ours. He operated his own meager operation of assistance to men and their families in Africa, Russia, Haiti, Europe, and campaigned for the smaller, newer churches around the world desperately needing funds. At the real threat of bankrupting himself, he sent aid constantly, never recording where it was going. When his own pension was gone, he borrowed from VISA in order to keep some of them afloat. He was overwhelmed with guilt for having so much, while his brothers had so little.

At one point when it seemed as if the seminary might ask him to take an early retirement, he said, "If they do that, I will go about the world, like Paul, encouraging the brothers."

When the seminary was in debate over changing the curriculum, Kurt was very much opposed to the changes that would affect the teaching of Systematic Theology. The very subjects that are central to the education our pastoral students were being "integrated" into other classrooms and being assigned to professors of other fields to teach. (For those who don't know what Systematic Theology is, suffice it to say it covers the doctrines by which our Church lives.)

I'm not implying that the doctors of the church who specialized in Church History, or Old Testament Theology, or any other field, were inept. Nor did Kurt feel that way about most of his colleagues. I'm just saying that men who teach those subjects are "experts", each in his old area, and unless your area has been dogmatics, you're not going to give them the full weight they deserve.

Regardless of his opposition, and that of some of his colleagues, the new curriculum was pushed through, resulting in a noticeable drop in enrollment. Students who had planned to come to Fort Wayne primarily because of the strong Systematics courses, went to St Louis instead. In Kurt's mind, it was a terrible mistake. He felt so strongly about it that every day, when he returned from classes, he said he had to cover twice the material in one class to make sure his men received what they needed in that area.

There was, therefore, a stinging moment, during the last few days of Kurt's life, when one of the Seminary administrators came to pay a visit to him at home. Only one other faculty member had been concerned enough to visit him. Then suddenly, after Kurt's official farewell at the last faculty meeting, this person saw fit to come, unannounced.

Sitting across from Kurt, he asked, "Tell me, Kurt. You've been on the faculty a long time. Is there anything you think we might want to do to improve our seminary?"

Kurt just looked at me, and I knew what was on his mind. "I don't think so," was his reply.

Unlikely Reunion

"Hello, my name is Andrey Korolenko. Do you remember me?"

This was how it started, the mysterious phone call that set an amusing drama into motion for the Marquart family.

In the 1980's, my late husband had read just about everything published about the Soviet Union and Communism. Having fled that part of the world as a teenager and never convinced that the Party had been laid to rest, he continued to stay informed about current affairs in those countries that had been overthrown by the powerful Soviet Union in earlier years, and who were one by one slipping out from under the cruel fist of its madness.

An entire quarter of his extensive library was full of documentaries by Whitaker Chambers, Richard Wurmbrand, Richard Nixon, and many others on the evils of totalitarianism. Every newscast was understood in light of what he knew to be the real truth of occupied Europe. He brandished little, if any, trust in anyone on either side of the Atlantic, since all his life had been spent watching power-hungry politicians carve up whole countries into tiny slivers who could do nothing to defend themselves against the larger powers.

More importantly, he had been constantly vigilant, with his antenna up, aware of the potential danger in which he placed himself and his family by his outspoken opposition to Communism and anything that he saw that would lead our country into socialism.

At the time of this phone call, our family resided on the campus of Concordia Theological Seminary in Fort Wayne, Indiana. Safely nestled in the heart of the Midwest, one would not imagine that such issues would still be relevant. After all, we had been in Australia fifteen years and back in the States since 1975 with no problems.

Well, that's not entirely true either. We were a little dismayed when the US Treasury attempted to hit us up for back taxes for all the time we were out of the country. But since Kurt had been under the employ of an Australian church body and not an American missionary, and because we had paid taxes in Australia, we escaped prison that time!

In all the years we had been married, Kurt had not had any acquaintances who spoke Russian. When, then, this call came in the middle of our dinner hour, he was a little suspicious and guarded.

"No, I do not recall that name. Should I?" he asked.

"Well, I read your letter to the Editor in tonight's paper, and I recognized your name. I wondered if you were the same person I knew in Germany." The accent was heavy, but that of an educated Russian.

"Where in Germany would I have known you?", Kurt asked.

"We were in the DP Camp in Fischbach together. I was the scout master there, and you and your brother went on hikes with our group." He sounded confident of his information.

"I'm sorry, I have no recollection of a scout group, nor anyone with your name."

"I would like to ask you and your family to come to my home and meet with my wife and our sons. Do you think that would be possible?"

"Where do you live?"

"We live in Fort Wayne, out near Covington. I can give you directions."

In those days, Covington was not as developed as it is today. The place he was directing us to was out in a forested area off Highway 24. The directions were very complicated. But after much imploring, he persuaded Kurt to come on the following Saturday.

Kurt was very uneasy about this invitation out of the blue. Had the phone call not been such a surprise, had he had more time to think about it, perhaps he would have rejected the idea outright. He had been warned by the U.S. State Department that should he ever disappear mysteriously, there would be nothing they could do.

He gave it a lot of thought, trying to think of what he could do to safeguard the family should this invitation indeed be some kind of insidious trap. At long last, he wrote a letter detailing that he was going to such and such an address to meet with so and so. If he should not return, the police should be notified. He took this letter to his superior and told him the circumstances.

The day of our adventure came with dreary, leaden skies and cold misty rain. It was chilly enough to warrant jackets and shoes and warm socks.

Kurt had not said very much to the children about the visit, except that we were visiting a Russian family and that they should be polite and try to eat what was given them. Being European had never swayed Kurt in his distaste for fishy things or pastries stuffed with cabbage. He should have lived in Italy, where he could enjoy his pizza and spaghetti. But the children would, they promised, try to be good guests.

We were still relatively new to Fort Wayne, and the home of our hosts was in an area totally unfamiliar to us. After a long drive and several mistaken turns, we happened across our destination, a large home, set in the woods, with a large reservoir visible in the not-too-distant brush. A friendly German Shepherd bounded out to greet us, resulting in five children crawling back into the car in panic.

Our hosts bustled out the door to greet us and rescue us from the dog, and invited us into a cozy room with a big fire blazing. I imagine we were treated to tiny glasses of wine, but before too long, we were settled around their large dining room table, where we were to meet two of their three sons. Vladimir and Basil showed typical signs of embarrassed teenagers belonging to parents with accents. Sergey was absent for the day.

Andrey and Irene were very gracious hosts. I can't recall what was on the menu, but I am sure it had cabbage. Most Russian dishes do! Andrey attempted to explain to Kurt where they had in fact been together, in a camp outside of Hamburg. But while Kurt could recall the camp, he had no memory of Andrey, who would not have been married at that time. Conversation was stilted and for once, Kurt seemed at a loss for words.

After hot tea in beautiful glass cups in Russian silver cup holders, it was announced that "now we were to go out on the boat on the pond". Presumably, this was a premiere sign of hospitality, to go out in a row boat, on a pond that was at least fifty feet deep, while it was raining, miles from other civilization.

A slippery path led down to the pond where a metal rowboat was tied up. It was obviously not big enough for everyone to board, but I know Kurt and I were helped to get into it with Irene, who was to be captain. Our youngest son recalls Irene attempting to teach him to row. "She was only a little thing," he recalls, "but she was rowing so hard and fast, that we were out in the middle of the pond in no time." Mmmm. What a perfect place in which to dispose of bodies!

The water was clear, and we could see how very deep it was. The boat tipped a little with our every motion, and we were very uncomfortable. It was difficult to make reasonable conversation in such a situation, even taking the language barrier into consideration. But we sat there, in the middle of the silly pond, trying to appreciate the effort.

From the rowboat, we could see an unexpected delegation of gentlemen coming down the path towards the pond. They were obviously Europeans, dressed in their gray, double-breasted, more than slightly out of date suits. They were broad across the shoulders, and moved with determination and purpose. O, my. What had we gotten ourselves into?

The three of them stood on the bank, talking with Andrey, all with their backs toward us. They paced and looked at their feet as they talked among themselves, every once in a while, looking out at us on the boat. No one was smiling or waving. Irene tried to keep us distracted by pointing out places along the shoreline that she thought significant. At last, the men wandered off. We didn't know if they were in the house or if they had left.

By this time, the rain was growing serious, and we were starting to feel it soak through to our skin. It didn't seem to worry Irene, but when we brought it to her attention, she agreed to take us back to the shore. My impression was that it was the most normal thing in the world for her to be out in a boat in the rain and that it had not dawned on her that we were indisposed at all.

After the necessary pleasantries, we managed to disengage ourselves to leave for home. Yes, yes, it was all great fun. Yes, we must do it again sometime, etc. The children did not have to be coaxed back into the car. Russian farewells were extended, and off we went, in as decent a manner as we could, to escape on to the main road that would take us back home!

Shortly after we left their driveway, our car started to emit a very strange odor. We were genuinely afraid some noxious gas had been planted in our car that would make us sick. We rolled all the windows down and hurried home, making every attempt to breath as little as possible. Since the children had no ill effects that night, we had to assume all was well, and that our catalytic converter had somehow malfunctioned.

Reaching the safety of home, confident that we had escaped a possible disaster, and feeling just a little silly that we had been worried at all, we were dismayed when later in the evening, Andrey called again. He told Kurt that there was a meeting the next night in the home of a friend, where a trade delegation of Russians was meeting. He said they were anxious to meet him, and would he be free to come? O brother! Now the plot really thickens! It would be so much easier to get rid of him on his own than with his whole family! Should he go, or not?

Well, he did go. And I guess it was all pretty boring. Although, he said, there was a rather buxom woman there wearing a blouse with a huge ruffle down the front that would have been plenty big enough to hide a microphone! At any rate, he came home safe and sound, and it was some time before we heard from Andrey again.

In the meanwhile, Kurt had managed to contact his brother, George, who was working for Polaroid in Moscow and was able to ask him about this Andrey Korolenko. Naturally, George remembered him. He told Kurt that they had both gone on a hiking trip with the scouts in Fishbach, but that Kurt had not wanted to go, so probably blocked it out of his memory.

Apparently, Andrey was the priest of a small Russian Orthodox Church in

Fort Wayne and outlying areas. He was a worker priest, holding down another job as an engineer in one of our local factories. Irene was a teacher at the local university, a brilliant woman, who later became a good friend with our eldest daughter who has always had an affinity with the Russian culture.

Andrey was to develop dementia in his later years, but could be counted upon to call from time to time to discuss theological matters with Kurt on the phone. In time, he was not able to shepherd his little flock, and on March 9, 2011, he died and was buried from the little Russian Orthodox Church over on Smith Street.

My daughter and I attended his funeral, and there was Irene, by now old and frail. She didn't recognize us at first, but when she did, her eyes lit up as she related how she had been at Kurt's funeral in 2006. She had taken a bus to the campus, walked all the way to the chapel, and then on the way to the bus stop had suffered a heart attack. Someone picked her up and took her for help. We never knew.

Irene is still living in her big house, with her youngest son in attendance. She is frail, but still bright and full of interesting stories from her early years. One day, Irene was entertaining a friend from New York who was supposedly an authority on Russian icons. She asked Cindy to take ours for her to look at. Our icon had been painted by Kurt's step aunt for our wedding. The art of icon painting had been taught her in a prison camp in Russia before she was able to come to the States. Apparently, it is very high quality.

The icon will remain in the family, with whom is yet to be determined. It will always be a testament of the bond of Faith that transcends time and distance. Interestingly, the icon was three days late for the wedding date, but so was the bride!

The irony is not lost on me. Two men, one an engineer, who volunteered to lead a pack of young scouts in a displaced persons camp, to give them some relief from their boredom; the other a teenager, totally unrelated, watching the atrocities of one branch of the human race against another, trying to make sense of a world gone mad. Each of them, after many years end up in the very same city, each of them servants of the church. Andrey a priest in the Russian Orthodox Church, shepherding a handful of scattered sheep throughout the tri-state region; Kurt a professor, preparing virtually thousands of men for the public ministry in the Lutheran Church Missouri Synod.

Then one day, the one sees a name in a local newspaper that he actually recalls from all those years ago. He picks up the phone, hoping to reconnect with a part of his past and reconnects this unlikely relationship. What world politics had put asunder is reunified, a friendship ignited, and a family bonding begun. Irene was to attend my Kurt's funeral, and I was to attend her Andrey's funeral. It began with two men. It ended with two women who remain to cherish this unlikely reunion.

Erik Christopher

Every time a difficult trial comes and goes, we tend to imagine that it can't get much worse. We approach and survive our fiftieth birthday, thinking that most of life has happened and that it will be clear sailing, kids grown up and marry, retirement on the horizon, home paid off, etc. *The Table of Contents* of my life belies that mirage. Looking back, it seems as if life was punctuated by more grief than happiness. That's not to say life was not full of blessings; but sometimes blessings come in the form of hardship. In fact, nearly always.

In a parish, the pastor and his wife are well acquainted with the illnesses, deaths and pain of their members. One weeps with them, one sits with them, one listens to them as they try to sort out the rationale of what they are enduring. You think you know all about the process of grief and healing after two suicides, many heart attacks, strokes, still births, cancer, young people in car smashes.

Nothing prepares you for death in your own family. It was always someone else's pain. Then it struck my family, my son, my grandson.

In 1992, Erik Christopher was born to my middle son and his wife. Following an exciting pregnancy, baby showers, and happy anticipation, this beautiful little boy came into our lives. For the first time in a long time, something happy was happening in the life of my son, who seemed to be a magnet for mishaps and let downs. Erik was named after his grandfather Marquart and his great-grand-father Martens. He had a lot to live up to.

Everything was going normally, and Erik and his mother were due to be released from hospital. The nursery was ready. The young couple were bracing for sleepless nights. But everyone was happy. Towards the evening of his second day, the nursing staff noticed that Erik was lethargic. He was not easily roused for meals, and he didn't cry much. The doctors decided to keep him an extra day for observation. They took him to the NIC unit where there was a very good doctor at that time, and as the day passed, his concern became the concern of my son as well. Instinctively, he called his father and asked him to come to the hospital to baptize Erik, which we did.

Not many hours passed before the doctor recommended that Erik be sent to Riley Hospital in Indianapolis. He was sent ahead in an ambulance, and the rest of the family sorted itself out, and several of us caravanned down with my son and his wife. I recall my son saying, "I think I have some idea how Abraham felt when he went up the mountain with his son."

In our society, we tend to think that everything can be fixed, once we find the problem. I think we initially thought the same. I lost track of time once we got to the hospital, but I do recall realizing that the staff was leading us down a dark path, giving little pieces of hope here and there, but the underlying truth was not good.

The female doctor tried to explain that Baby Erik had ATC, a genetic condition passed on to him by his mother, who was an unknowing carrier. In simple terms, he had two enzymes missing which meant that he could not process protein properly. The protein turned to ammonia and was killing his brain stem.

A couple was brought in to talk with my son and his wife, parents of a child with this condition. They told us that their own little boy would probably live a couple of years, but only with very careful feeding and only certain kinds of care. They talked about how hard it was, but how they loved him anyway. Another lady who had lost a child to ATC brought in an angel doll that she had made, with Erik's name on it, and tried to show sympathy. It was an interesting process to watch from the outside. The hospital knew Erik was dying, and they were gradually preparing these young parents to let him go, giving a little hope, and then a little fear and dread, and then a bit more hope, and on and on. My son said, "My biggest dread is that they will ask my permission to pull the plug on Erik. I don't think I can do that." I told him, "Maybe God will spare you that."

The fourth day, after the entire family had gathered there for mutual support, the doctors told us that Erik's brain stem was effectively dead, that only the respirator was keeping him alive. So that was God's decision. My husband asked to be alone with Erik. We all watched, as this 6' 4" grandfather, dressed in his clerical black, hovered over the crib of that tiny little boy, offering up last prayers. The staff allowed the family to go into the little room by couples to say our goodbyes, and the mother and father were allowed to hold him one last time. Then my son, his father, his wife and I circled the crib, recited the 23rd Psalm and the Lord's Prayer. His grandfather gave him the Benediction. My son's parting words were, "Erik, I love you more than anything in the world. But I have to let you go. See you in Heaven." We left the little room. That was the last time we saw Erik.

The following days, I felt totally helpless to give any real comfort to the grieving couple. Funeral plans were necessary, and they were in no condition to do it. I took a baby shawl that I had made for Erik to the funeral home and asked if they would wrap him in it. The cemetery arranged for us to have a plot in their baby section. And somehow, we all managed to get through agony of watching my 6' 5" son carry that tiny white coffin down the aisle of the church for the service.

Can one call that a celebration of life? I've often wondered. Erik would be over twenty years old now. His brother, sister and cousins are all towering, beautiful young people. I cannot imagine his ghost with them, since he will always be an infant in my memory. His photo hangs with the rest of the grandchildren. I tell people I have fifteen grandchildren here and one in heaven.

He didn't have much of a chance to leave memories of himself behind. He didn't have time to learn to smile. But as a family, we will most assuredly never forget the four days he was with us, and the lasting bond our family shares because of him. The little angel doll still lives with me on the bed in my guest room as a reminder that Erik is alive, living a better life than any of us. That is giving real hope. For if Christ is risen from the dead, then all who are baptized in His Name are also alive.

Hands

Not that I have a fetish for hands, but I cannot recall a time when I didn't notice the hands of most of the people in my life. Whether they be attached to the lady at the checkout register, or a toddler just learning to grab unobtainable objects for the first time, hands say almost as much to me as the words coming from their counterpart, the mouth!

For instance, there are some hands that I would have a difficult time holding. That sounds silly, doesn't it? It wouldn't be due to their rough, weathered or even dirty skin, but possibly more the fact that their owner is not genuinely forthcoming. I also find it hard to think about holding a hand with two-inch-long fingernails, shaped like cockroaches, and painted with stars and stripes and flowers.

How many times have we had to shake the hand of someone who has a refrigerated fish on the end of his arm? There's absolutely no grip, no welcoming return grasp. Just an obligatory act of custom, most likely reflecting the inner reluctance of the owner to be touched. Or perhaps that person is one whose hand was crushed, with his ring on sideways, by someone determined to be remembered for his vice grip, the little elderly man who is hoping to be thought of as still having his virility if he can break your fingers. Me thinks the genteel kiss on the hand preferable myself.

Shaking hands is a very personal action, when you come to think about it. How many other socially acceptable forms are there for touching a perfect stranger? I dare say some cultures frown on it as distasteful and rude.

After we get past the initial handshake, however, it is impossible for me to be oblivious to people's hands. Hands speak, when the rest of the person doesn't. They are either calm, confident, happy in their own skin, or anxious, or impatient, or very animated, lending emphasis to their owner's speech. Watch a politician sometime.

One of the first things I noticed about my late husband was his hands. His fingers were long and slim, like the rest of his body, the skin unscarred from physical labor. I was trying to recall why they were so special, and I believe it was because they reflected his inner control over his mind and actions. When he preached a sermon or lectured or debated, there was no sense of desperation, but rather an impression of conviction and the ability to back up what he was saying. . . non-threatening, but compelling. . . non-intrusive in company, but always ready to reach out to someone with an attitude of common humanity to all, soul to soul.

I believe it's a faulty assumption that people with lovely manicured nails are lazy lie-abouts. Some people just love beautifully manicured hands like others love a manicured yard or garden. The opposite might be said of yet others who care a great deal about lovely hands, but cannot attain them, no matter how hard they try.

My Mother's hands were very beautiful. I don't recall ever seeing her without nail polish. When I was a little girl, her polish was always a bright red, which seemed in such contrast to her shy disposition. As she aged, the colors softened and often included that lovely pearl finish. Regardless of the color, her nails were always filed, buffed, sporting an undercoat and top coat, and never a chip was to be seen!

Like so many little girls, I sat in church with my Mother's hand in mine, twisting her rings around, and tracing the veins that always stood out on the top of her hands. My Mother worked hard all her life. She cleaned her house, dug in her garden, washed the car, cleaned windows and polished furniture with the best of them. She waited tables, carried heavy trays, poured hot coffee, clapped for boring speakers, cooked meals for thousands of thankless people, and folded them in quiet prayer. But throughout it all, her hands remained soft and inviting, sitting calmly in her lap when she was at rest. She made amazing things with those hands, and when all the other parts of her body failed, and they lay neatly posed on her chest in death, they were a lovely testimony to her intrinsic femininity.

My Mother's funeral took place on a July day following a week of storms and driving rain. As we gathered on the water-logged lawn of the cemetery, we waited for the committal service to commence. My arm was resting on the back of the chair next to me, around the shoulders of my son. Someone behind me was overheard to say to her companion, "Look, Barbara has her mother's hands."

2000 or Y2K

During the very last years of the Twentieth Century, a very strange phenomenon took place in our world. People who were very young, or not yet born, will never realize the fear, nor the reason for it, that pervaded much of our civilization at the time when we were preparing to enter the year 2000, a time when we had, as it were, a foot in two different centuries.

How did our great-grandparents react, I wonder, when they left the 1800's and entered the Twentieth Century? I think it's safe to say they probably had grand parties, singing "O God, Our Help in Ages Past", and took time to reflect on the changes they had seen. In contrast, as a population, generally proud of our world of information and wisdom, much of our nation became almost paralyzed with speculation and dread.

Formidable prophecies were given, primarily through those whose job it was to accomplish high ratings, which resulted in behavior heretofore unheard of in this country, and throughout other progressive parts of the world. There was such a preponderance of so-called scientific evidence floating around. Y2K became the topic of every broadcast and panel discussion, and the man on the street was gradually, against his better judgement, convinced that he needed to prepare for great calamity, that he was a fool if he did not prepare for his survival and that of his family.

Naturally, this whole charade provided opportunity for profit for those who were quick to take advantage of the contagious desperation of customers who came to believe that they needed to stockpile food, rush out and grab generators, squirrel away cash, write their wills. Every day, there was a new fear tossed out, in case the old one wore thin. It was thought that the air traffic control systems would be compromised and that airplanes would be flying blind and crashing. We were told it was a perfect time for terrorists to make a move, to poison our drinking water, or our economy would crash due to the sudden loss of our entire electrical grid.

Every creative person was producing memorabilia, and you could buy T-shirts and cocktail napkins, you name it, with something to do with Y2K. A new Barbie doll was introduced. I'm not sure why. Was this supposed to be consoling? Did she lead the way to faith in a new century? No, she and all the other nonsense made money off the fear of the population. For many people in America, Y2K remains almost as big a news story as 911. Whether it affected people directly or not, many people believed it would.

Why, some religious bodies even took this whole issue as a sign of the Apocalypse and were preparing their members for the end times. Church attendance rose in relation to how much Law was preached, and how much fear could be generated. Some people might have even turned their lives around, but it would be short lived.

Psychologists reported an upswing in patients who were suffering from what would be called "Millennial Delusion", a fear that catastrophe was looming.

New Years Eve parties were cancelled across the country. 8000 police were patrolling Times Square that night, on alert for terrorists. While "the show must go on", Dick Clark was trotted out to count down the final seconds of 1999. Plans for this event, intended presumably to take our minds off the coming doom, took place at the same time it is rumored that New York City had ordered 250,000 body bags and had planned to use the ice rink in Madison Square Garden as a temporary morgue in the event of a terrorist attack.

The source of the problem? The computers around the world had been calibrated to function in such a way using the last two digits in a year, that they would not be able to cope with four digits all of a sudden. Despite some of the best minds in the industry insisting that it was not going to present a problem, the facts were largely ignored by the media. No doubt, this was because "this is news, Baby!" This sells papers. This gives us ratings. This is what people want to hear.

I recall those days quite well. Every year, during the Christmas break in his teaching schedule locally at the Seminary, Kurt always flew to Haiti to teach at the seminary of our sister church there. It was the highlight of his winter, anticipating the warm weather, swimming in tepid waters, seeing his friends again. While the rest of us were Christmas shopping for the family, he would be stashing away dozens of small gifts to take along to his impoverished brothers in the Caribbean. He was with us, but not really, as he was packing his bags, getting his tickets, his suntan lotion and mosquito repellant ready. It was as if he was literally counting the seconds until he could leave this "wretched winter" and get into the sun for a couple of weeks.

No one wanted him to go this particular year. With all the warnings about cancelled flights and potential air disaster, it seemed as if he might take just this one year off. But he would hear nothing of it. "Stuff and nonsense", he said. "Nothing is going to happen. And if it does, I know where I'll be landing and spending eternity." New Year's Eve found him in friendly skies heading South.

So it was that January 1, 2000 came and went. The world remained intact. Some people got a lot of mileage out of all this hysteria. The news managed to terrorize us more than any enemy, with pregnant women wondering if their babies would survive, the elderly worried whether they would make it on their own if loved ones were somehow lost. Businesses worried that their equipment would not work, or that they would be bankrupted if they had to replace or upgrade it all. A few people started to look at life a little differently, when they thought there might not be much of it left. This was good for some, bad for others.

What a strange culture we are, when you think of it. The world held its breath, didn't it? On the strength of rumors and projections, threats and fear. It seems strange to me that few of us think of life as fragile every day, not just under such foreboding circumstances. With world travel bringing ancient plagues and incurable diseases to our shores, illegal, helpless youngsters being dumped on our borders with nowhere to go, carrying who knows how many new horrors with them, with the weather so erratic and fickle so that rich crops are truly in the hands of God, tornadoes sweeping away entire cities, and tidal waves washing whole populations out to sea, why do we not think of each day as a survival of sorts?

It would not surprise me if people in the poor countries of the world were laughing at us all along. After all, the disasters we were imagining, happen to them every day. Do the rest of us, fellow members of the human race, care?

How Do I View Retirement?

All the Memoir Manuals strongly suggest including retirement in one's writing. Since it seems as if I'm still in that state, it seems more like an on-going struggle than something I have successfully achieved.

While we hear that retirement is when you finally have the luxury to do what you like, and sleep as late as you want, I find all that grossly exaggerated. I suppose it is conceivable that one could develop self-serving habits and pursue the day with more leisure. One cup at a time. Tune in the morning TV news if desired. Or play music to make the necessary adjustment to facing tasks that await. One could sit and watch non-stop movies on TV, or scan Face Book posts for hours. Getting one's fill of reading non-relevant books until saturated, or checking out travel brochures might help fill the empty hours.

In my experience, however, the same household chores are required during retirement as were there before. What's more, when I first retired, it seemed as if there was a lot of backed-up cleaning staring me in the face, things I had found it convenient to put off before, that simply had to be dealt with.

At any rate, almost as soon as retirement is official, one discovers the sad truth about how unimportant one's job was, in the scheme of things. The work faced day in and day out at a job can just as easily, and in some cases more so, be done by someone else. One begins to regret the excessive energy and emotion expended over the thing for so long, and gradually, it comes to you that your family is really the only part of your life that matters. It was an easy matter to pretend you were needed on the job, more than you were by anyone who was actually related to you. As time is taken to visit with and listen to your grown children and their offspring, it sinks in how much you have missed, and you become painfully aware of how much you might have had to offer them during their struggles.

The clock, however, cannot be wound back, and one begins sorting and filling one's life, one's remaining life, in a different way than before. Different areas of life become priorities and things that **were** vastly important simply don't matter any longer. Possibly it is different for men than for women. I cannot say.

While totally absorbed with my job at Ascension Lutheran Church and School (ten years), I gave little thought to retirement. The prevailing mentality in the office was that we would all work until we dropped, or died. My homelife had ceased to require much of my time and attention after our youngest left, and my late husband was out of town so frequently that I was already a grass widow. My sense of worth and contentment were pretty much found in my daily hours in my little office, tending to the students, their parents, visitors who came to investigate our school for their kids, and doing what I could to be the bridge between Pastor and congregation. In my interview for the position, I was told that my main job was to make the Pastor look good. That was not hard, since he was a hardworking, God-fearing servant of the Church, and it was a pleasure to do things to make his job render good results.

My position was born together with the birth of the preschool and grew year by year in complexity and responsibility. The job gradually grew under my care and as new tasks arose, I implemented them the only way I knew how. I more or less created my own "job description" based on what I knew needed to be done. Few, if anyone, realized how complex it was.

My goal was to put a cheerful face on relations with the children, their families, the faculty, and all members of the congregation. I was the first person many met when they came to the church, and often the impression people gained would either welcome or turn them away. In other words, I was a salesman, and the product I sold was the opportunity for families to know God. What could be boring about that?

The running joke was that all the little kids thought I was the Principal. I can't think why, unless it was because I stood at the front door every morning and greeted the kids as they came in. I figured that some of them might have had rough beginnings to their day, didn't hurry enough to find all their stuff, maybe got fussed at all the way to school, or forgot to eat breakfast. That's not a great way to start a long day, but I know it happens. Eventually, I knew most of the children, and which little girls were besties, and which little boys were not all that happy to be there, and it was fun to get them laughing before they went down the hall to their classroom. Years after I retired, a mom told me that she used to watch this interaction and wonder just what was going on. She was never game to introduce herself to me, because "she thought I was too important"! Ha. Anyway, one day, she asked her little boy, "What does that lady do every day when you go in?" His response was, "She smiles at me." What greater reward is there!

God blessed the congregation and school, and both grew very quickly. After six years, during which the Pastor served as Principal, the job was separated, and the new principal was installed in an office adjacent to the work room. New faculty gradually replaced the original people, and the operation adopted more and more technology to deal with the added work and State requirements. Additional tasks were handed to my position, many of which were either outside of my technical proficiency, or they presented stressful conflicts with regard to the amount of time I had at my disposal. Budget restrictions prevented us from hiring help with new tasks that were being dumped on us by the State, and with the new accrediting demands. I was, as a result of these changes, unable to spend time with the things I felt important, including dealing on a more personal level with the children and people who were frequently in the building to volunteer with repairs, cleaning. There was so much traffic in the building that we needed a central point where at least someone knew where everyone was at any given time. While I had been part of the original staff, helping with decision-making, etc., more and more, I felt excluded, and my input was not requested.

At some point, it became obvious to me that my role, as it had been, was slowly being redesigned, and without my consent. Rather than continue to feel trapped in a place where I no longer felt needed, I decided to announce my retirement and gave them a year to find a replacement. My hope was that they would split the job, and have someone dedicated to the Pastor/Congregation and someone dedicated to the school. That has not yet happened, and most likely due to lack of funding.

Jokingly, I had told the Pastor that I expected a big Retirement Party when the time came. I was not disappointed, and despite the worst thunderstorm of the season, there were over 150 people there, and many expressions of gratitude were expressed. The ladies went to great lengths to make it very special.

Since my tenure at Ascension lasted ten years, I knew everyone. Every baptism, every confirmation, every wedding, every funeral . . . each was processed by me. There can be few lives more interesting than when one is allowed to witness the birth of Faith, the growth of Christian affection among His children, advancement into Heaven by His saints.

At my desk, many women sat and cried over their children, and sought advice. Some confessed they were on the road to divorce and asked for prayers. Some were lonely and looking for direction in their lives as their little ones started school, leaving the house suddenly silent every morning. What an opportunity to pour oil on troubled waters and often attempt to keep peace between parents and teachers. My desk was the buffer zone where many antagonisms melted, and problems which could have exploded were diffused. I enjoyed a wonderful fellowship with other women, young and old.

Thus, it was, when I retired, that I was suddenly alone. For a long time, I had dreams that I went to the school to help out, and as I prowled the halls looking for jobs, I was told I no longer belonged there. From that, one might assume retirement came too early and that I was not really emotionally ready for it.

Because most people recognized how much I enjoyed my job, I was often asked why I was retiring. My response was that I had lots of pictures to paint and many books to write. As it turned out, the first year, I goofed off as much as I wished, before Kurt was diagnosed with ALS. From then on, all my time and energy were consumed by attempts to take care of him and his affairs, Had I not retired, my sudden need to vacate my post would have resulted in administrative chaos. As it was, retirement became a time of concentrated effort to keep Kurt going, both in the classroom and in his travels. For a long while, his health was failing, but we didn't know from what. He had a stent put in his heart arteries, and that was supposed to give him renewed energy, but didn't. He had surgery for sleep apnea. That didn't help. In the meanwhile, he travelled to Africa, where he spent an entire six weeks in Kenya teaching. I suspect the warmth didn't hurt him any, since it was our winter.

Gradually, it became necessary for me to drive him to St Louis for his CTCR meetings, and anywhere else he had to go. He was unable to feed, dress, or bathe himself, as his arms were useless. Shortly after my retirement, I attempted to convince Kurt to spend an hour every-once-in-a-while to work in the study to create some kind of order. It was a large room, completely full of piles of papers and books from years of neglect. I knew eventually I would have to get it done, and it seemed as if it would be a good occupation for him to be somehow involved. But he resisted with vigor, and I was left with a task that ended up taking over six years and many hours of labor by myself, as well as Robert Paul, a seminary student who came three afternoons a week to sort and file documents which ultimately went to the seminary archives. . . all 59 boxes!

Spare time? I spend a lot of time thinking about what I *might* do. Bob, my husband now of eleven years, and I have few social connections, so our company consists primarily of family. In the early years of our marriage, I discovered a class where seniors were instructed how to write memoirs. The dream of publishing a book for clergy wives has surfaced and vanished, and resurfaced and vanished so many times. The effort has been interrupted many times; energy and circumstances have come and gone. The fact that it is happening is giving me pleasure beyond expression.

So then, Retirement. The only thing I can deduce is that it is a critical time in one's life when it becomes necessary to employ everything one has learned along the way in order to continue to be a valid contribution to some aspect of somebody else's life. While there is nothing wrong with a person living day to day exactly the way she wants to, in the end, it is not satisfying to be cut from the herd, so to speak. It becomes vital to remain an active piece of the puzzle of life, and apparently, one has to initiate that oneself. Rarely does it happen that I am invited, for instance, to anything. If I don't think of it, it doesn't happen. Having been in the work force full time for so many years, other women who might have stayed in touch, finally discounted me, and it was as if I became invisible. One prays that if there is something special the Lord wishes one to do, He will make it evident and possible. Since the urge to write is ever before me, I must assume that is what He is wanting me to do. Right now, looking after Bob and giving him a comfortable and happy life each day is enough. He makes me very happy and has provided opportunities for me to achieve in many areas heretofore nonexistent. He gives purpose in his quiet unassuming way. He is, like everything else, a gift from God.

And so, it becomes necessary to distinguish between retiring from gainful employment and retiring from life. It seems to me as if there is a huge difference.

International Year of Women - 1975

"International Year of Women"! Ah, you might say, that sounds like a good thing!

Mandated by the United Nations back in 1975, at first glance, one might imagine that this was a world-wide celebration, a move to encourage countries to treat their women with more decency, to give them a place in the human race which would assign more value than a slave or farm animal. In the very least, such a mandate would require that the amazing contributions of past womankind would be recognized.

A packed carload of us pro-lifers arrived on the campus of the University of Queensland for what was to be a sad revelation as to the inroads feminism had made in Australia. Surrounded by congregational life and protected by our Christian society, none of us could have been prepared for the deliberate staging of how our western civilization was to be unraveled, and that life as we knew it would be manipulated by the very people we wanted to protect. . . women. The most grievous part is that I have had to watch those plans come to fruition through the years, step by step.

The initial impact came in the sheer numbers of women attending this extravaganza. Australian women were known for being at home, baking, scrubbing floors, hanging out laundry and getting tea on for the family. I estimate two thousand women were registered. It was a beautiful, typical Queensland day, sunny and inviting, so that our meals were taken outside at picnic tables, and the atmosphere was very jolly, at first.

After lunch, the massive crowd was herded into a gymnasium, welcomed by an enthusiastic greeting, and sounded pretty innocuous in the beginning. While pantsuits were still considered quite daring, and not many women had given in to them yet, the leaders were all wearing them. Each had large name tags, leaving no doubt that the "equality" speeches were for everyone but themselves. There was no question as to who were the ranking, and who were the "rank and file".

The group I was with broke up into four pairs, in an attempt to cover all the sectionals. My group set out to climb up into the rows of seats in a large auditorium classroom. Almost the instant the lights dimmed, the happy- clappy atmosphere changed and the agenda became boldly outlined.

Our presentation followed these topics:

Women unite! We must fight for equality.

Men are not necessary, and we will gradually be free of them.

If you MUST have children, you need not be married to a man. Our sperm banks will keep the world populated for a long time. (I didn't think of it then, but this must have been the precursor to same sex marriage, which has recently been legalized.)

Get rid of male doctors. They exploit women. Finance street clinics for women where we can do pelvic exams and abortions for each other.
Politicians who do not agree with our agenda will be done away with by slander and rumors.

Identify brilliant women and finance their university degrees, so that we can later vote them into power.

Everything was couched in vulgar language. Family values, Christian schools, traditional families and most forms of common decency were ridiculed. I had the sense that Satan was unleashed and that he was poised in his lair, rubbing his filthy claws together, while these women did his work.

As the day progressed, we were subjected to films which made some of us avert our eyes. Unnatural sexual behavior was shoved down our throats in nothing short of pornography. Everything was calculated to instill fear and defeat into anyone who was not in the feminist camp.

We left for home before the seminar was over because we could stomach no more.

It was reported that at the national gathering, hosted in Canberra by the Prime Minister's wife, Mrs. Whitlam, every form of lewdness was employed, including the use of little girl greeters who passed out printed porn!

Younger readers may not be too shocked by all this. But in 1975, this open defiance of all that had been civilized life seemed to be sliding down a ravine. Sadly, my generation has had to watch as the goals of this movement have been met in many places and ways.

After our two hour drive back to Toowoomba, each of us was in a state of exhaustion. I was met at home by Dr. Marquart, who had warned me for years that this was coming, that the feminists and gay community were well financed and were well on their way. I would laugh at him and say, "Surely women are too intelligent to fall for that guff!" But as surely as I write this, everything we ever believed about family structure and life changed that year.

Are we then paralyzed by anxiety at the thought of such a wretched movement loosed on us? Our motherly instincts make us want to run and find our chicks and wrap them in safety, protecting them from horrible things. In our present 2000"s, we know that these things are officially taught at many of our universities in "Women's Studies". Many young women have come to believe these teachings. Maybe you have met some of them.

The good news in all this is that our Survival Manual, God's revealed Word, is stronger and wiser than all their machinations. The burden becomes ours, then, to be so immersed in that Word that all we do for and with our children is taken from the "playbook" of God.

Women's magazines, health bulletins, movies, TV shows depict women as some kind of superior race, while reducing the men to look like beer swilling idiots, who care for nothing but their football. O, I hope they're wrong. How I pray our men are better than that. Mine was.

Readers, please be conscious every waking minute that your children are little souls, not just runny noses, dirty laundry, hungry tummies. These little people, given by God for you to nurture for Him, will end up in heaven or hell. There is no in-between. We do not have time to play at this business of parenting. Dr. Marquart used to say that he knew he would stand at the Throne of God one day and give an account for his parish. But more importantly, he would have to give an account for the souls of his children. He could not bear the prospect of any one of them not remaining in the Household of Faith, and thereby not being with him in eternity.

What is your prayer before you retire? What is your prayer on waking?

+

Below is a small part of the legacy left in the archives of Dr. Marquart. The rest of it may be googled at Mother Shipton's Prophecies. She wrote these in the 1500's:

> *For in those wondrous far off days*
> *the women shall adopt a craze*
> *to dress like men, and trousers wear*
> *and to cut off their locks of hair.*
> *They'll ride astride with brazen brow,*
> *as witches do on broomsticks now.*
> *And roaring monsters with men atop,*
> *do seem to eat the verdant crop.*
> *And men shall fly as birds do now,*
> *and give away the horse and plow.*
> *Then love shall die and marriage cease*
> *and nations wane as babes decrease.*
> *And wives shall fondle cats and dogs,*
> *and men live much the same as hogs.*

V
LAST STRUGGLE

The Emperor's New Clothes

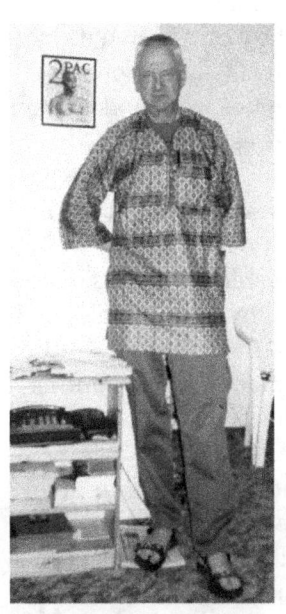

Recently, I ran on to a modern version of "The Emperor's New Clothes". I think it was produced in 2012. I couldn't tell you the name of the lead actor, and unfortunately I missed the beginning. It seems that the real emperor had gone into hiding and an impostor was taking his place in the palace. No doubt, some part of his government was taking advantage of this arrangement. I'm not sure.

At any rate, Napoleon had chosen Eugene as his name and vanished into the slums of Italy where he was able to board with a widow and her son. During his sojourn with her, he had to drop his imperious behavior in order to make everyone believe he was just another peasant. In the process, he became quite likable and even the workers off the street began to admire and follow his leadership as he helped them improve on their marketing skills.

The widow's husband had been a soldier under the emperor's command on many deployments, and she hated the emperor as a result, since her husband had been killed, leaving her alone. But she fell in love with Eugene, and they were beginning to build a nice life together when the impostor died, and the country believed that Napoleon was dead.

Eugene was frantic to let the people in charge know that he was actually not dead, but he could not get in to see anyone who would listen to him. The widow and her friends thought he had gone insane and had delusions of grandeur. After many futile attempts to have himself recognized, he finally gave up and reconciled himself to living the happy life of the peasants.

While I was watching this movie, I had to think of Kurt. Many instances, the emperor said things that sounded just like Kurt. I thought of the many times he moved about the world in the company of the common people, those he loved the most. I know he had to cover his own refinement many times to avoid making them feel uncomfortable with him. He wanted to fit in, and thus was continually looking for ways to make himself look like "the rest of the guys".

In the early stages of his illness, he began to wear clothes that were out of character with his public image. He got a crew cut. And he went out of his way to dress down whenever he was not in the pulpit or classroom.

Initially, it troubled even me. Only recently, as I recall the stages of deterioration he endured, have I become convinced that he was having symptoms of ALS long before the rest of us knew about it. I recall seeing him put his foot up on the vanity in the bathroom, propping his elbow on his knee, while he used the hair dryer. At the time, it annoyed me, because I could only imagine what that was doing to the surface of the vanity. I had no idea that he could no longer hold up the hair dryer. Little by little, he wore sports clothes that he had never really admired. His colleagues were making fun of him, and even criticized me for not making him "dress decently".

Now I realize that already he was having difficulty with the buttons, zippers, collar buttons, etc. The slippery materials were easily put on, and the crew cut required no fussing.

I was already noticing a slight tremor when he rested his hands on the bottom of the steering wheel. When I would comment on it, he blew me off. I can't believe he drove over six thousand miles that last year, in that condition. But he was always conscious of "saving money for the church", and preferred to drive so that he could take boxes of books along on his speaking tours or extension classes.

I have come to believe that while most of us thought Kurt was living his second childhood and trying to be youthful, he was in fact coping as well as he could to not distress anyone who might uncover his true condition. He wasn't consciously attempting to be someone he wasn't, but in an effort to protect the family from the truth, and to delay the inevitable termination of his career, he donned "the emperor's new clothes."

What Do You Feel Like Doing?

We are all familiar with the expression, "What goes around, comes around." Some of us get that in spades. Tony is one of them!

When Tony was a little boy, he had a serious aversion to anything that smacked of vomit. I suppose in our big family, he had seen the ramifications of nausea more than a few times, and it was just one of those things he could not handle.

It was so bad with Tony, that if anyone said, "I don't feel well.", Tony immediately asked, "What do you feel like doing?" and made to run off if necessary. In his experience, anyone who didn't feel well was bound to go one step farther, and it would not be pleasant.

But as if that wasn't bad enough, Tony also had a disliking for wiping his own bum! Whoever was closest to the bathroom at the time was cornered into helping him, and more than once, the patrons at our favorite Pizza Hut were amused by a little voice calling out from the restroom, "Somebody help me!" Thankfully, he outgrew that weakness as well!

The irony was not lost then, when the seminary sent Tony with his Father, on three trips. Kurt was suffering the physical deterioration that comes with ALS and could not possibly manage on his own. Each trip included a week of teaching in-service theological courses to pastors in the field. Everyone tried to talk him out of pushing himself to complete these obligations, but he knew there were men signed up for the courses, and he did not want them to be disappointed. One was in Texas and two were in California.

Tony, who by then had undergone multiple surgeries, due to his deteriorating spine disease, had passed the point of being squeamish. Out of his understanding of what it means to be on the receiving end of care giving, he could sympathize with his father's embarrassing and unavoidable needs.

So it happened, that they flew together, stayed in hotels together, shared meals together, slept together, laughed and cried together. Tony bathed, dressed, fed and assisted his father in numerous ways, many of which were quite disagreeable. That being said, it was an enviable time shared by a grown son and his dying father.

If you ever saw the two of them together, it would be easy to imagine the hysterics that went on during those adventures. I can hear the uncontrollable giggling, and squealing as showers and bathroom duties were necessary. When I would bath Kurt, he was not amused. It was embarrassing and humiliating. But I can easily imagine Tony making a bit of a comedy out of it all, and the two of them exhausted after the final clean up! It was a time when Tony had to solve logistical problems, making connecting flights with a man who didn't want to use a wheel chair, but who could hardly stand under his own weight. It was a time when difficult things had to be explained to people who stood in their way. It was a time of practicing the greatest diplomacy, while keeping it light for both of them.

During those days, Tony was witness to the priceless interaction his father enjoyed with his students. He relived those days of sitting in his daddy's class as a little boy, before he started school, scribbling notes. He recalled the conventions they attended together, the *"thousand island dressing"*, the elevator encounter with *"the little shiatsu"*.

It was THEIR time, and a time that was given them only.

Talking about these times with his father is difficult for Tony. All the memories surface once again, and the peace that he has been able to achieve gets mingled with deep grief once more. Having been at Cleveland Clinic when his father was told he had ALS, it was destined that he would help him carry this heavy burden.

While Kurt's ALS was not as drawn out and dreadful as we know it can be, it did rob him of his body. When we say he was just a skeleton of himself, we are being quite literal. The tall, strong, essential man that we all knew melted away until there was only his mind left, with a pumping heart. The heart belonged to God. It pumped until all was finished. When the three intensive courses were finished, he was at peace.

On September 18, after his family dispersed from having had Holy Communion together, and his having been able to administer the Sacrament of Holy Baptism to his great-grandson, Evan, he reluctantly lay down his body and his load on the hospice bed. After a few restless hours, Tony was privileged to be by his deathbed to say their last good-byes. The press of the hosts of heaven was palpable. It was time. Tony led us in the Lord's Prayer, we assured Kurt we would be all right, and that he should go and be with God. With prayers for his godsons barely escaping his lips, he took his final, weary, earthly breath at 2 a.m.

Being that sick, really sick unto death, and continuing in one's duty is difficult. Being a loving caretaker is equally hard. To share the pain, the anxiety, anger and disappointment with another human being is one of the greatest acts of mercy any of us can give. Taking care of his dad was his last gift to him, and his dad's last gift to Tony. It was painfully beautiful.

Always in His Shadow

Periodically, through the decades, this same little black and white snapshot surfaces. It was taken with an old Brownie camera in the back yard of our first parsonage in Toowoomba.

The unique thing about this photo, the thing that finally made it one that I will always keep, is the clear, undeniable shadow of Kurt, my husband, who was behind the camera. It actually means more to me today than it did when I was still youthful and unafraid to share a broad smile. More profound to me than the actual photo is the fact that Kurt's shadow is superimposed over my image. Thus, the title of this chapter.

Anyone who has walked beside another who is so huge will tell you how effortlessly one's identity, one's individuality, can vanish. Through no fault of anyone, one or the other seems to have to live in the shadows cast by the more dynamic of the two.

I had imagined myself as a pretty strong character. That is to say, I was not timid about setting out to achieve objectives. When I married Kurt, I was thrown into company that was, for the most part, at least ten years my senior. I was twenty, they were thirty. At least. From the beginning, then, it seemed at the time as if there were those who were always attempting to mold me to fit into that age group. Everyone else had children. (You know the feeling.) Every time we went somewhere socially, the first question was "Do we have good news yet?"

But it was not the parish that changed me. It was the desire to become what Kurt wanted me to be, because, let's face it, realistically, he was right about just about everything. Though an inexperienced bachelor, and precious little experience with a sister, he somehow believed how a lady should dress, speak and behave. It is not difficult to understand how a young, willful woman would quickly find it quite dreary when the highest compliment tended to be, "Ah, you look just like Queen Elizabeth"!

I recall saying to him once, "I am what I am. People need to take me the way I am." His reply was simple and indisputable, "No one is so perfect there is no room for improvement." Mind you, as his colleagues all knew, he could say something like that and make it sound kind.

Once we started providing the wished-for children, I felt as if I was finally receiving the satisfaction and approval I was wishing for. Our first son was received into Christ's Family through Holy Baptism on our first wedding anniversary, and an open house was held at the parsonage. (I challenge any church member to have "better timing"!)

To reassure everyone once again that all was well, we produced our little girl eighteen months later. This achievement tended to allow folks to back off and trust us for a while. No more questions. Mind you, we neglected to tell you about the foster children we had in between!

When our little boy was one month old, twelve and thirteen year old brothers came to live in our home. Their family had been splintered by the evils of drink, and the five children were split up. These brothers helped bring out the best and worst in me over the years and testing my character in unimaginable ways you can't fathom unless you have opened your home to total strangers – strangers with deep wounds of their own.

But I digress. Five years into our marriage, I produced another son, followed four years later by another little girl. Even by Australian standards, our family had gown quite large. After our last little boy came along, whenever we were all together, we were nine! Little wonder dinner invitations dried up!

You're probably thinking this is pretty negative. Well, there were some rugged days, for sure. But in the process of dealing with this growing family, I found that I was indeed formed into a lady of substance. Instead of a kid in the manse, I became a seasoned mother, a somewhat gifted art teacher at our college, and a person who was not timid about ministering to those poor souls languishing in the epileptic and mental hospitals in Toowoomba. They didn't nickname me Mrs. Margate for nothing! While it was considered poor judgement to acquire personal friends in the congregation, I was surrounded by many women and girls of all ages with whom I enjoyed great fellowship.

Daily struggles, challenges and successes form each of us. I, thank God, had a great mentor as well in my husband, who thankfully didn't give up on me. No, he kept up with his tutorials until the day he died. What a gift!

Few women can admit that nearly everything they know about history, theology, psychology, cooking, music and literature came from a life with a husband for whom these things were important. Because he loved these things, they soon became part of my life as well, and they are things for which I have learned to be thankful.

While living with a prominent public figure requires the spouse to live in the shadow of his greatness, it also means that some of life is lived with the reputation that accompanies such a person. Some of the spotlight overflows occasionally onto the spouse and it is fun to bask in that light, knowing it is the result of that person's goodness and specialness. It is an experience that actually elevates the spouse and provides opportunities that would not be possible otherwise. It is a sheer gift, unearned and singularly exciting.

And so, rather than resenting having lived in Kurt's shadow for over forty years, I thank God so very often that I had such a rich and exciting life with one of the most unique, fascinating and truly good men in all of history (And for the cynics who were forever questioning his authenticity,

I can only say, "What you see is what you get." He was the most humble, sincere man I've ever known.)

It cost me a bit of compromise, a bit of patience, a bit of disappointment, and more than a bit of change in my approach to life. I learned what Alec Guiness said to Grace Kelly in "The Swan" is true. When a person has been groomed to be a swan, to glide along the water gracefully, with dignity, then dares to step out onto the banks, she cannot help looking like a goose. Just another way to say, "We may be in the world, but we are not part of it." When we try to emulate the culture around us, rather than living Christ's way, we will always flounder.

Last Moments

"You have the conscience of a saint."
"I love you. I need you. I want you."
"Hypocrite."

All statements made to me by my dear late husband. Can I reconcile them? It took a long time.

From our first nights together on our honeymoon trip to the North Coast of Queensland, my life with Kurt Marquart was, as Scripture says, a preparation of the bride to enter heaven pure and holy. It was a bit of a surprise to find myself listening to Compline before retiring. Goodness! I didn't even know what Compline was at that time. But before falling asleep every night, there was a reading of the Psalms. While it was a new practice for me, it seemed as if it filled a chasm, a deep void, from the beginning. Before long, I was anticipating our devotions, much like one looks forward to a coffee break from life.

We were as different as two people can be, my husband and I. He was this educated, refined gentleman, and I was a cowgirl from Texas with a high school diploma in business education. As luck would have it, it was his wish to not be coupled with someone, whom he said, would constantly be challenging his intelligence. I was surely the answer to that wish!

While I was not a Bible scholar or extraordinary Christian, I was never in doubt of God's love for me. I fumbled my way through a bad marriage, unevenly yoked, some would say, to a young airman I had met at the church. Having survived somewhat unscathed, but a little more tolerant, I was pretty good material for a pastor's wife, understanding how good people can fall onto hard times and emerge whole again through God's mercy. As we muddled our way through those first years of marriage, I was less than perfect, in many respects, and I admire his patience with my lack of social graces. But when I did inflict pain, as a wife can and does, I would go to him and repent and ask his forgiveness. And that was when he told me I had the **conscience of a saint.** He could not have spoken more loving words to me.

My dear husband's background had not given him much mentoring in functional family life. His father deserted the family when he was young. His step-father had shown nothing but jealous cruelty. He had no lessons in how to express those deep emotions that humans feel towards one another. And so it was difficult for both of us. He didn't know how to receive love, and I didn't understand why he couldn't express it. Many years went by when each of us was lonely, and we didn't know how to fix it.

We filled our life with children. And there was never a better father! Perhaps recalling all the missing factors of his own childhood, he understood instinctively what kids needed. It was a mystery to me how a young man, so recently a bachelor, could know how to parent. Eventually, it dawned on me that he dealt with his children as God deals with us. There were rules. Rules for safety and order. When the rules were broken, there was sorrow and contrition. There was forgiveness. It was forgotten. This was unconditional love in action.

Our first born, Danny, came along and was baptized on the date of our first wedding anniversary, August 12, 1962. When Danny was a month old, Kevin and Colin, local brothers from a broken local family, came to live in our home as foster children. Then Cindy was born on March 5, 1964, and not too much later, Barry arrived February 11, 1966.

With so much work to do, and parish life to keep up with, my personal needs were not an issue most of the time. I did the best I knew how, and while I was not perfect, I suspect no other woman could have done better. It often occurred to me that God had chosen me from conception especially for this unique man, and that whatever was needed would come from Him.

Four years after Barry was born, God answered our prayers with the gift of Angela Maria, who arrived February 9, 1970. She was a dear little girl, and I thought our family was complete. Kevin had gotten married and moved to Dalby to share farm, and Colin had moved up North to work. It seemed as if we were at peace at last. Even though Kurt was out of town a lot on church business, we were coping pretty well.

Then we were surprised by another baby, Tony. I was not ready for another baby. I had been teaching art at the college and felt as if I was actually good at something besides washing diapers. It was a difficult pregnancy, and I really didn't know if our marriage would hold up with yet another child.

When it was time for Tony to be born, March 11, 1974, Kurt took me to the hospital. Dropping me off at the hospital, his parting words to me were **"I love you. I need you. I want you."** It was the first time he had said that to me in our married life. Those words got me through the delivery and sustained me for a long time. Tony won the heart of Kurt right away, and they were best friends for the rest of Kurt's life.

When we reluctantly returned to the States, after fifteen years in the parish, for Kurt to teach at the seminary, things were different and exciting on every level. Kurt had to create new courses and was distracted and busy. Dr. Preus had him doing special things for him as well, which took time and energy. We lived on campus, and the children had free run most of the time. Eventually, I went to work at Redeemer Church part time to enable us to buy a station wagon, as the boys were not getting any shorter.

One thing and another seemed to pull us apart, with my becoming involved with the resettlement of Asian refugees, and Kurt's work becoming more and more consuming.

When my Mother's illness became serious in 1989, I went back to Texas to take care of her for ten weeks. After she died, with the inheritance she left me, we were able to put a down payment on a home of our own, and we moved off campus after fifteen years. It took a long time to find the right house, since we needed a study for Kurt's books. Kurt realized it was a good financial move, but he regretted the loss of the grounds crew and maintenance men that had been so good about taking care of the house and yard on campus. He also missed being able to walk to class every day. I believe he felt guilty living in what he perceived as being such a "flash" house, when he knew so many people around the world who were struggling just to survive. Eventually, he reconciled himself to the fact that we had a home of our own, that he had a huge study in which to store his books and papers. But finally, I think he thought of the house as "her house", for my pleasure, as he was not in it very much. It was a place he came to when he returned from other duties, but he never seemed to take pleasure in the ownership of it.

Not too long after our move, I was hired at Ascension as a teacher's aide for their new preschool with Sharon Ryan, an old friend from Redeemer. That job turned into a full-time job in the church office which lasted ten years before I took an early retirement.

Tensions arose when Kurt began sending massive amounts of money to Haiti to people he had met there, and who harassed us weekly by phone for help. We had terrible disagreements over this. He was spending his pension and his Social Security, borrowing money to send them when that ran out. No one could reason with him, and we were on the point of separation because it was bankrupting us. In one three month period, he sent $12,000 to Haiti alone. It was an obsession out of control. What few normal attitudes he might have had towards stewardship evaporated. Our debts grew.

After I had retired for a year, Kurt was diagnosed with ALS. It was a profound shock to him that he would, as he said "just unravel" bit by bit. His own father lived to be almost 100, and he expected the same would happen to him. Reluctantly, he became more and more dependent on me for eating, dressing, bathing, etc. It was a blessing that I retired when I did, since keeping him going was a full time job. I drove him everywhere, once he could no longer drive. I ended up doing about everything other than teach his classes. He hated being dependent on anyone. He had never allowed me to help him with anything before, and this was extremely vexing to him that he needed help.

When he finally agreed to hospice care, after a rigorous summer of three intensives, it was obvious that he was drawing to his end in this world. I alerted our grandson that if he wanted his grandfather to baptize his little boy, he'd better get it together, because Kurt had told me he would die that night. This was September 18, 2006.

Kyle gathered his friends, and our family, and together with Pastor David Petersen, we communed, after which Kurt baptized Evan. It was such a memorable time, one of those events where joy and grief were intertwined, as the children and I knew it would be his last official act, and likely the last time they would see him alive. He was losing his voice and wanted to retire, so the kids all left, with the exception of Tony, and my son-in-law, John Hill, who was in town.

The hospice bed had arrived earlier that day and it was the first night Kurt had lain in it. It was set up in the family room, and for a short time, Kurt watched TV. But he was very restless, thrashing about under the sheet, as those nearing death always seem to do. The men retired upstairs. I kept vigil in the family room. I sat and read the Psalms, his favorite Scripture, to him in semi darkness, knowing that before long he would no longer be with us. Suddenly, out of nowhere, in a strong voice, he said, *"Hypocrite!"*

I was crushed. How was it possible that his last thoughts of me would be that I was a hypocrite?

I continued to read. It was apparent that he was slipping away very quickly, so I called the men down. Standing around the head of his bed, I told him it was ok for him to go to God, that Tony and I would be ok. He had been distressed that Tony would not cope with his death. Tony led us in the Lord's Prayer. We could hear prayers on behalf of his godsons, Winston and Emelio, escape his weary lips, as he drew his last breath.

For some time, I confess that I was wounded at the thought that my husband of 45 years, the one person who really knew me, thought of me as a hypocrite. Of all the words one leaves with a loved one, why those? Finally, one day, my son Barry said, "Mum, don't you know that Satan was trying one last time to pull Dad away, and that they were arguing? He wasn't talking to you. He was shouting down the devil."

Shortly after that, I read something from Luther about the deathbed struggles Satan has with the faithful, giving it his last effort to steal their souls to himself. In speaking with other Christians, I have heard so many stories of loved ones in Christ who had this horrible battle on their death beds, and how the Lord has sustained His own.

It has become quite important to me to share with others who will ultimately sit with a dying loved one that this battle does take place. I'm certain Satan would be most gleeful if he could deceive and bring down especially those who have been in the service of the Church, to create doubt about their vocation and love of God, to remind them of all their sinful past and demoralize them as much as possible. Even during long illnesses, Satan tempts us to deny our Lord and blame Him for our pain. We are all weak and helpless at some point of life, and Satan is only too eager to utilize those times to snatch us away from God. If we are aware of that, we can comfort and encourage one another in these dread times.

I thank God every day for the life of my dear Kurt. It was not always a happy life for him, but he did take great joy in his faith and never doubted God's mercy and might. He loved humanity and gave his life to sharing the wonderful message of the Gospel to everyone who crossed his path, whether it was from the pulpit, or on a plane flying over the ocean, sitting over a meal, or hanging out with the kids.

During one of his final days, as he rested in front of the window in his big chair, he said, "I'm so overwhelmed by the many opportunities the Lord has given me to serve His church. I have not had time to think much about it until now, and I am so humbled."

I, too, am humbled to have shared that life with him. He was God's gift to the Church, and His treasured gift to me. Because I love the Office of the Ministry and all the foot soldiers who do daily battle for the Gospel, perhaps my biggest hypocrisy has been my feeble attempt to uphold their virtues in the eyes of the people. After all, there's a bit of hypocrite in each of us.

Give to Him Who Asks of You . . .

Some of us are born predisposed to share. Some are just naturally more generous towards those around us than others. Those who hang on to their resources carefully often think of the givers as just plain stupid.

"Don't you know he's just going to waste what you give him?"

"She should have to work for it like everyone else."

"They wouldn't be in this mess if they had used any sense."

We attempt to deal with what we have in an intelligent manner, so as to not become a burden to others. We spend carefully, save as much as we can, and invest in what we hope will prove to be sound, either materially or by giving good service. All this effort tends to make turning loose of our assets painful, unless we have set apart a special portion of it that we don't feel we really need, the "just in case" fund.

When we were living in Australia, we managed fine, through the good graces and generosity of our members, some more than others. Our salary when we left, after fifteen years, and with five children was $150 a week. From the beginning of our marriage, then, it seemed as if I learned to function with what we had, and the idea of saving was simply not part of the scheme. In fact, our salary was deposited into our account, and bills were paid directly from that by check. So that cash rarely crossed our hands.

Had it not been for the fact that one of our members owned a hatchery and provided us with "chook" and eggs, and another owned a market garden, providing us with endless fresh veggies, we would not have made it. We wore hand-me-down clothes offered up by people as their children outgrew things, including school uniforms. And I, with my little portable Singer sewing machine made all the clothes for the girls and myself.

Fortunately for me, this was not considered living in poverty. Many of our young families dealt with expenses the same way. So we never felt deprived. The occasional birthday check would come from my parents, but more often than not, I was tickled to have extra so that I was in a position to do something nice for someone else.

When we returned to the States, many things changed for our family. While the salary was higher, so were expenses. There were no car allowances, nor folks dropping off goodies from their garden. While we were blessed with campus housing for the first fifteen years in Fort Wayne, we had kids in three different schools requiring us to be on the road a lot. While Kurt didn't need a car to get to class, when he would leave town to teach somewhere, I would be left without transportation. Honestly, I don't remember what I did. The car pool folks I was with must have filled those gaps. Because we never had a second car.

In order to accommodate our long-legged teen-age boys, we had to get a larger car, which meant I had to go to work, part time. But until then, I used public transport to get to and from Redeemer Lutheran Church over on Rudisill, where I was church secretary for three years. The response to the need for a second car was always, "When we need a second car, it will mean you are running around too much."

We had our children in Lutheran schools all over town, and I seem to remember counting one day and realizing I was going in and out the front entrance of the campus twelve times a day.

At any rate, I digress. While all this was going on, Kurt was developing his classes while going about lecturing, while preparing resolutions and papers for Dr Preus. There was no time for self-pity, so we just got on with things.

They say couples argue over money more than anything else. Guilty!

In fact, I don't think we argued about much of anything else. I fought for an allowance, even if it was only $5 a week, just so I could have a little savings account and occasionally buy something that was outside the budget. But because he was so inept with finances, never having had any, Kurt kept a tight rein on our resources. More than once he had to rob Peter to pay Paul, and when we finally bought our own home, I know it was refinanced more than once in order that we would have sufficient money to do what we needed to do.

And yet, and yet, if anyone asked him for help, he never refused.

It sometimes really hurt me to watch this. It didn't matter whether he had known the person for a long time, had any hope of getting his money back, or could even be sure what the loan was for. If someone asked, he gave. And yet, if I wanted to make home improvements or give something to one of the kids, he refused. Plus, the fact that he gave so much away left me without the option to do any giving of my own to folks I knew could use help.

I have written elsewhere where this spending really came to a head toward the end of his life, when he was already receiving his pension and spending funds we didn't have in order to send money to Haiti, Africa, Selma. It was so bad, that at one point, I feared we would lose our home.

Over the years, since his death, I have been reading the Old Testament more and more, and even in the Gospels, I am finding texts that are quite clear about what we are to do when someone asks for help. We have been taught that "if you give someone cash they will just go buy booze or drugs." And so, when the old lady approaches us in the parking lot of the local grocer and begs for "loose change" to help with her rent, we back off and manage to have no cash at all, thinking it's bound to be a scam.

If anyone understood Kurt's devotional life, they would know that he was in the Word continuously. Even on the first night of our honeymoon, we could not retire without Compline! When you find, therefore, texts like Matthew 5:42, and Acts 20:35, and know that God's Word is final in all matters, it is easy to understand why Kurt could not help giving. Even giving what he didn't have, when someone asked.

"Give to him who asks of you, and do not turn away from him who wants to borrow from you." Matt.5:42

"In everything I showed you, that by working hard in this manner, you must help the weak and remember the words of the Lord Jesus, that He Himself said, "It is more blessed to give than to receive." Acts 20:35

This man was simply trying to live by God's commands in a world with a different belief system. So how could anyone ever understand him when he bought nothing for himself, carried a burden of guilt for living in a house with a roof that didn't leak, bought nothing that was not absolutely critical for existence, (except chocolate). He had friends and colleagues in all parts of the world who were living in poverty, hunger and persecution.

Then when he came back to his home and had to endure the luxury of wall to wall carpeting, running water, central heating and air conditioning, and balanced meals, he could but ache for the rest, all the hundreds he could not help.

Recently, I was vacationing in the South and had the pleasure of spending some time with Kurt's brother, George. We were recalling stories about their life as children, and it was clear to see that there was great affection between them as they lived through the uncertainties that were at that time for anyone trying to escape the war. When I mentioned Kurt's interesting generosity and how annoying it had often been, he looked me right in the eye and said, "But he was right, you know."

Yes, he was right.

Into His Nearer Presence

The duration of Kurt's illness, after the diagnosis was made in Cleveland Clinic, was relatively short. Many victims of ALS suffer for years. Of course, none of us really knew when it all began. There were some signs along the way that we should have picked up on, but didn't. No one among our families had ever been sick with anything like this, so we didn't know what was going on until they performed specific tests which indicated that, yes, he did indeed have ALS. Amyotropic lateral sclerosis.

Initially, his trusted family physician suggested he go to a class for diabetic nutrition. He was losing weight and strength in his limbs. Perhaps neuropathy? But giving up class time to do anything so trivial was not in the cards for him, and he refused that advise. When the doctors at Cleveland Clinic set him up to be under the Multiple Sclerosis umbrella, for financial assistance towards what most likely lay ahead, he went for one appointment. After waiting hours to see the actual physician and listening to him say that it was a waste of money to take vitamins, he stood, with some effort, and said, "I'm sorry, Doctor. I'm afraid we are taking up too much of your time." And we left.

When the suggestion was made that he undergo various drug programs to see if his condition might be retarded, he would simply say, "If I'm on the path to meeting my Lord, don't anyone get in my way!"

Stubbornly resisting, but gradually accepting the idea that he would just simply unravel, as he put it, he still drove himself most places, and held classes as if nothing was wrong. In time, since I was retired at the time, I was able to snatch the keys and become his driver to nearly everything he needed to do, including attending CTCR meetings in St Louis.

His affliction was basically the loss of all strength between his shoulders and his fingertips. He could still walk. Showering, grooming, dressing, and eating became actions he could no longer perform. It was most vexing to him to have to accept help in these matters, but he had little choice in the end. He had frequented Pizza Hut hundreds of times with family and friends, but the chairs became intolerably uncomfortable for him, when the muscles in his back became so depleted that he was virtually all bone.

The last meal we had in St Louis together with the members of the CTCR was attended by our good friend, Charlie. By then, Kurt could no longer hold a drinking glass with just one hand, and so he would grasp it with both hands and manage relatively well. His colleagues were unaware of how ill he was and began to stare. Typically supportive, Charlie whispered to me, "Let's both hold our glasses that way." We did, and then everyone at the table began to do so as well. It was this kind of moment that allowed us all to laugh a little and endure the isolation that was to come.

The summer before his death, Kurt had three intensives to teach in other cities. The classes had been booked for some time, and while we exhorted him to cancel, he insisted that these men were expecting him to be there, and he was going. Since he was unable to travel alone, some kind soul provided what was necessary for our son to accompany him. Since our son was employed by the seminary, he had the kind of insurance that would cover him, should he endure any kind of back injury or physical problem as a result of the lifting that was necessary to assist his dad.

So it was that they made these three trips together, giving them this special time in both their lives. This story is written elsewhere in this book.

The fall quarter began in early September of 2006, and Kurt was very sick and quite weak. But there was a wheel chair at the door of the classroom block, so when I would drive him to the campus, we would put him in the chair, and someone would take him to his class where he was able to deliver his lecture. I cannot say how well he did, but it had to leave an impression on his students that he loved them and the classes they shared enough to make that final effort.

In attending his final faculty meeting, he thanked his colleagues for their support and said his "goodbyes". Even then, many of them had no idea that in the next few days, he would be dead.

After about three days of teaching, he developed an infection of some sort, resulting in his being too sick to return to class. He had already been assigned to a Hospice Program, and the nurses told me that they feared his time was drawing close. On the morning of September 18, Kurt told me that he was going to die that day.

Our grandson's infant son had been born sometime before this and had not yet been baptized. I contacted my grandson and alerted him to arrange for his sponsors to gather that night, along with the rest of the family. Together with those he loved, we all received the Sacrament one last time, after which, he was strong enough to baptize his great-grandson. It was his last official act as a pastor.

At two a.m. on the 19th, Kurt went to His nearer Presence forever. His battle was over and at last he was at peace, in his heart, mind and body. His youngest son, our son-in-law, and I were at his side, and assured him we would be ok, that he needed to go Home. As he took his last breaths, whispered prayers for his Godsons slipped through his lips, and he was received into the arms of Christ.

Perhaps you have heard of cases where angels filled the room when someone was taken to Heaven? I can tell you that in this case, it was true. Whatever hosts they were, they pressed in around us, and the peace and joy in the room was palpable.

When we knew Kurt's illness was terminal and imminent, it fell to me to meet with the folks at the funeral home to make arrangements. This I did alone, since I knew what I wished to do. Besides, when I asked him if he wanted to be part of the planning process, he refused and said to do what I thought best.

After he died, I also met with Kantor Resch, who was kind enough to assist with the service. The Church was in turmoil, with many fearful that we might be facing a split among our dear people. I worried that the loss of this man who had, in many respects, been the leader of the men in the field, the crisis might seem insurmountable. I wanted a service that would comfort, but also encourage the brethren, hymns and readings that would say in every possible way that the Lord of the Church was still with us, and that as He had taken away, so likewise would He provide.

I was pleased that it was possible to have a black casket, with three white lilies on the top, for the Trinity. Since he always wore his black suit, there was no other color that would do. Since the funeral facility was already booked for the funeral of a local celebrity, we were allowed to have the visitation in Luther Hall on Campus. The people at the seminary were very helpful and cooperative in our attempts to provide for the many folks we knew would be coming.

Hundreds of pastors came from all over the country, many of whom had been his students, others who were colleagues. Friends from Redeemer congregation as well as Ascension were there, too. As the chapel began to fill up that morning of the 22nd, I kept advising folks to go on over, so they would be able to be seated. I was told that there was an estimate of eight hundred worshippers, plus the many who were watching the service being broadcast live across the country.

The video shows some hundred and fifty vested clergy up front. The singing was wonderful. "We All Believe In One True God" was the opening hymn, followed by the Venite and then Psalm 130. The Office Hymn was

"The Strife Is O'er, the Battle Done", and the sem choir sang verse three of "Lord, Thee I Love With All My Heart".

Our son-in-law, Rev. John Hill, gave the Homily, "The Son Gives Light".

Healy Willan's "Te Deum" was beautiful with the male voices, organ and brass. And the service ended with "A Mighty Fortress Is Our God". As the coffin and family began leaving the chapel, a piper could be heard playing "Amazing Grace" outside on the steps. It was Kurt's favorite hymn.

As we left the chapel, it was starting to rain lightly once again, but we were warmed by the honor guard provided by the sea of vested clergy. The procession led us to Covington Memorial Gardens, where the ground was said to be too mushy to hold the committal. The service was held in their chapel there. Once again, we were surrounded by our life-long friends and colleagues, as we said our final farewell, placing red carnations on his casket.

For me personally, one of the most difficult parts of any funeral is when the coffin leaves the safety of the sanctuary to go to the cemetery. The other has to be driving away from the cemetery, leaving the one you love behind. However, after being surrounded by love by so many, I experienced a sense of joy. The love his friends had for him overflowed onto me and the children, and we received such comfort from it. As a family, we had been given time to prepare for this separation, and because we understood Kurt's devotion to his Lord and his eagerness to be with Him, we could only rejoice that his suffering on this earth was finished, that he had been renewed to the perfect person that God had created him to be in the beginning. The formidable yet tender, brilliant but humble, terminally ill, now perfectly healthy man is there, waiting for us.

Final Reunion

One night recently, when sleep would not come, after a hectic day with too much coffee, I lay there, in an attempt not to panic over the realization that in a few hours I would be required to be up and functioning. Sometimes, the sheer anxiety of not achieving sleep just makes it worse. On those occasions, it has been fun to work on the next chapter of my book in my head.

Somehow, the most extraordinary ideas are born in the still of the night. Just the right words seem to fall together, expressing all the things you have been struggling with for days. More often than not, this happens at totally inconvenient times, when the computer is housed in the study, where the puppy is sleeping in his kennel. Does one risk waking him up, in order to avoid yet another brilliant thought slipping away? No. We tie a knot in the corner of the sheet instead, hoping to regain the flavor of the idea the following morning.

Earlier that day we had received news of another dear friend having died, and I was imagining her bliss, having come face to face with her Lord. Finally, in her new self, totally free of her painful illness, she would be walking in the heavenly gardens, perhaps running into many of those who had preceded her. She had been a pastor's wife for decades and had said "good-bye" to many who were, no doubt, walking in that same garden.

It is impossible for me to think about heaven without recalling my late husband, Kurt Marquart. For most certainly, I know he is there waiting for me. Kurt was the most Christ-like person I ever knew. When we said our farewell that early morning in September of 2006, there was no question about a reunion down the line.

I attempted to strike a deal with him several times, trying to get him to promise that if he got to heaven before I did, he would be there waiting for me when it was my turn. The best he could offer was, "I imagine God might have something to say about that."

It is exciting for me to think that when I am called Home, I will immediately recognize him. He will be perfect, as God intended him, healthy, happy. The fragile, impotent skeleton of a body that lay there that night would be changed, fleshed out again, hands doing what he wanted them to, his mind sharp and full of humor and joy. The attributes God gave him in order that he could serve the Church so very well will be even more honed. The human character flaws, shyness, insecurities, loneliness, all those things that thwarted him in this life will be gone, and he will stand before me as I believed him to be when we first met.

And, thankfully, I too will be perfect, as God intended me. All the unattractive personality weaknesses and sinful disposition will dissolve, and I will become the perfect match for this perfect man. No, we will not be married, as we were in this life. Pure love, however, will be there, and we will rejoice in it throughout eternity. The gift God gave us in this life will go on forever.

We often wish for signs, after someone leaves this life, signs that they are somehow still connected to us. From the moment Kurt died, I thought of him as simply being in another dimension. He was not dead. He traveled all our married life together. This was just another trip, one that would separate us for a time. Still, I longed for a sign. I had dreams of looking for him, to discover that he was nowhere to be found. Waking with an aching heart, I kept hoping that someday I would have just something that would comfort me during my wait.

One night, as clearly as if he was sitting on my bed, I heard him say, "I love you. I have always loved you. Soon, we will be together again. This time it will be forever."

O perfect Love, all human thought transcending
Lowly we kneel in prayer before Thy throne.
That theirs may be the love that knows no ending,
Whom thou for evermore dost join in one.

O perfect Life, be Thou their full assurance
Of tender charity and steadfast faith,
Of patient hope, and quiet brave endurance,
With childlike trust that fears nor pain nor death.

Grant them the joy which brightens earthly sorrow.
Grant them the peace which calms all earthly strife.
And to life's day the glorious unknown morrow
That dawns upon eternal love and life.

Our Wedding Hymn
Dorothy Frances Gurney,
Australian Lutheran Hymnal

Students Recall Dr. Marquart

Even today, when I run into former students of my dear late husband, there always arises a story about their experience with him. It is comforting to me to realize that his memory lives on in the hearts of those for whom he cared so much.

I'm not sure if the site went up while Kurt was still living, while dealing with his illness, or if it was put on line upon the announcement that he was gone. Pastor David Petersen from Redeemer gave the friends of my husband a chance to post memories of class time with him, and following are some of them:

One Sunday at Redeemer, Prof. Marquart was preaching on the parable of the man without the wedding garment. Afterwards, in my arrogance, I thought I would enlighten him about my then-theory that the parable was really about Judas. He instantly responded, "But is there not a little Judas

Prof Marquart in Class

in all of us?" I have never been able to forget those haunting words, and their utter truth. As much as I learned from him in his classes, that was one of the most beneficial lessons I learned. I will always be thankful to God for His servant, Kurt Marquart, a true Doctor of the Church.

I remember something about sermon writing and not letting your mind go walkabout. But it isn't the quotes that stuck with me. It was the man. He would gladly take time to talk with you, explain things to you. There was the gentleman pastor enfleshed. He was a regular guest at our home when we would have a mid-quarter open house. There was always a gracious demeanor about him. I don't know where this saying started, but that which I have received, I deliver unto you. It was said among some fourth-year students at the Fort, "Scaer taught me how to think. Weinrich taught me how to study. Marquart taught me what to believe." There were never negative jokes about Prof. Marquart, as I remember. If there were, the students must have been ashamed to tell them. The only jokes about him that I heard compared his "level of sanctification" to perfection. This testifies to the piety he exuded, which surely had a salutary effect on his students. He takes theology and the mysteries of God seriously, and he encouraged all of us to do the same.

When I preach, I try to speak with Prof. Marquart's clarity.
When I visit the sick, I hope to display his obvious compassion.
When I deal with a misled parishioner, I try to be as patient as he was with class after class of ignorant students.
I learned from all my professors, but I want to BE like Professor Mar-

quart – mainly because he would call that idea "RUBBISH!" and say rather that I should look to our Lord.

I do not have any good quotes to add to the list here, but from having Prof. Marquart in class and from having him as a guest in my congregation, I most appreciate his pastoral heart. His quiet grace and dignity, and the way he treats everyone, from the least to the greatest—with honor and respect, remains a model for me that I will always aspire to. To do that while yet standing firm in the faith is, I think, a true pastor. He has the ability to completely dismantle your errors and false theology, and have you thank him for it! Though I would never come near to being the theologian he is, I pray that someday I may become half the pastor. Thank you, Kurt. I will always consider you a mentor and a friend.

Back in the 80's when I was considering seminary education, Prof. Marquart spoke at a conference in Lansing, Michigan. Earl Elowsky, a neighboring pastor, told my brother and me, "You've got to come and hear this guy!" So we did.

As he so often did, Prof. Marquart seemed to zero in on the obvious "new guy", the visitor, especially the younger ones. At one of the breaks, he came right up and talked to us. We were honored and humbled.

Then, somehow, we were seated directly across from him at the lunch table. Having seminary on my mind and the growing desire to become a pastor after hearing the professor, I asked him the stupidest question I could come up with. Remember I was a total fundie. Ready? Here goes.

"Professor Marquart, why attend one of the two LCMS seminaries? I mean, what's to stop me from attending, say, Dallas Theological Seminary, and then becoming an LCMS pastor?"

To which he politely replied, "I suppose one could, but then he would have to go through a bit of delousing." Everone laughed. I'm embarrassed to this day.

The point is, this says volumes about "the most popular professor" at the Fort, according to earnstwhile Admissions Counselor, George Lange. Though I had said one of the stupidest things in my life, he was somehow able to answer in such a positive and lighthearted way that I ended up going to the Fort. My brother and I are both pastors now. There will never be anyone like Professor Marquart.

I use my Tappert BOC rarely. But in the inside front cover of it are quotes from Prof. Marquart. These quotes are from LCII, Fall Quarter, 1999.

"What is the recipe for Holy Water? Boil the hell out of it."
"We install three things: Refrigerators, Televisions, and Pastors."
"God created us to be happy in Him."
"Preaching is to comfort the afflicted and afflict the comfortable."

"Calvinism is nothing but high-church Zwinglianism."
"Priests are born. Pastors are made."
"The sermon is a spiritual battle for the hearts and minds of the people."
"There is no such hymn as "Clown Him with Many Clowns."
Thank you, Professor Marquart

My first Systematics class was with Marquart. I relished going to class. Theology was life. It healed my soul. It spoke to my sins, my condition. Far from boring or abstract, Marquart made theology matter to me. During class, I copied down a few quotes. Here they are:
"The Gospel saves some and infuriates others."
"The Catechism is the layman's Bible."
"Strive in your preaching to bring light rather than heat."

I first met Professor Marquart at some presentation he was giving on apologetics in a Chicago suburb in the mid 1980's. I was a college kid trying to decide what to do with the rest of my life. I had a vague idea to go to the seminary, but I wasn't sure about it.

Professor Marquart greatly impressed me with his presentation. He was smart, crisp, funny and devastatingly sharp with his analysis and critiques of theology and culture. And that accent!

After that I began picking up CTQ's in the Concordia RF library and reading articles and such he had written. I read "Anatomy of an Explosion". Marquart's ability as a writer and a theologian were one of the reasons I went to the seminary and became a pastor. His intelligence and sharp wit convinced me that being a pastor and studying at the seminary could be exciting and invigorating.

At seminary, Prof. Marquart's love of the Confessions and systematics imprinted themselves on my brain and led me into the depths of Lutheran theology. At seminary, his churchly approach, his sacramental focus, his evident piety all deeply impressed me. He intimidated the heck out of me, frankly, with his learning and stature in the church. He seemed great then, he still does today.

In one class, we were talking about the "prattling and rattling" of prayers that go on and on for no reason, and our highly esteemed Prof said, "If you're tired and have had a long day, don't try to force yourself through lengthy prayers. Simply pray the words of the Fourth Psalm, 'Now I lay down to sleep in peace, for you alone. O Lord, maketh me to dwell in safety", make the sign of the cross and go to sleep. A night doesn't go by in our household when that prayer isn't prayed, the sign of the holy cross isn't made, and our family doesn't lie down and sleep in peace. Thank you Professor Marquart.

During my second year, I worked for seminary security. There was a dirt loop behind the Marquart house that we would drive through every now and again to check. I was doing that one Sunday morning when I got the little Datsun pick-up stuck. For about thirty minutes, I tried to rock back and forth to get it out. Then Prof. Marquart, in clerical garb, appeared and asked if I needed a hand. I said I did, expecting him to get his vehicle to tow me out. Instead, he opened the door and said, "Let me give it a try." I presumed the mild mannered professor would be mild mannered in driving, too. Well, no sooner did he shut the door when he had put the pedal to the metal—all the way to the metal and then some. The engine roared, the tires spun, and smoke bellowed from the back. Finally, the truck lurched free. I stood there, mouth agap. Pro. Marquart opens the door, dusts himself off, and walks away, saying, "Sometimes you're just got to show the old girl who's boss!"

Final favorite quotes:
Re "decision theology" I am in support of infant baptism: "A child needs to eat long before he can read a menu."
"Avoid Ku Klux Klannery."
"Heresy always likes to dress up in the vestments of the historic Church."
"The ears of the people are holier than the mouths of the priests."
"Hatred is simply chilled and hardened anger."
"You can teach a monkey to do liturgy, but you can't teach a parrot to preach."
You are a treasure, Prof. Marquart, and we love you. I shall never forget you!

VI

MORE NEW BEGINNINGS

It All Began With A Christmas Card

"I was going through some old Christmas cards today, and I ran across one from your family. Thought I'd give you a call to see how you're doing. Kurt's been gone about eighteen months now, right?" I recognized the deep voice right away, even though it had been quite some time since I'd heard it. It was Bob Johnston, a good friend of ours, a voice from the past.

Bob was at that time a retired pastor from the Wisconsin Evangelical Lutheran Synod, living in Florida, the location of his last congregation. His first wife, Esther, and all his children had been in Australia at the same time as our family, and through the decades that followed, we had been in touch from time to time as our children graduated, married, and moved about the country.

Esther had died of a sudden heart attack some years before, and he had married a widow from his congregation, whose name was Cecelia. They were together nine years when she died after fighting pancreatic cancer.

I remember the exact spot I was when the call surprised me. There were two friends helping me organize the chaos of the study, and they happened to also be friends of Bob's from days in Australia. I took the phone down stairs and carried on a bit of a visit, sitting on the sofa, looking out the living room window. It was just a friendly, rather innocuous conversation, one of those times when you go down the list of all the kids to say what each is doing, etc. We exchanged email addresses, and that was about it.

To make a long story short, there began a flood of letters back and forth, as we renewed our friendship and caught up on what had happened to each of us over the years. Bob had actually been the pastor who officiated at the wedding when Kurt and I married in Australia. We had many friends in common, and it was fun to dredge up the memories of late night pinochle parties, and dinners in days gone by.

During one of our phone calls, Bob suggested I might enjoy coming to Florida for a few days to visit. I had never done anything like that before, and I had a dog to consider. For some reason, it just sounded like a fun thing to do. My children were a little surprised.

Actually, that's putting it mildly. They were not used to their mother just taking off to visit a man for a week. The youngest, in particular, was still in the mourning process from the death of his father, and I think he was actually angry with me for even thinking of such a thing. Even though it had been almost two years since he died, my son could not believe I would even dream of having a relationship with another man.

The idea of marrying again had not really entered my mind until then. I was adjusting to the single life, and there was still much to do to get Kurt's study under control. It was my problem, and I simply had to do it. I sure was not going to do a pub crawl to find a man.

But I did pray to God that if there was an elderly gentleman out there that He wanted me to look after, that He would have to lead the way. And then there was Bob.

My wardrobe consisted primarily of left-over outfits from having worked ten years in a church office. I had been told that attire in general was very informal in Florida, even at church. It was difficult to pack. I did pick up a pretty cream satin blouse with a black pattern in it to wear with black slacks and found a cute little quilted black jacket to go with it. That would be my travelling outfit and the first thing he would see when I landed in Tampa.

I always have an anxiety attack before flying. Not because I'm afraid of flying, but I just think about all the possible things that can go amiss on a trip, sleep evades me, and by the time I get out the door, I wonder what on earth I'm doing. But I found a good dog sitter, someone took me to the airport, and off I went.

My first date began, then, as I rode down the escalator in the terminal and locked eyes with this gentle soul who was waiting for me at the bottom. He was very handsome in his short sleeved checkered shirt. Tanned and smiling from ear to ear. I told him he looked much younger than his photo, and he said I was prettier than mine. Having been married to two women in his past, he knew to enquire whether I needed to stop at the ladies' room before we set out on our two hour drive to Citrus Springs, where he lived.

He also knew there were no eating places on the highway, and so he had picked up two subway sandwiches, at my request, had put them in a cooler, for us to eat on the way back. The idea was that we would go to his son's home, where I would be sleeping while I was there. Pete, his son, would take me to work each morning, where Bob would pick me up, and we would spend the days together.

The reception I received at Pete and Kay Lynn's was welcoming, but a little guarded. I suppose they were as surprised by this nonsense as my own children. Nevertheless, I had a pleasant room there, and they made me as comfortable as they could.

Next morning, Bob picked me up and we went to his house. It was a nice little three-bedroom bungalow that he and his late wife had built some years before. The neighborhood was quiet, isolated in a new addition, with other small, scattered houses. He introduced me to his neighbors in the back and on one side.

I don't remember all the things we did those days. But our outings would have included lunch, visiting the manatees, going to the waterfront, and going to his church. His home was located on the Gulf side of Florida, about 80 miles north of Tampa. There was nothing spectacular about it, boasting of small shopping centers, a movie theater and lots of little breakfast places, where it seemed all the seniors ate most of their meals.

I met a few of the members of his church and there was much speculation in the air about what would happen with this new woman. They had all known both his late wives, and it is hard to imagine what they were thinking.

About the third day I was there, we went to a mall that had a jewelry island. We stopped to look at the rings! He asked me what kind of rings I liked the best, and I asked to see a few. One set in particular was really lovely. Nothing was said after that, but we continued to stroll around, and then went back to the house.

Upon my arrival the first day, there had been a dozen long-stemmed red roses in a beautiful red glass vase on the coffee table. We sat down on the couch there, where I assume he had thought he created a romantic atmosphere, and he summoned the courage to ask if I would consider marrying him. There had been a great deal of communication between us before this trip, and we knew the mind of the other pretty well by then. I knew Bob was a gentle, kind, and selfless fellow, and that while he was a bit older than I, he was still sharp and clever and a deeply devout Christian man. I could see, from the beginning, the handsome young man that I had known in years gone by, tall, black hair, deep voice. I saw no red flags flying up from anywhere, with the exception of his difficulty in always getting his legs to carry his weight when he stood up too fast. It seemed to me that it would be a good thing to have a life of my own with a stable man who would take care of me, so that my children could get on with their own lives and not worry about me.

When I said yes, he pulled out the rings that he had already purchased, and they were exactly the same as the ones I had admired at the store. He was so terribly happy, and I was relieved that the indecision was behind us.

Bob planned to come to Fort Wayne for the Easter that was coming soon and spend some time with us, so that the children would feel easier about this decision. When I departed on my flight home, then, I knew the separation would not be long. I was a little weary of the constant company by the time we got to the airport and thought I would be glad to be leaving. When the time came that I had to go to the gate and leave him behind, I was surprised how lonely I suddenly felt without him. That revelation, more than any other moment, confirmed my decision to take this new walk in life.

Note: From time to time, we get "signs" in our lives that seem to give some kind of cohesion to our ongoing saga. In my case, it has been a Psalm. As a teenager, I attended a gathering at our church where a special District Youth Director was a guest for the day. We did a lot of rather innocuous things that day, but while we were in our "circle", he asked two questions. First was: "Who are you?" That was easy, in that company. I am a child of God. Second was: "What is your favorite Bible verse?" Ooops! I didn't have a favorite Bible verse! Is that something people have? I'd always liked "I must do the works of Him Who sent me while it is day, for the time cometh when no man can work." But, that being a quote from Christ, somehow it seemed a bit egotistic of me to claim it as my own.

While the others were quoting theirs, I scrambled to find a text that I could call my own. I had never noticed it before, but my eyes fell upon Psalm 27, and I liked it very much. From then on, that was my favorite verse.

Years later, the pastor who officiated at our wedding, a man I had not yet met, selected that text as our wedding text. Even more years later, at the funeral of my husband, the man who put together the service found that Psalm 27 was the Psalm for that week. When my funeral is observed, that Psalm will be read one more time, as it applies to me. The circle will be complete.

www.ingramcontent.com/pod-product-compliance
Lightning Source LLC
Chambersburg PA
CBHW050629300426
44112CB00012B/1723